Study Guide

MICROECONOMIC THEORY:
AN INTEGRATED APPROACH

Study Guide

MICROECONOMIC THEORY: AN INTEGRATED APPROACH

Stephen A. Mathis ▲ Janet Koscianski

Shippensburg University

Upper Saddle River, New Jersey 07458

Executive editor: Rod Banister
Assistant editor: Marie McHale
Production editor: Wanda Rockwell
Manufacturer: Victor Graphics

ISBN 0-13-011419-7
10 9 8 7 6 5 4 3 2 1

TABLE OF CONTENTS

CHAPTER 1: REVIEW OF BASIC CALCULUS TECHNIQUES

SUMMARY

Our purpose in this chapter is to provide a review of those basic calculus techniques that are frequently used in microeconomic analysis. At the outset, we briefly discuss the basics of model building, defining the concepts of independent and dependent variables, while distinguishing between univariate and multivariate functions. Next, we discuss the concept of a derivative and review several of the rules for differentiating functions, providing a specific mathematical example for each case. The computation of higher order derivatives is also discussed.

After the basic rules for differentiation are reviewed, we direct our attention to optimizing univariate functions. First, a critical value of a decision variable is defined in terms of the first order condition for a maximum, a minimum, or an inflection point for a univariate function. Next, we define second order conditions and discuss the role they play in determining whether a function is at either a maximum, minimum or an inflection point. To avoid simply reviewing calculus techniques, per se, we note that derivatives represent marginal functions in economic analysis, and present some optimization problems applying concepts used in microeconomic analysis.

The last part of this chapter focuses on derivatives of multivariate functions. Our primary attention is on partial derivatives. Specifically, we discuss what they represent conceptually, how they are computed, and how they can be applied to solving economic problems. Essentially, this discussion of partial derivatives provides the foundation for optimizing multivariate functions, a topic we present in Chapter 2. Finally, Chapter 1 concludes with a brief discussion of total derivatives as they are applied to multivariate functions. The main topics covered in this chapter are as follows.

- A univariate function contains only one independent variable, such as y = f (x).

- The average slope of a univariate function, such as y = f (x), is measured as $\frac{\Delta y}{\Delta x}$, where ƛy and ƛx represent discrete changes in the variables y and x, respectively.

- The instantaneous slope of a univariate function, such as y = f (x), is equal to the derivative $\frac{dy}{dx}$ = f' (x).

- In economics, the first derivative of a total function is referred to as a marginal function. For example, the first derivative of a total revenue function is a marginal revenue function.

- Higher-order derivatives are determined by taking the derivative of a derivative. For example, the second-order derivative of the univariate function y = f(x), denoted $\frac{d^2y}{dx^2}$ or f'' (x), is equal to $\frac{d\left(\frac{dy}{dx}\right)}{dx}$.

- The second order derivative measures the slope of the marginal function.

- One of the most important applications of derivatives is in solving optimization (maximization or minimization) problems.

- An optimization problem for a univariate function, such as y = f(x), involves finding the solution value for the independent variable, x, that corresponds to an optimal value (maximum or minimum) for the dependent, or objective, variable, y.

- Given a univariate function such as y = f (x), a critical value for the independent variable, x, exists if at this value of x the first derivative of the function is equal to zero, that is, $\frac{dy}{dx} = 0$. This is also known as a first-order condition for an optimum.

- Once a critical value is found, it is necessary to examine the value of the second-order derivative of the function, $\frac{d^2y}{dx^2}$ = f'' (x), in order to determine whether the function is at a maximum, a minimum, or an inflection point at the critical value of the independent variable.

- If the second-order derivative is negative, then the function is at a maximum at the critical value.

- If the second-order derivative is positive, then the function is at a minimum at the critical value.

- If the second-order derivative is equal to zero and the third-order derivative is not equal to zero, then the function is at an inflection point at the critical value.

- A multivariate function contains more than one independent variable, such as $y = f(x_1, x_2, x_3)$.

- A partial derivative measures the change in the dependent variable in a multivariate function due to a change in one of the independent variables, while holding all of the other independent variables constant.

- Partial derivatives are used to compute the marginal functions relating to a multivariate total function. For example by taking the partial derivatives of a multivariate production function, such as Q = f (K,L), you can determine the marginal product of labor function, $MP_L = \frac{\partial Q}{\partial L}$, and the marginal product of capital function, $MP_K = \frac{\partial Q}{\partial K}$.

- A total derivative measures the change in a function due to an infinitesimally small change in an independent variable, when all independent variables are allowed to vary.

KEY TERMS

- critical value
- dependent, or objective, variable
- higher-order derivative
- independent, or decision, variables
- marginal function
- model
- partial derivative
- partial slope
- total derivativc
- univariate function

EXERCISES

1.1 Determine $\frac{dy}{dx}$ for each of the following functions.

a. $y = 6x^0$

b. $y = 12x^3 - 9x^2 + 15x + 40$

c. $y = 330x^{-3} + 20x^{-2} + 15x^{-1} + 2x + 75$

d. $y = (8x^2 - 4)(9x^3 - x^2 + 12x)$

e. $y = (18x^2 + 5x) / (3x - 14)$

1.2 Determine $\frac{dy}{dx}$ and $\frac{d^2y}{dx^2}$ for each of the following functions.

a. $y = 1800x + 500$

b. $y = \frac{12}{x^3}$

c. $y = (7x^2 + 20) / 8x^3$

d. $y = (20x)(5x^3 + 14x^2)$

1.3 Assume a univariate function of the form

$$y = 4000x - 10x^2.$$

a. Determine the value of the independent variable, x, that optimizes the value of this function.

b. Is this function at a maximum, a minimum, or an inflection point at the value of x you determined in part a.?

c. Determine the optimal value of y.

1.4 A firm's total revenue, TR, is a function of its level of output, q, where its total revenue function is

$$TR = 400q - 5q^2.$$

a. Determine the firm's marginal revenue function.

b. How much output must the firm produce in order to maximize its total revenue?

c. Determine the maximum amount of total revenue earned by the firm.

1.5 A firm's total cost, TC, is a function of its level of output, q. Assume its total cost function is

$$TC = \frac{1}{3}q^3 - 4q^2 + 16q + 20.$$

a. Determine the firm's marginal cost function.

b. How much output must the firm produce in order to minimize its marginal cost?

c. Determine the minimum value of marginal cost.

1.6 Assume a multivariate function of the form,

$$y = 10x^3 z^2.$$

a. Find $\frac{dy}{dx}$ and $\frac{\partial y}{\partial z}$.

b. Evaluate the partial derivates you found in part a. when x = 2 and z = 3.

c. Now assume that a relationship exists between x and y such that $z = 12x^2$.

Determine the total derivative, $\frac{dy}{dx}$, and evaluate it when $x = 2$ and $z = 3$.

1.7 A firm produces output, Q, using capital, K, and labor, L. Its production function is

$$Q = 24K^{\frac{3}{4}}L^{\frac{1}{4}}.$$

a. Determine the functions for the firm's marginal product of labor, MP_L, and the marginal product of capital, MP_K.

b. Compute the values of MP_L and MP_K when the firm uses 16 units of capital and 81 units of labor.

CHAPTER 2: UNCONSTRAINED AND CONSTRAINED OPTIMIZATION OF MULTIVARIATE FUNCTIONS

SUMMARY

The material we present in Chapter 2 consists of an extension of the discussion of multivariate functions and partial derivatives presented in Chapter 1. First, we analyze the process of optimizing a multivariate function in the absence of a constraint. Specifically, we show how to use partial derivatives to compute sets of first order conditions, and then how to solve these first order conditions to obtain optimum values for the decision and objective variables in the function. We also include an optional section describing how to compute and solve the second order conditions in order to determine whether the associated solution values constitute a maximum, minimum, or a saddle point.

Next, we introduce the concept of a constraint involving the decision variables in an optimization problem, and describe the important roles played by constraints in economic analysis. We briefly describe how constrained optimization problems can be solved using the substitution method. Our major focus, however, is on the method of Lagrangian multipliers as constituting the most useful approach to solving these types of problems. After describing this method in detail, we use it to solve a problem containing the same objective function as an earlier problem used to demonstrate an unconstrained optimum. Thus, we are able to compare the solution values for both problems, demonstrating the effects of a binding constraint. Finally, we discuss the concepts of primal and dual analyses, describing how the roles of the included functions are reversed across the two approaches. Specifically, the objective function in the primal problem is treated as the constraint in the dual, and the constraint in the primal is treated as the objective function in the dual. The main topics presented in this chapter are as follows.

- Partial derivatives are used in solving optimization (maximization or minimization) problems involving multivariate functions.

- Given a multivariate function, $y = f(x,z)$, the first order conditions for an unconstrained optimum value for y are:
- $\frac{\partial y}{\partial x} = f_x = 0$ and $\frac{\partial y}{\partial z} = f_z = 0$.

- Given a multivariate function, $y = f(x,z)$, the second-order conditions for a maximum are:
  $f_{xx} < 0, \quad f_{zz} < 0$
  and
  $[f_{xx} \quad f_{zz} - (f_{xz})^2] > 0$.

- Constrained optimization is the process of optimizing (maximizing or minimizing) some objective function subject to the limitations imposed by some predetermined factors affecting the values of the decision variables.

- The most common technique for solving constrained optimization problems is the Lagrangian multiplier method.

- The Lagrangian function, $\mathcal{L}$, is comprised of the objective function and a created variable, λ, multiplied by the constraint, which is solved to equal zero.

- The first-order conditions for a constrained optimization problem consist of the partial derivatives of the Lagrangian function with respect to each of the decision variables and the Lagrangian multiplier, λ, each set equal to zero. This system of partial derivatives is solved to determine the values of the decision variables that correspond to a constrained optimal value for the objective function.

- The optimal value of the Lagrangian multiplier, λ^*, measures the effect on the value of the objective function when the value of the constraint is changed by one unit.

- It is conventional in economics to refer to the original constrained optimization problem under analysis as the primal problem. The primal can either be represented by a constrained maximization or a constrained minimization problem.

- If the primal is a constrained maximization problem, then the dual to this problem is a constrained minimization problem, and vice versa.

- In formulating the dual constrained maximization problem, the constraint used in the primal becomes the objective function in the dual, while the objective function used in the primal becomes the constraint in the dual.

- The optimal values of the decision variables in the primal problem are the same as those which optimize the dual.

- The optimal value of the Lagrangian multiplier, λ^*, which is computed by solving the primal problem, is equal to the reciprocal of the optimal value of the Lagrangian multiplier computed by solving the dual problem, λ^{D*}.

KEY TERMS

- constrained optimization
- Lagrangian function
- Lagrangian multiplier
- primal problem
- dual problem

EXERCISES

2.1 Assume a multivariate function of the form

$$y = 252x + 6xz - 3x^2 - 6z^2.$$

a. Determine the values of x and z that optimize the value of y.

b. What is the optimal value of y?

2.2 Using the same function given in exercise 2.1, assume a constraining relationship now exists between the independent variables. Specifically, assume a constraint of the form

$$x + z = 36.$$

a. Using the Lagrangian multiplier method, determine the values of x and z that optimize the value of y, given the constraint.

b. What is the optimal value of y?

c. How does the optimal value of y you computed in part b. compare with the optimal value of y you computed in exercise 2.1? Explain why these values are different.

2.3 a. Compute the value of λ^* associated with the constrained optimization problem in exercise 2.2.

b. Interpret the value of λ^* you computed in part a.

2.4 a. Using the Lagrangian multiplier method, determine the values of x and z that optimize the following constrained minimization problem.

Minimize $y = 5x^2 + 2xz + 3z^2$
subject to $x + 2z = 380$.

b. Determine the minimum value of y.

2.5 a. Determine the value of λ^* for the constrained optimization problem in exercise 2.4.

b. Is the constraint in this problem binding? Explain your response.

c. Interpret the value of λ^* you computed in part a. as it specifically applies to this problem.

2.6 a. Using the Lagrangian multiplier method, determine the values of x and z that optimize the following constrained maximization problem.

Maximize $y = 200\, x^{.5}\, z^{.5}$
subject to $10x + 5z = 1000$

b. What is the maximum value of y?

c. Determine the value of λ^* and interpret this value as it specifically applies in this problem.

2.7 a. State the dual to the constrained maximization problem in exercise 2.6.

b. What are the values of the decision variables, x and z, that optimize the dual problem?

c. Compare the value of λ^{D*}, associated with the dual problem, to the value of λ^* you computed in exercise 2.6 for the primal problem.

CHAPTER 3: UTILITY THEORY

SUMMARY

In Chapter 3, our focus is on developing the background and concepts related to consumer preferences. Initially, we establish the goal of a rational consumer, and specify the critical assumptions underlying her consumer preferences. Specifically, these are: completeness, transitivity, continuity, and for some cases, nonsatiation. Also discussed at the outset, are the two types of utility analyses: cardinal and ordinal. Once we develop the utility function, we mathematically and graphically derive the related utility and marginal utility curves. The concept and significance of diminishing marginal utility is also discussed at this point. We should note that these concepts are presented for utility functions exhibiting a bliss point and also for those reflecting nonsatiation.

Next, we focus on indifference curves, demonstrating their development both graphically and mathematically. Considerable attention is directed toward the negative of the slope of an indifference curve, or its associated marginal rate of substitution. This measure is developed mathematically, but with a particular emphasis on its conceptual significance regarding the role it plays regarding consumer choice. We should note that our initial analysis of consumer theory is cardinal in nature. However, once the marginal rate of substitution is developed, we discuss the importance of utility functions that are monotonic transformations of each other, and thus make the conversion to an ordinal analysis.

The remainder of this chapter is spent discussing the characteristics of indifference curves, specifically, that they are everywhere dense, non-intersecting, typically negatively sloped, and usually strictly convex toward the origin. The majority of this discussion focuses on the important implications of these characteristics regarding consumer choice. Finally, we present and analyze some of the important exceptions to some of these general characteristics. Notably, we discuss situations for which two goods represent perfect substitutes, perfect complements, and combinations where one good is desirable, and the other is considered undesirable. Some of this discussion regarding exceptions is relegated to the chapter appendices. In summary, this chapter provides much of the background for solving constrained utility optimization problems that we present in Chapter 4. The main topics covered in this chapter are summarized below.

- A utility function expresses the level of utility an individual receives in terms of the amounts of goods and services he consumes.
- Two methods of measuring consumer utility are cardinal utility analysis and ordinal utility analysis.
- Cardinal utility analysis assumes that a consumer has the ability to accurately measure the level of utility she receives from consuming a particular combination of goods and assign a actual (cardinal) number to it, measured in terms of a fictitious unit known as a util.

- Ordinal utility analysis is less restrictive than cardinal utility analysis, since ordinal utility analysis only requires an individual to rank consumption combinations from best to worst, rather than actually assigning a particular numerical value to the amount of utility he receives from consuming a combination of goods.

- A rational consumer uses all prevailing information to choose among various goods and services that yield the maximum amount of utility.

- In consumer theory, we assume that a rational consumer's preferences for goods and services abide by the axioms of completeness, transitivity, continuity, and in some cases, nonsatiation.

- The marginal utility of a good measures the change in a consumer's utility resulting from an infinitesimally small change in his consumption level of that good, while holding his consumption of all other goods constant.

- If we assume that a consumer chooses between two goods, X and Y, and her utility function is U = f (X,Y), then the marginal utility she derives from an additional unit of good X, while holding her consumption of good Y constant, denoted MU_X, is computed as the partial derivative of her utility function with respect for good X and is represented mathematically as $MU_X = \frac{\partial U}{\partial X}$.

- Given a consumer's utility function, U = f (X,Y), then the marginal utility a consumer receives from an additional unit of good Y, while holding her consumption of good X constant, denoted MU_Y, is computed as the partial derivative of her utility function with respect to good Y and is represented mathematically as $MU_Y = \frac{\partial U}{\partial Y}$.

- The marginal utilities of goods represent the partial slopes of the utility function.

- The law of diminishing marginal utility states that as an individual consumes additional units of a good, while holding his consumption of all other goods constant, the resulting increments to his utility will tend to diminish.

- An indifference curve is the set of combinations of two goods that yield the same level of utility to a consumer.

- An entire mapping of indifference curves, plotted in goods space, demonstrates that those indifference curves lying further to the "northeast" correspond to increasingly higher levels of utility since they contain larger combinations of goods, given the assumption that consumers always prefer more goods to less.

- The marginal rate of substitution, denoted MRS, measures the rate at which a consumer is willing to substitute units of one good for units of another good while maintaining the same level of utility.

- Mathematically, the marginal rate of substitution is defied as the negative of the slope of an indifference curve, or,

  $$MRS = \frac{-dY}{dX}.$$

- The marginal rate of substitution is also measured as the ratio of the marginal utility of good X to the marginal utility of good Y, or,

  $$MRS = \frac{MU_X}{MU_Y}.$$

- A positive monotonic transformation of a function is one that preserves the ordering associated with the original function.

- Indifference curves possess the following characteristics: they are everywhere dense, nonintersecting, typically negatively sloped, and usually strictly convex toward the origin.

- Two exceptions to the characteristic that indifference curves are negatively sloped occur when two goods are perfect complements, or when one of the two goods the consumer chooses between is an economic "bad".

- When two goods are perfect complements, the associated indifference curves are L-shaped.

- When one of the two goods a consumer chooses is an economic "bad", the associated indifference curves are positively sloped.

- An exception to the strict convexity characteristic of indifference curves occurs when the two goods are perfect substitutes.

- When two goods are perfect substitutes the associated indifference curves are downward sloping, but linear, therefore the marginal rate of substitution does not diminish as more units of one good are substituted for the other good, while maintaining the same level of utility.

- Ridge lines for an indifference curve contain combinations of goods, such as X and Y, where the marginal utility of good X or the marginal utility of good Y is equal to zero. These ridge lines designate the economically meaningful ranges of an indifference curve, where $MU_X > 0$ and $MU_Y > 0$, from those ranges of an indifference curve that a rational consumer would not choose to consume goods combinations.

KEY TERMS

- cardinal utility
- indifference curves
- law of diminishing marginal utility

- marginal rate of substitution
- marginal utility
- ordinal utility
- positive monotonic transformation
- rational consumer
- ridge lines for an indifference curve mapping
- util
- utility
- utility curve
- utility function

EXERCISES

3.1 Steve consumes soda pop, X, and pizza, Y, and his utility function is $U = 160X^{.25}Y^{.75}$.

a. Determine Steve's marginal utility function for soda pop.

b. Determine Steve's marginal utility function for pizza.

c. Does Steve's marginal utility from soda pop consumption diminish as he consumes more soda pop? Justify your response mathematically.

d. Does Steve's marginal utility from pizza consumption diminish as he consumes more pizza? Justify your response mathematically.

3.2 Refer to Steve's utility function in exercise 3.1.

a. Determine Steve's marginal rate of substitution of soda pop for pizza.

b. Does Steve's marginal rate of substitution of soda pop for pizza diminish as he substitutes more soda pop for pizza? Justify your response mathematically.

c. Determine the value of Steve's marginal rate of substitution when he consumes 2 sodas and 12 pizzas.

d. Interpret the value of Steve's marginal rate of substitution you computed in part c., as it specifically applies in this problem.

3.3 Donna consumes shoes, X, and dresses, Y, and her utility function is $U = 20X^{.5}Y^{.5}$.

a. Determine Donna's marginal rate of substitution of shoes for dresses.

b. Plot Donna's indifference curve when she is consuming three alternative combinations of shoes and dresses that give her 40 units of utility.

c. Determine the value of Donna's marginal rate of substitution of shoes for dresses at each of the three points you plotted on her indifference curve in part b. Does Donna's marginal rate of substitution of shoes for dresses diminish?

3.4 Samantha consumes steak, X, and lobster, Y, where her utility function is $U = 200X + 800Y$.

a. Determine Samantha's marginal utility of steak. Does her marginal utility diminish as she consumes additional units of steak? Justify your response mathematically.

b. Determine Samantha's marginal utility of lobster. Does her marginal utility diminish as she consumes additional units of lobster? Justify your response mathematically.

3.5 Refer to Samantha's utility function in exercise 3.4.

a. Determine Samantha's marginal rate of substitution of steak for lobster, and interpret this value as it specifically applies to Samantha.

b. Does Samantha's marginal rate of substitution of steak for lobster diminish as she substitutes more steak for lobster? Justify your response mathematically.

c. Plot Samantha's indifference curve when she receives 2400 units of utility from consuming alternative combinations of steak and lobster.

3.6 Olga derives utility from consuming soft pretzels, X, and packs of mustard, Y. She only receives utility from consuming each soft pretzel with two packs of mustard.

a. Mathematically state Olga's utility function.

b. What type of relationship exists between soft pretzels and packs of mustard for Olga?

c. Plot Olga's indifference curve when she receives 16 units of utility from consuming alternative combinations of soft pretzels and packs of mustard.

d. Does Olga receive more utility from consuming 3 pretzels and 8 packs of mustard than from consuming 3 pretzels and 6 packs of mustard? Justify your response mathematically.

3.7 George consumes cheddar cheese, X, and broccoli, Y, where his utility function is $U = 5X - 15Y$.

a. Determine George' s marginal utility from consuming cheddar cheese and interpret this value as it specifically applies to him.

b. Determine George's marginal utility from consuming broccoli and interpret this value as it specifically applies to him.

c. How does George regard these goods?

d. Plot George's indifference curve that contains the goods combination of 6 units of cheddar cheese and one unit of broccoli. Also determine the level of utility he receives when he consumes this combination of goods.

3.8 Why do economists typically use strictly convex indifference curves to analyze consumer behavior?

CHAPTER 4: CONSUMER OPTIMIZATION

SUMMARY

Our primary focus in Chapter 4 is on developing and solving the fundamental constrained optimization problems faced by a typical consumer. Specifically, these are the constrained utility maximization problems, that we treat as the primal, and the expenditure minimization problem, that we consider to be the dual. At the outset of this chapter, we develop a consumer's budget equation, treating it as a constraint. Next, we mathematically and graphically demonstrate the various shifts and rotations of this constraint caused by changes in a consumer's income and by changes in the prices of the goods included in the constraint.

Once we have familiarized the student with the budget constraint, we use it, along with the utility functions and associated indifference curves that were introduced in Chapter 3, to solve the consumer's constrained utility maximization problem. In this problem, we treat the consumer's utility function as the objective function and the budget equation as the constraint. This analysis is first conducted intuitively and graphically to demonstrate that a constrained utility maximum is achieved by an individual selecting amounts of two goods where the marginal rate of substitution between these two goods is equal to the ratio of their prices. Next, we demonstrate how to solve this problem using the method of Lagrangian multipliers, generating and interpreting solution values for the consumption levels of the two goods, the utility index, and the Lagrangian multiplier itself. Two numerical problems are solved, where the second involves an additive utility function such that the solution values for the goods contain the prices of both goods, as well as income. We have solved such a problem in order to lay the groundwork for the derivation of both own-price and cross-price demand curves, as well as Engel curves, that is conducted in Chapter 5. The main topics covered in this chapter are summarized below.

- A consumer's budget equation represents the set of combinations of goods an individual can purchase, given the predetermined prices of the goods and his predetermined level of money income, where the individual's expenditures on these goods is exactly equal to his money income.

- Given that a consumer can choose to buy goods X and Y, where the predetermined unit prices of these goods are $\overline{P}_{X,1}$ and $\overline{P}_{Y,1}$, respectively, and his predetermined money income is denoted $\overline{I}_1$, then this consumer's budget equation is expressed mathematically as $\overline{P}_{X,1}X + \overline{P}_{Y,1}Y = \overline{I}_1$.

- A consumer's budget set represents the set of combinations of goods that are affordable to the individual, given the predetermined prices of the goods and his predetermined level of money income, where his expenditures on these goods is either less than or equal to his money income.

- Given that a consumer can choose to buy goods X and Y, where the predetermined unit prices of these goods are $\overline{P}_{X,1}$ and $\overline{P}_{Y,1}$, respectively, and his predetermined money income is denoted $\overline{I}_1$, then this consumer's budget set is expressed mathematically as $\overline{P}_{X,1}X+\overline{P}_{Y,1}Y\leq\overline{I}_1$.

- An increase in a consumer's income, *ceteris paribus*, causes his budget equation to shift to the right in a parallel fashion, thereby increasing the size of his budget set.

- A decrease in a consumer's income, *ceteris paribus*, causes his budget equation to shift to the left in a parallel fashion, thereby decreasing the size of his budget set.

- A change in the price of one of the two goods a consumer can buy, *ceteris paribus*, will alter the slope of the budget equation, $\frac{-\overline{P}_{X,1}}{\overline{P}_{Y,1}}$, as well as the one of the two intercept values.

- An increase (decrease) in the price of good X, *ceteris paribus*, makes the budget equation steeper (flatter).

- An increase (decrease) in the price of good Y, *ceteris paribus*, makes the budget equation flatter (steeper).

- In the primal, constrained optimization problem of the consumer, the goal of the consumer is to determine the consumption levels of goods that yield the maximum amount of utility while exhausting the consumer's predetermined level of money income, given the predetermined prices of the goods.

- The primal, constrained utility maximization problem of the consumer is stated mathematically as

  Maximize U = U (X,Y)

  subject to $\overline{P}_{X,1}X+\overline{P}_{Y,1}Y=\overline{I}_1$.

- In the dual to the consumer's constrained utility maximization problem, the goal of the consumer is to determine the consumption levels of goods that minimize her expenditures while yielding a predetermined level of utility.

- The dual, constrained expenditure minimization problem of the consumer is stated mathematically as

  Minimize E = $\overline{P}_{X,1}X+\overline{P}_{Y,1}Y$

  subject to $\overline{U}_1=U(X,Y)$.

- The necessary condition that must be satisfied at the optimal goods combination, (X^*,Y^*), for both the primal and dual consumer constrained optimization problems, states that the marginal rate of substitution for these goods must equal the ratio of their prices.

- The necessary condition for the consumer's primal and the dual constrained optimization problems is expressed mathematically as

$$\text{MRS} = \frac{\overline{P}_{X,1}}{\overline{P}_{Y,1}}.$$

KEY TERMS

- budget equation
- budget set

EXERCISES

4.1 Dave has $12 to spend on popcorn, good X, and peanuts, good Y.

a. If the unit price of popcorn is $1.00 and the unit price of peanuts is $1.50, formulate and plot Dave's budget equation.

b. Assume the unit price of peanuts increases to $2.00, *ceteris paribus*. Formulate Dave's new budget equation and plot it in the graph you drew in part a.

c. Assume Dave's income triples and the prices of the goods are the same as those reported in part a. What effect will this change in Dave's income have on his budget equation and his budget set?

4.2 Assume initially a consumer faces the following income and prices for goods X and Y, respectively, $\overline{I}_1 = \$80{,}000,\ \overline{P}_{X,1} = \$100,\ and\ \overline{P}_{Y,1} = \$500.$

a. Mathematically state the consumer's budget equation and the consumer's budget set.

b. What are the values of the slope, and X- and Y- intercepts of the budget constraint?

c. What will be the effect on the consumer's budget equation and budget set, if, simultaneously his income is reduced by one-half and the prices of goods X and Y are reduced by one-half? Justify your response mathematically.

4.3 Jan's utility function for goods X and Y is

$$U = 7200X^{.75}Y^{.25}.$$

She must pay $90 for a unit of good X and $30 for a unit of good Y. Jan's income is $1200.

a. Determine the amounts of goods X and Y Jan purchases to maximize her utility given her budget constraint.

b. Determine the maximum amount of utility Jan receives.

c. Determine the value of λ^* associated with this problem.

d. Interpret the value of λ^* you computed in part c. as it specifically applies to Jan.

4.4 a. Formulate the dual constrained expenditure minimization problem associated with 4.3 and determine the optimal amounts of goods X and Y Jan should purchase.

b. Determine the minimum amount of expenditure made by Jan.

c. Determine the optimal value of λ^D and provide a written interpretation of this value as it specifically applies to Jan in this problem.

d. Compare the optimal values of X, Y, and λ you computed in exercise 4.3 with those you computed in parts a. and c. of this exercise.

4.5 Matt derives utility from consuming bacon, good X, and eggs, good Y, where his utility function is

$$U = \text{minimum}\left(\frac{X}{4}, \frac{Y}{1}\right).$$

Assume Matt's income is $360 and that he must pay $1.00 for each egg and $0.50 for each slice of bacon.

a. Determine the optimal amounts of eggs and bacon Matt should buy to maximize his utility given his budget constraint.

b. Determine the maximum amount of utility Matt receives.

4.6 Stewart derives utility from his consumption of mozzarella cheese, good X, and cheddar cheese, good Y, where his utility function is

$$U = 140X + 140Y.$$

Stewart must pay $4 for each unit of mozzarella cheese and $2 for each unit of cheddar cheese. He has $280 in income to spend on these goods.

a. How does Stewart regard these goods?

b. Determine the amounts of mozzarella cheese and cheddar cheese Stewart should buy to maximize his utility given his budget constraint.

c. What is the maximum level of utility Stewart can attain?

4.7 Refer to exercise 4.6. In the same graph, plot Stewart's budget constraint and the indifference curve associated with the maximum amount of utility he receives. Also indicate his optimal combination of goods in the graph.

CHAPTER 5: INDIVIDUAL DEMAND FUNCTIONS AND RELATED TOPICS

SUMMARY

Our focus in Chapter 5 is on the development of individual demand functions. More specifically, we extend our interpretation of the results generated by the consumer's constrained optimization process to derive individual Engel, own-price demand, and cross-price demand curves. Initially, we allow income to vary, while holding the prices of the goods constant, to develop an income consumption curve and its related Engel curve. We also discuss the implications of the slope of the Engel curve regarding whether a good is normal or inferior, and even more specifically, if the good is a luxury or a necessity.

Next, we allow the price of one of the goods to vary, *ceteris paribus*, and by so doing, derive a price consumption curve and its associated own-price demand curve. Then, we decompose the effects of a change in the price of a good on the quantity demanded of that good, into the associated substitution and income effects. This decomposition is demonstrated for normal, inferior, but not Giffen, and Giffen goods. Although the majority of this analysis is done graphically, we also rely on the mathematical development of compensated demand curves, demonstrated in Chapter 4, to derive the expenditure function. Ultimately, this enables us to develop the Slutsky equation and demonstrate substitution and income effects mathematically. We should note that this mathematical analysis is presented in sections that are considered optional.

The remainder of the chapter is devoted to developing and analyzing cross-price demand curves by focusing on the relationship between the quantity demanded of a good and the price of another. This analysis is conducted both graphically and mathematically. We give considerable attention to discussing goods that are either gross substitutes or gross complements, and describe how these relationships are reflected by the slopes of the cross-price demand curves. The mathematical decomposition of cross-price demand curves by applying the Slutsky equation is reserved for an appendix. In addition, another appendix is provided to discuss net substitutes and net complements, since this analysis must be accomplished mathematically. The main topics covered in this chapter are as follows.

- A consumer's demand function expresses her optimal level of consumption of a good, also known as the quantity demanded of a good, in terms of the prices of all goods in the constrained utility maximization problem, and her money income.

- If a consumer chooses optimal amounts of only two goods, X and Y, the individual's demand functions for goods X and Y are, respectively,

  $$X^* = X(P_X, P_Y, I)$$

  and

  $$Y^* = Y(P_X, P_Y, I).$$

- An income consumption curve represents the set of combinations of goods corresponding to constrained utility maximum solutions for different levels of money income, while holding the price of the good constant.

- An Engel curve expresses an individual's optimal consumption level of a good for different levels of his income, while holding the prices of all goods constant.

- If the consumer chooses optimal amounts of two goods, X and Y, his Engel curve for good X is expressed as

$$X = X\left(\overline{P}_{X,1}, \overline{P}_{Y,1}, I\right),$$

and his Engel curve for good Y is expressed as

$$Y = Y\left(\overline{P}_{X,1}, \overline{P}_{Y,1}, I\right).$$

- The slope of an Engel curve indicates whether the good under analysis is normal or inferior.

- If the slope of the Engel curve for good X is positive, $\frac{\partial X}{\partial I} > 0$, then good X is normal and the consumer's optimal consumption level of good X increases as the consumer's income rises.

- If the slope of the Engel curve for good X is negative, $\frac{\partial X}{\partial I} < 0$, then good X is inferior and the consumer's optimal consumption level of good X decreases as the consumer's income rises.

- A price consumption curve represents the set of optimal combinations of goods corresponding to alternative levels of the price of one of the two goods, while holding the price of the other good and the consumer's money income constant.

- An individual's own-price demand curve relates the quantity demanded of a good as a function of its own price, while holding the prices of the other goods and the consumer's money income constant.

- If a consumer chooses optimal amounts of two goods, X and Y, his own-price demand curve for good X is

$$X = X\left(P_X, \overline{P}_{Y,1}, \overline{I}_1\right),$$

and his own-price demand curve for good Y is

$$Y = Y\left(\overline{P}_{X,1}, P_Y, \overline{I}_1\right).$$

- The total effect of a change in the price of a good on the optimal consumption level of that good can be separated into its two subcomponents, the substitution effect and the income effect.

- The substitution effect measures the impact that a change in the own-price of a good has on the quantity demanded of that good due solely to the resulting change in the relative prices of the goods.

- The substitution effect reflects the tendency for a consumer to substitute away from the good that is becoming relatively more expensive in favor of the good that is becoming relatively cheaper.

- The income effect measures the impact that a change in the own price of a good has on the quantity demanded of that good due to the resulting change in the consumer's real income.

- The directionality of the income effect depends on whether the good is normal or inferior.

- If a good is normal then a decrease (increase) in the own-price of the good causes the consumer's real income to rise (fall) thereby inducing him to buy more (fewer) units of the good.

- If a good is inferior then a decrease (increase) in the own-price of the good causes the consumer's real income to rise (fall) thereby inducing him to buy fewer (more) units of the good.

- A good that is exceptionally inferior is known as a Giffen good. In this rare case, the income effect dominates the substitution effect.

- An individual's compensated demand function expresses his optimal consumption level of a good, also known as the quantity demanded of a good, in terms of its own-price, the prices of the other goods, and the individual's level of utility.

- If a consumer chooses optimal amounts of two goods, X and Y, his compensated demand function for good X is
  $$X' = X(P_X, P_Y, U),$$
  and his compensated demand function for good Y is
  $$Y' = Y(P_X, P_Y, U).$$

- An individual's expenditure function expresses her expenditures, say on goods X and Y, as a function of the prices of these goods and her level of utility, stated mathematically as
  $$E = E(P_X, P_Y, U).$$

- The Slutsky equation is used to mathematically decompose the total effect of a change in the price of a good on the quantity demanded of that good, into the summation of the subsequent substitution and income effects.

- A cross-price demand curve expresses the quantity demanded of a good as a function of the price of another good, while holding the own-price of the good and the consumer's money income constant.

- If a consumer chooses optimal amounts of two goods, X and Y, the cross-price demand curve for good X is expressed as

$$X = X\left(\overline{P}_{X,1}, P_Y, \overline{I}_1\right),$$

and the cross-price demand curve for good Y is expressed as

$$Y = Y\left(P_X, \overline{P}_{Y,1}, \overline{I}_1\right).$$

- Two goods are gross substitutes (complements) if the quantity demanded of one good is directly (inversely) related to the price of the other good, while holding its own-price and the consumer's money income constant.

- Two goods are net substitutes (complements) if the quantity demanded of one good is directly (inversely) related to the price of the other good, while holding its own-price and the consumer's utility constant.

KEY TERMS

- compensated demand curve
- compensated demand function
- cross-price demand curve
- demand function
- Engel curve
- expenditure function
- Giffen good
- gross complements
- gross substitutes
- income consumption curve
- income effect
- individual's own-price demand curve
- inferior good
- net complements
- net substitutes
- normal good
- price consumption curve
- Slutsky equation
- substitution effect

EXERCISES

5.1 Raymond derives utility from consuming goods X and Y, where his utility function is

$$U = 80X^{.25}Y^{.25}.$$

He spends all of his income, I, on his purchases of goods X and Y, and he must pay prices of P_X and P_Y for each unit of these goods, respectively. Assume that his income is $3200, the unit price of good X is $100, and the unit price of good Y is $100.

a. Determine the amounts of goods X and Y that Raymond should purchase to maximize his utility given his budget constraint.

b. Determine the maximum amount of utility Raymond can receive.

5.2 Refer to your response to exercise 5.1.

a. Derive Raymond's own-price demand curve for good X.

b. Derive Raymond's own-price demand curve for good Y.

5.3 Refer to your responses to exercise 5.1.

a. Derive Raymond's Engel curve for good X.

b. Is good X a normal good or an inferior good? Justify your response mathematically.

c. Derive Raymond's Engel curve for good Y.

d. Is good Y a normal good or an inferior good? Justify your response mathematically.

5.4 Assume an individual's own-price demand function for good X is

$$X = X(P_X, P_Y, I) = 200 - 4P_X - 1.5P_Y + 0.008I$$

where P_X and P_Y denote the unit prices of goods X and Y, respectively, and I denotes the consumer's money income.

a. Compute the individual's cross-price demand curve for good X when the unit price of good X is $2 and the consumer's income is $40,000.

b. Are goods X and Y gross substitutes or gross complements? Justify your response mathematically.

5.5 Recall from exercise 5.1 Raymond's utility function, when he consumes goods X and Y, is

$$U = 80X^{.25}\,Y^{.25}.$$

Once again, assume the unit price of good X, P_X, is $100, and the unit price of good Y, P_Y, is $100. Determine the quantities of goods X and Y Raymond should purchase that will minimize his expenditures on these goods and yield 320 units of utility to him.

5.6 Refer to your response to exercise 5.5.

a. Determine Raymond's compensated demand curve for good X.

b. Determine Raymond's compensated demand curve for good Y.

5.7 a. Using strictly convex indifference curves and linear budget constraints graphically illustrate the substitution, income, and total effects of an increase in the price of good X, which is an inferior, but not a Giffen good.

b. In a graph, beneath the one you drew in part a., derive the individual's corresponding own-price demand curve for good X.

5.8 Is it possible for an individual's demand curve for a good to be positively sloped? Support your response with an appropriate graphical analysis.

CHAPTER 6: MARKET DEMAND CURVES

SUMMARY

This is a relatively short chapter in which we have focused on generating the market wide counterparts to the individual Engel, own-price, and cross-price demand curves derived in Chapter 5. More specifically, we demonstrate the process of constructing a market own-price demand curve from a set of individual such curves with the understanding that similar processes can be conducted for Engel and cross-price demand curves. Initially, we demonstrate, both graphically and mathematically, a basic horizontal summation process of individual own-price demand curves to derive the market own-price demand curve. Once this is accomplished, we stress the point that this simple process reflects our assumption that consumers' preferences and quantities demanded of a good are independent of one another.

Next, we introduce the concept of a network externality by analyzing a bandwagon effect, where one consumer's quantity demanded of a good is directly related to another consumers consumption level of that good. Using both a graphical and mathematical analysis, we derive a market own-price demand curve, employing this assumption of a bandwagon effect. Afterward, we make a comparison of the results generated by a horizontal summation process that includes a bandwagon effect to those results generated in its absence. Within the context of this comparison, we pay special attention to the different slopes associated with the two different market own-price demand curves.

Finally, we briefly discuss another type of network externality, specifically, a snob effect, noting how the introduction of this effect impacts the market own-price demand curve in a manner opposite to that we have demonstrated for the bandwagon effect. The primary topics presented in this chapter are as follows.

- An individual's demand function for a good expresses her quantity demanded of that good in terms of the own-price of the good, the price of another good(s), and the individual's income.

- By holding constant all but one independent variable in a demand function, we can derive relationships between the quantity demanded of a good and its own price, the price of other goods, and a consumer's income. These resulting curves are known as an own-price demand curve, a cross-price demand curve, and an Engel curve, respectively.

- The market own-price demand curve for good X, X_m, can be derived by summing the quantities demanded by all consumers of good X at alternative prices for the good.

- A network externality exists when some consumers' own-price demand for a good are dependent on other consumers' demand for that good. Two types of network externalities are the bandwagon and snob effects.

- If some consumers' quantities demanded of a good are directly related to other individuals' consumption levels of that good, then a bandwagon effect exists. Graphically, a bandwagon effect alters the slope of the own-price market demand curve by making it less steep and thus more quantity-price sensitive.

- A snob effect exists if, as some consumers change their quantities demanded of a good, others will change their quantities demanded of that good in the opposite direction so as to avoid being identified with the consumption choices of the other consumers. Graphically, a snob effect influences the own-price market demand curve by making it steeper, and therefore less quantity-price sensitive, than a market own-price curve not containing a snob effect.

KEY TERMS

- bandwagon effect
- market own-price demand curve
- snob effect

EXERCISES

6.1 Suppose the market for good X consists of two consumers, designated 1 and 2, where their respective individual own-price demand curves for good X are

$$X^D_1 = 200 - 2P_X \text{ for } P_X \leq 100$$

and

$$X^D_2 = 100 - 4P_X \text{ for } P_X \leq 25.$$

The terms X_1 and X_2 are the quantities of good X demanded by consumers 1 and 2, and P_X represents the price of good X.

a. Determine the market own-price demand curve, $X^{D,M}$, for good X.

b. If $P_X = \$20$, compute the quantities of this good demanded by each consumer. Also, compute the market quantity demanded at this price.

6.2 Refer to the information provided in exercise 6.1.

a. Derive the inverse own-price demand curves for consumers 1 and 2. Also, determine the inverse market own-price demand curve for the market own-price demand curve that you developed in exercise 6.1

b. Determine the price, P_X, and market quantity demanded, $X^{d,M}$, intercepts of this inverse market own-price demand curve, as well as its slope.

6.3 Refer to the information provided, as well as your computations, in exercises 6.1 and 6.2.

a. Illustrate the inverse market own-price demand curve.

b. Observe, this curve has a kink in it. Why? At what output-price combination does this kink occur?

6.4 Assume the market for good X consists of two consumers designated 1 and 2, where their respective individual own-price demand curves for good X are

$$X^D{}_1 = 200 - 2P_X \text{ for } P_X \leq 100$$
$$X^D{}_2 = 100 - 4P_X + X_1 \text{ for } P_X \leq 25$$

and

$$X^D{}_2 = 0 \text{ for } P_X > 25,$$

where X_1 and X_2 are the quantities demanded for good X by consumer's 1 and 2 respectively, and P_X is the price of good X.

a. What type of effect has been introduced into the analysis? Explain.

b. Compute the market own-price demand curve in this case.

6.5 Refer to the information given in exercise 6.4. However, now assume that the own-price demand curve for individual 2 is

$$X^D_2 = 100 - 4P_X + X_1 \text{ for } P_X \leq 25$$

and

$$X^D_2 = X_1 \text{ for } P_X > 25.$$

Note the qualifier that $X^D_2 = 0$ for $P_X > 25$ has been removed. Now compute the market own-price demand curve. Explain the difference between this curve and the one you derived in exercise 6.4.

6.6 What is a network externality? How does this term relate to the concepts of bandwagon and snob effects? Give some real world examples.

CHAPTER 7: DEMAND-RELATED ELASTICITIES

SUMMARY

Our focus in this chapter is on developing the elasticities associated with the market wide demand function constructed in Chapter 6. These are the own-price, income, and cross-price elasticities, corresponding to the own-price demand, Engel, and cross-price demand curves, respectively. Initially, we discuss the concept of an elasticity in general, demonstrating how it represents a modification of a slope coefficient that links two variables. We stress the advantage of using an elasticity over a slope coefficient, in that an elasticity value is independent of the units of measurement.

The first elasticity presented is the own-price elasticity of demand. After deriving the associated working formula, we discuss the interpretation corresponding to the different potential values of such an elasticity. Specifically, we discuss the meaning of elastic, unitary, and inelastic own-price demand. We also separate those own-price demand curves that yield a constant elasticity from those possessing a variable elasticity. The related topics of total and marginal revenue associated with the sales of a good are introduced and related to the own-price elasticity concept. Then, we provide a lengthy discussion of the determinants underlying different elasticity values for different goods, and also include some tables containing real world computations of these elasticities for different types of goods.

Next, we derive the formula for an income elasticity and demonstrate how it is related to an Engel curve. This concept is demonstrated for both Engel curves possessing constant elasticities and those yielding variable elasticities. Special attention is paid to the various interpretations of the computed values of these elasticities, thus enabling us to classify goods as either normal or inferior, as well as luxuries or necessities. Again, we provide a table containing some real world calculations of income elasticities for various goods.

Finally, we derive the formula for a cross-price elasticity and demonstrate how this concept relates to a cross-price demand curve. A discussion of how the sign and magnitude of these computed values can be used to classify goods as either gross substitutes or gross complements is provided. Once again, we include a table containing some real world calculations of cross-price elasticities for various goods, in order to demonstrate the applicability of this concept. The main topics covered in the chapter are summarized below.

- Own-price elasticity of demand measures the percentage change in the quantity demanded of a good resulting from a percentage change in the price of that good.

- The own-price elasticity of demand for a good, such as good X, denoted E_{X,P_X}, is mathematically stated as

$$E_{X,P_X} = \left|\frac{\%\partial X}{\%\partial P_X}\right| = \left|\frac{\partial X}{\partial P_X}\frac{P_X}{X}\right|.$$

- If $E_{X,P_X} > 1$ then we classify demand for good X as unit elastic, meaning that for some percentage change in the price of good X, there is an equivalent percentage change in the quantity demanded of good X in the opposite direction.

- If $E_{X,P_X} < 1$ then we classify demand for good X as inelastic, meaning that for some percentage change in the price of good X, there is a smaller percentage change in the quantity demanded of good X in the opposite direction.

- Along a negatively sloped linear demand curve the value of the own-price elasticity of demand varies. At the midpoint of the demand curve $E_{X,P_X} = 1$. For values of X and P_X that lie above the midpoint, $E_{X,P_X} > 1$ and for values of X and P_X that lie below the midpoint $E_{X,P_X} < 1$.

- Along a constant elasticity own-price demand curve, the value of E_{X,P_X} is independent of the values of X and P_X.

- Total revenue, TR, is the value of consumers' expenditures associated with the sale of a good.

- The total revenue associated with the sale of good X, TR_X, is expressed mathematically as $TR_X = P_X X$.

- Marginal revenue, MR, measures the change in total revenue resulting from a change in the quantity of that good sold.

- The marginal revenue associated with an infinitesimally small change in the sales of good X is represented mathematically as $MR_X = \frac{dTR_X}{dX}$.

- In the elastic range of a demand curve, marginal revenue is positive, and total revenue increases (decreases) as the price of the good decreases (increases).

- When demand is unit elastic, marginal revenue equals zero and total revenue is maximized.

- In the inelastic range of a demand curve, marginal revenue is negative and total revenue decreases (increases) as the price of the good decreases (increases).

- The own-price elasticity of demand for a good is affected by the availability and closeness of substitutes for the product, the length of the time period under analysis, and the percentage of households' total expenditures attributed to that particular good.

- Income elasticity, $E_{X,I}$, measures the percentage change in the quantity demanded of a good resulting from a percentage change in consumers' money income.

- The income elasticity of good X is stated mathematically as $E_{X,I} = \frac{\%\partial X}{\%\partial I} = \frac{\partial X}{\partial I}\frac{I}{X}$.
- If $E_{X,I} > 0$ we categorize the good as normal.
- A subcategory of a normal good is known as a luxury good, when $E_{X,I} > 1$.
- The other subcategory of a normal good pertains to $0 \leq E_{X,I} \leq 1$, where we categorize the good as a necessity.
- If $E_{X,I} < 0$ then the good is classified as inferior.
- The cross-price elasticity of demand, E_{X,P_Y}, measures the change in the quantity demanded in good X resulting from a percentage change in the price of good Y.
- If $E_{X,P_Y} > 0$ then we classify goods X and Y as gross substitutes.
- If $E_{X,P_Y} < 0$ then we classify goods X and Y as gross complements.

KEY TERMS

- cross-price elasticity of demand
- elastic
- elasticity
- income elasticity
- inelastic
- marginal revenue
- own-price elasticity of demand
- total revenue
- unit elastic

EXERCISES

7.1 Assume you are an economic analyst for United Airlines. Using your knowledge of own-price elasticity of demand, suggest three pricing strategies for the airline that will increase the company's total revenue.

7.2 The annual market own-price demand function for good X is estimated as

$X = 142 - 5.0\ P_X - I - 3.5\ P_Y$

where

X = quantity demanded of good X in units/year

P_X = price of good X in dollars/unit

I = per capita income in dollars/year

P_Y = price of good Y in dollars/unit.

a. Calculate the market own-price demand curve when $I = 25$ and $P_Y = 12$.

b. Using your results from part a. calculate the quantity of good X demanded in the market when $P_X = 10$.

c. Calculate the own-price elasticity of demand for good X when $P_X = 10$, $P_Y = 12$, and $I = 25$.

d. Interpret the value of own-price elasticity of demand calculated in part c.

e. Refer to your response to part c. Would it be a rational business decision for a revenue maximizing seller of good X to increase the price of this good? Explain your response.

7.3 Refer to the market own-price demand curve for good X in exercise 7.2.

a. Calculate the cross-price elasticity of demand for good X assuming $P_X = 10$, $P_Y = 12$, and $I = 15$.

b. Interpret the value of cross-price elasticity of demand you computed in part a.

c. How can a seller of goods X and Y use the cross-price elasticity of demand value you calculated in part a?

7.4 Refer to the market own-price demand curve in exercise 7.2.

a. Calculate the income elasticity when $P_X = 10$, $P_Y = 12$, and $I = 25$.

b. Interpret the value of income elasticity you calculated in part a.

c. How can a seller of good X use the income elasticity value you calculated in part a.?

7.5 Assume the market own-price demand curve for good Z is
$Z = 1000 - 100\ P_Z$,
where Z denotes the market quantity demanded of good Z and P_Z represents the own-price of good Z.

a. At what values of P_Z and Z is the value of own price elasticity of demand equal to one?

b. What is the value of marginal revenue when $E_{Z,P_Z} = 1$?

c. What is the maximum amount of total revenue that can be earned from the sale of good Z?

7.6 Assume the market own-price demand curve for good W is
$W = 500P_W^{-1}$,
where W denotes the market quantity demanded of good W, and P_W is the unit price of this good.

a. Determine the value of own-price elasticity of demand for good W.

b. Interpret the value of own-price elasticity you computed in part a.

c. Using your result from part a., determine the value of marginal revenue.

d. Does the value of marginal revenue vary as the price of good W changes? Justify your response mathematically.

7.7 Assume the cross-price demand curve for good X is

$X = 8P_Y^2$,

where X denotes the market quantity demanded of good X and P_Y is the unit price of good Y.

a. Determine the value of cross-price elasticity.

b. Interpret the value of cross-price elasticity you computed in part a.

c. How are goods X and Y related? Justify your response using the value of cross-price elasticity you computed in part a.

7.8 The Engel curve for good Y is

$$Y = 2 + 2I^{.5}.$$

a. Determine the income elasticity of good Y.

b. If I = $1 (in thousands of dollars), what is the value of the income elasticity of good Y.

c. When I = $1 (in thousands of dollars) is Y a normal good or an inferior good? Also, if good Y is a normal good, is it a luxury good or a necessity? Justify your response mathematically.

CHAPTER 8: PRODUCTION IN THE SHORT RUN

SUMMARY

Chapter 8 is the first of five chapters that we have devoted to the theory of the firm. The initial part of this chapter dwells on defining the concepts of a production function, fixed versus variable inputs, technology, and the short and long run time periods. After these preliminaries are discussed, in the remainder of this chapter we focus on a firm's production in the short run. Accordingly, we treat one of the firm's inputs as fixed, and develop total product of input curves. Although these curves are derived for both inputs, our major focus is on treating capital as the fixed input and labor as the variable input. Next, we develop marginal and average product functions, both graphically and mathematically, carefully establishing the relationship between these two types of functions, as well as the relationships between each of these functions and the total product curve from which they are derived. In addition, we define the law of diminishing marginal productivity and explain its significance as it relates to a firm's input usage. Finally, we employ the marginal and average product functions to define the three stages of production regarding the use of an input and to provide a rationale as to the stage in which a rational firm will choose to operate. The main topics presented in this chapter are as follows.

- We assume that firms act rationally, employing all relevant information, when engaging in the production of goods and services for the purpose of generating revenue and profit. Therefore, the rational firm is expected to use inputs such as labor, land, and capital in the most efficient manner in order to maximize its profits.

- Another important factor affecting a firm's production of output is the state of technology, defined as society's pool of knowledge concerning the industrial arts.

- A production function expresses the maximum quantity of output that can be produced when employing various combinations of inputs, given the prevailing state of technology. Assuming only two inputs, capital, K, and labor, L, a production function for some output, Q, can be mathematically represented as $Q = f(K,L)$.

- Depending upon whether the firm has sufficient time to vary some of its inputs, it is possible to categorize inputs as being either fixed or variable. In particular, a fixed input cannot be altered by a firm during the time period under analysis, while a variable input can be changed during the time period under consideration. Over relatively shorter time periods, it is typically convention to regard capital as a fixed input and labor as a variable input. Moreover, as the length of the time period under analysis becomes longer, the greater will be the number of variable inputs.

- In economic analysis, it has become convention to designate time into two distinct periods, the short run and the long run. Specifically, the short run is a time period during which at least one of a firm's inputs remains fixed, whereas the long run is a sufficiently long enough period of time whereby all inputs used by the firm are variable.

- A total product curve expresses the maximum level of output, or total product, which can be produced by a firm as a function of one variable input, while holding all other inputs and the state of technology constant. Since at least one input, typically capital, is held constant, the concept of the total product of labor is applied only to the short run. Mathematically, the total product of labor curve, TP_L, is derived from the production function, Q = f (K,L), by setting capital constant at some level. For example, if capital is fixed at the level $\overline{K}_1$, then the total product of labor curve may be expressed as $TP_L = Q = f\left(\overline{K}_1, L\right)$. If the amount of capital is held constant a higher level, say $\overline{K}_2$, then the total product of labor curve shifts upward to the right.

- The marginal product of an input measures the change in the production of output, or total product, arising from a change in the use of that input, while holding all other inputs and technology constant. If capital is held constant and the level of labor use is allowed to vary, then the marginal product of labor, MP_L, is computed as $MP_L = \frac{\partial Q}{\partial L} = \frac{dTP_L}{dL}$. *The* marginal product of labor also measures the slope of the total product of labor curve. Analogously, the marginal product of capital, MP_K, is computed by holding labor use constant, while varying capital, and determining the effect on output, hence, $MP_K = \frac{\partial Q}{\partial K} = \frac{dTP_K}{dK}$.

- The level of labor use where TP_L reaches a maximum corresponds to the level of labor at which the marginal product of labor is equal to zero.

- The Law of Diminishing Marginal Productivity of an Input states that as additional units of an input are used in a production process, while holding all other inputs and technology constant, the resulting increments to output, or total product, become successively smaller.

- The average product of an input measures the amount of output produced per unit of that input employed in the production process, holding all other inputs constant. More specifically, we compute the average product of labor, AP_L, as $AP_L = \frac{Q}{L}\Big|K_1$ and the average product of capital, AP_K, as $AP_K = \frac{Q}{K}\Big|L_1$.

- We can compute the average product of labor by measuring the slope of a ray drawn from the origin to a point on the total product of labor curve.

- The level of labor use at which the average product of labor curve reaches its maximum corresponds to the level of labor use at which the average product of labor is equal to the marginal product of labor.

- The marginal and average product of labor curves, when analyzed simultaneously, can be used to designate three distinct stages of production for a firm. Specifically, when treating capital as fixed and letting labor be the variable input, the Stage I area of production includes that range of production for which increases in the use of labor cause the average product of that input to increase. Stage I also corresponds to the range of labor use over which $MP_L > AP_L$. The Stage II area of production constitutes that range of production for which increases in the use of labor result in a decrease in the average product of that input, but for which the corresponding value of the marginal product of labor remains nonnegative. Finally, the Stage III area of production constitutes that range for which the use of labor corresponds to negative values for the marginal product of that input.

- A rational firm would never choose to produce in Stage III because the marginal product of the variable input is negative. Thus, by increasing its use of this input, the total product of labor will decline. A rational firm will not choose to operate in Stage I due to the fact that the marginal product of the fixed input is negative. Thus, the only stage of production which remains viable to a firm is Stage II, within which the marginal products of both inputs are nonnegative.

KEY TERMS

- average product of an input
- fixed input
- input
- Law of Diminishing Marginal Productivity of an Input
- long run
- marginal product of an input
- market period, or immediate run
- production function
- short run
- Stage I area of production
- Stage II area of production
- Stage III area of production
- state of technology
- total product curve
- variable input

EXERCISES

8.1 Suppose a firm has the production function

$$Q = 4K^{\frac{1}{4}} L^{\frac{3}{4}},$$

where Q is the firm's production of output, K represents the capital input, and L is the labor input. Assume capital is fixed at $K_1 = 16$ units.

a. To what time frame does this production function pertain? Why?

b. Derive the firm's total product of labor, TP_L, curve in this case.

8.2 Refer to the information given in exercise 8.1

a. Derive the firm's marginal product of labor curve, MP_L.

b. Derive the firm's average product of labor curve, AP_L.

8.3 Refer to the curves you computed in exercise 8.2.

a. Compute the values of the marginal and average products of labor if L = 81 units.

b. Now, compute the values of the marginal and average products of labor if L is increased to L = 256 units. Regarding the marginal product of labor values you have computed in parts a and b, what law is being exhibited? Define this law.

c. Suppose the amount of capital is increased to K = 81 units. Now compute the marginal and average product of labor values. How do these compare to the values you computed in exercise 8.3? Conceptually, explain why they are different.

8.4 Assume a firm has the production function

$$Q = 4K^{\frac{1}{2}} + 8L^{\frac{1}{2}},$$

where Q is the firm's output, K is its capital input and L is its labor input. Suppose that capital is fixed at $\overline{K_1}$ units.

a. Derive the firm's total product, TP_L, of labor curve.

b. Derive the firm's marginal and average product of labor curves.

c. Compute the marginal product of labor values if L = 4 units and then if L = 9 units.

d. Does the MP_L curve obey the law of diminishing marginal productivity in this case? Will a change in the fixed level of capital affect the marginal productivity of labor?

8.5 Suppose a firm has the production function

$$Q = KL,$$

where Q is output and K and L represent the capital and labor inputs, respectively. Assume capital is fixed at some level, $\overline{K}_1$.

a. If $\overline{K}_1 = 2$ units, determine the MP_L curve.

b. Now determine the MP_L curve, if $K = \overline{K}_2 = 3$ units.

c. Does the MP_L obey the law of diminishing marginal productivity?

d. Will a change in the level of capital affect the marginal productivity of labor?

8.6 Assume a total product of labor curve, TP_L, where output increases at an increasing rate, as labor increases, up to some inflection point. Beyond this point, further increases in labor cause output to increase at a decreasing rate, up to some point of labor use at which output achieves a maximum value. Thereafter, any further increases in labor use result in decreases in output.

a. Illustrate this TP_L curve and label this figure panel (A).

b. In another figure, labeled panel (B), placed just below the figure you constructed in part a, illustrate the associated MP_L and AP_L curves. Link the two figures, noting the labor values at which $MP_L = AP_L$ and $MP_L = 0$.

8.7 Refer to the information provided in exercise 8.5. Construct another figure containing the MP_L and AP_L curves, and designate the ranges of labor use pertaining to the Stage I, II, and III areas of production. Define these three stages. In which stage will the firm operate? Explain why it will operate in this stage and not in the other two stages.

CHAPTER 9: PRODUCTION IN THE LONG RUN

SUMMARY

In this chapter, we extend the initial discussion of production theory presented in Chapter 8. Now, however, we treat all inputs in a production function as variable, enabling us to conduct a long run analysis. Initially, we discuss the different conditions underlying production processes, specifically, variable proportions and fixed proportions. Once this discussion is completed, our major focus in the remainder of the chapter is on those production functions representing the condition of variable proportions. First, we hold output constant at different levels and construct an isoquant map. This is accomplished both graphically and mathematically. Special attention is paid to the slope of any such isoquant, and by so doing, we develop and interpret the associated marginal rate of technical substitution. The remainder of the chapter dwells on the characteristics pertaining to isoquants and isoquant maps. Specifically, isoquants are everywhere dense, cannot intersect, generally have negative slopes, and generally are strictly convex.

We discuss the important implications associated with each of these characteristics, while noting some important exceptions for which these characteristics do not hold true. The most noteworthy exception is a situation where two inputs constitute perfect complements in a production process. In summary, this chapter essentially provides the foundation for a firm's constrained cost minimization process that we analyze in Chapter 10. The key topics covered in this chapter are as follows.

- Production processes differ on the basis of whether the inputs can be substituted for each other, or whether they must be used together as complements.

- The condition of variable proportions refers to those production processes for which it is possible to produce a given level of output from an infinite number of input ratios.

- The condition of fixed proportions refers to those production processes for which it is possible to produce a given level of output from a finite number of input ratios.

- The extreme case of fixed proportions exists when it is possible to produce a given level of output from only one input ratio. In this case, the inputs are perfect complements in the production process.

- The set of input, usually capital-labor, combinations capable of producing a particular level of output is known as an isoquant.

- The negative of the slope of an isoquant measures the marginal rate of technical substitution, a term indicating the rate at which one input can be substituted for the other while producing the same level of output.

- The characteristics of isoquants are that they are everywhere dense, cannot intersect, generally have negative slopes, and generally are strictly convex.

- An exception to isoquants having the characteristics of negative slopes and strict convexity occurs when the inputs used in a production process are perfect complements. In this case the isoquants acquire right angle shapes.

- Another exception to the isoquant characteristic of strict convexity occurs when the inputs used in a production process are perfect substitutes. In this case, the isoquants are linear.

KEY TERMS

- ❑ condition of fixed proportions
- ❑ condition of variable proportions
- ❑ isoquant
- ❑ marginal rate of technical substitution
- ❑ ridge lines for an isoquant mapping

EXERCISES

9.1 Suppose a firm produces its output, Q, using capital, K, and labor, L, where the inputs must be combined in a ratio of one unit of capital to three units of labor.

a. What condition underlies the production process in this case?

b. Formulate the production function that represents this process. What type of production function is this?

9.2 Refer to the information in exercise 9.1.

a. If the firm uses six units of labor and two units of capital, how much output can it produce?

b. If the firm uses seven units of labor and two units of capital, how much output can it produce?

c. What is the minimum amount of labor that must be combined with four units of capital in order to produce four units of output?

d. Illustrate the isoquants associated with the production function in these examples.

9.3 A firm produces output, Q, according to the production function

$$Q = 2K^{\frac{1}{4}} L^{\frac{3}{4}},$$

where K and L represent the capital and labor inputs, respectively.

a. If Q = 4 units, determine the corresponding isoquant.

b. If the firm uses L = 2 units of labor, how much capital must it use to produce Q = 4 units of output?

c. Without computing the marginal products of the two inputs, directly derive the formula for the marginal rate of technical substitution, MRTS. Evaluate the MRTS for L = 2 units.

d. Define the MRTS in terms of the marginal products of the two inputs. Again, evaluate the MRTS for the K and L values given and computed earlier.

9.4 Suppose a firm has the production function

$$Q = 10K^{\frac{1}{2}} + 20L^{\frac{1}{2}},$$

where Q is output, K represents the capital input, and L is the labor input.

a. Derive the expression for an isoquant associated with this production function.

b. Derive the marginal rate of technical substitution, MRTS. Does this MRTS diminish as labor is substituted for capital?

9.5 A firm produces its output, Q, using labor, L, and capital, K, in accordance with the production function

$$Q = 10K + 20L.$$

a. What is the relationship between capital and labor in this production process?

b. Determine the marginal rate of technical substitution and interpret its meaning. Does the marginal rate of technical substitution diminish as the firm substitutes labor for capital?

c. Plot the isoquant that contains an input combination with 4 units of capital and 3 units of labor. Also determine the number of units of output the firm can produce using this input combination.

9.6 Determine whether each statement below is true or false and justify your answer.

a. It is possible for isoquants to intersect.

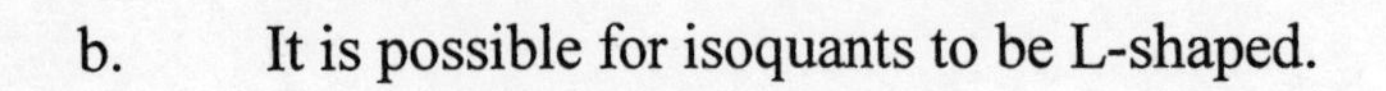

b. It is possible for isoquants to be L-shaped.

c. It is impossible for isoquants to be linear and downward sloping.

d. If a firm doubles its use of all inputs its output must increase.

9.7 Mathematically state a production function, where output, Q, is a function of capital, K, and labor, L, which is theoretically consistent for each of the production processes described below.

a. Good X is produced always using two units of capital with one unit of labor.

b. Good Y is produced using units of capital and units of labor where four units of labor are always substituted for one unit of capital.

c. Good Z is produced using units of capital and units of labor where the rate at which units of labor can be substituted for units of capital always diminishes.

9.8 Plot isoquants that correspond to each of the production processes described in exercise 9.7.

CHAPTER 10: LONG-RUN OPTIMIZATION FOR THE FIRM

SUMMARY

Our focus in Chapter 10 is on analyzing the long run optimization process for a typical firm. More specifically, this process consists of a constrained cost minimization procedure, where both the capital and labor inputs used in a firm's production process are treated as variable. Initially, we develop a firm's isocost equation and emphasize the economic importance of its slope and intercept coefficients. We also demonstrate how shifts in this curve reflect different levels of cost. Once we have developed the isocost equation, we use it along with the isoquants, derived in Chapter 9, to demonstrate a firm's constrained cost minimization procedure. Special attention is paid to analyzing the necessary condition that establishes a solution for this process. Next, we analyze this constrained cost minimization procedure mathematically by applying the method of Lagrangian multipliers. This process is first developed using generalized notation and then demonstrated with a specific numerical example.

The final topic presented in this chapter is a firm's expansion path, which we develop both graphically and mathematically. Within this context, we discuss the related concepts of constant, increasing, and decreasing, returns to scale in order to determine whether a firm experiences advantages or disadvantages from expanding or contracting its production of output. To facilitate this discussion, we introduce the concept of degrees of homogeneity associated with production functions, a topic that we will develop further in Chapter 11. The main topics covered in this chapter are as follows.

- An isocost equation represents a set of input combinations that a firm is able to purchase for a particular level of expenditures, given a set of input prices.

- If a firm purchases two inputs, labor, L, and capital, K, where the unit price of labor is $\overline{P}_{L,1}$, and the unit price of capital is $\overline{P}_{K,1}$, then the isocost cost equation representing a total expenditure level of $\overline{C}_1$ is stated mathematically as $\overline{P}_{L,1}L + \overline{P}_{K,1}K = \overline{C}_1$.

- The slope of an isocost equation is measured as the negative of the ratio of the price of a unit of labor to the price of a unit of capital, or mathematically stated, $\dfrac{-\overline{P}_{L,1}}{\overline{P}_{K,1}}$.

- The slope of an isocost equation measures the rate at which a firm is able to substitute units of one input for units of the other input in its purchasing process.

- The vertical intercept of the isocost equation is measured as $\frac{\overline{C}_1}{P_{K,1}}$ and indicates the maximum number of units of capital a firm can purchase if it spends all of its budget, $\overline{C}_1$, on capital.

- The horizontal intercept of the isocost equation is measured as $\frac{\overline{C}_1}{P_{L,1}}$ and indicates the maximum number of units of labor a firm can purchase if it spends all of its budget, $\overline{C}_1$, on labor.

- An increase in the total expenditure on inputs, $\overline{C}_1$, *ceteris paribus*, results in a parallel, rightward shift of the isocost equation.

- A decrease in the total expenditure on inputs, $\overline{C}_1$, *ceteris paribus*, results in a parallel leftward shift of the isocost equation.

- A change in one of the input prices, *ceteris paribus,* results in a change in the slope and one of the intercepts of the isocost equation.

- Using the Lagrangian multiplier method we can solve the constrained cost minimization problem of the firm to determine the levels of inputs that minimize the firm's expenditures, or costs, of producing a predetermined level of output.

- The necessary condition for a constrained cost minimum for a firm is that at the optimal combination of inputs, the marginal rate of technical substitution must equal the ratio of the input prices.

- Assuming a firm produces output using labor, L, and capital, K, the necessary condition for a constrained cost minimum is expressed mathematically as
  $MRTS = \frac{MP_L}{MP_K} = \frac{P_L}{P_K}$.

- An expansion path is a set of optimal input combinations that pertain to constrained cost minimization solutions for different levels of output.

- Production functions that are homogeneous to the first degree exhibit constant returns to scale, indicating that a proportionate increase or decrease in the use of all inputs results, respectively, in a proportionate increase or decrease in output.

- Production functions that are homogeneous of a degree greater than one exhibit increasing returns to scale, indicating that a proportionate increase or decrease in the use of all inputs results, respectively, in a more than proportionate increase or decrease in output.

- Production functions that are homogeneous of a degree less than one exhibit decreasing returns to scale, indicating that a proportionate increase or decrease in the use of all inputs results, respectively, in a less than proportionate increase or decrease in output.

KEY TERMS

- ❑ constant returns to scale
- ❑ decreasing returns to scale
- ❑ degree of homogeneity
- ❑ expansion path
- ❑ increasing returns to scale
- ❑ isocost equation

EXERCISES

10.1 A firm produces output, Q, using labor, L, and capital, K, according to the production function

$$Q = 81K^{.70} L^{.35}.$$

The unit price of capital is $90 and the unit price of labor is $30, and the firm has $100,000 to spend on these inputs.

a. Determine the marginal rate of technical substitution of labor for capital in this production process.

b. Formulate the isocost equation if the firm has $100,000 to spend on capital and labor.

c. State the necessary condition for a constrained cost minimum for this firm.

10.2 Assume the unit price of capital is $100 and the unit price of labor is $25.

a. State the isocost equation when the firm has $250,000 to spend on these inputs.

b. Plot the isocost equation you determined in part a.

c. Now assume the firm has only $125,000 to spend on capital and labor. State the new isocost equation.

d. Plot the isocost equation you determined in part c. in the same graph you drew for part b.

10.3 A pasta maker produces ravioli, Q, using labor, L, and capital, K, according to the production function
$Q = 64K^2 + 16L^2$.
The firm must pay $120 for each unit of capital and $80 for each unit of labor.

a. Determine the optimal amounts of capital and labor the firm should employ to minimize its cost of producing 14,400 units of ravioli.

b. Determine the minimum cost incurred by the firm when it produces 14,400 units of ravioli.

10.4 a. Refer to your response to exercise 10.3 and determine the optimal value of λ.

b. Interpret the value of λ^* you computed in part a. as it specifically applies to the pasta maker.

10.5 Assume a firm's production function is
$Q = 200K^{.75}L^{.50}$,
where Q denotes the firm's level of production, and K and L represent the capital and labor inputs, respectively,

a. Determine the degree of homogeneity associated with this production function.

b. Determine the type of returns to scale this production process exhibits.

c. Provide a real work example of a production process for a good that exhibits the same type of returns to scale as the production function in this problem.

10.6 A green bean farmer uses capital, K, and labor, L, to produce its output, Q according to the production function
$Q = 400K^{.5} L^{.5}$.
The firm must pay $25 for each unit of labor and $2500 for each unit of capital.

a. Determine the amounts of capital and labor the firm should purchase to minimize the cost of producing 8000 units of green beans.

b. Determine the minimum cost incurred when the firm produces 8000 units of green beans.

10.7 a. Using the information in exercise 10.6, derive the equation for the green bean farmer's expansion path.

b. Determine the amount of capital the farmer must use to minimize the cost of producing 8000 units of green beans, when he uses 500 units of labor.

10.8 A baker produces donuts, Q, using capital, K, and labor, L, according to the production function

$$Q = \text{minimum}\left(\frac{K}{1}, \frac{L}{4}\right).$$

He must pay $100 for each unit of capital and $10 for each unit of labor.

a. Determine the amounts of capital and labor the baker must employ to minimize the cost he incurs when producing 400 donuts.

b. What is the value of the minimum cost incurred by the baker when he produces 400 donuts?

c. Plot the isoquant representing 400 units of donuts and the isocost equation representing the minimum cost of producing this amount of donuts. Also indicate the optimal amounts of capital and labor the baker employs.

CHAPTER 11: COSTS OF PRODUCTION IN THE LONG RUN

SUMMARY

In this chapter, we extend the concepts associated with long run production theory, presented in Chapter 9 and 10, to develop long run cost functions. Initially, our discussion focuses on the concept of cost, emphasizing that this broad term includes both explicit and implicit costs for a firm. By doing so, we establish the basis for defining the concept of economic profit that will be used extensively in subsequent chapters. Next, we define the terms, fixed and variable costs, emphasizing that, in the long run, all of a firms costs are variable due to the absence of any fixed inputs. Then, we demonstrate the derivation of a long run total cost function, both graphically and mathematically. Once this is accomplished, we show how to convert a long run total cost function into its long run average cost counterpart. At this point, we provide a rather extensive discussion of the shapes of various long run average cost curves. Specifically, we discuss these shapes within the context of increasing, constant, and decreasing returns to scale, while recalling the degree of homogeneity concept presented in Chapter 9. We also analyze the broader topics of economies and diseconomies of scale, as well as economies of scope.

Finally, we discuss long run marginal cost and demonstrate the derivation of its associated curve both graphically and mathematically. We also provide a rather detailed discussion of the relationship between long run marginal and average cost curves, proving that they must be equal where long run average costs achieve a minimum value. The key topics covered in this chapter are outlined below.

- A cost function represents a firm's costs of production in terms of its output, holding all input prices constant.

- In the short run, since at least one of a firm's inputs is fixed, the firm's costs of production includes those costs attributable to its fixed inputs, known as fixed costs, as well as those costs associated with its variable inputs, known as variable costs. Thus, a firm's short run total cost function can be expressed as SRTC = FC + VC. However, in the long run, since all of a firm's inputs are variable, the firm only incurs variable costs.

- A firm's explicit costs include those costs, that are associated with non-owner supplied inputs used in its production process, while implicit costs are those costs associated with the inputs supplied by the owners to their firm. Therefore, implicit costs are measured in terms of what the owner supplied inputs could earn if they were employed in their next best alternative use, and as a result, measure the owners' opportunity costs.

- A long run total cost function measures a firm's minimum cost of production in terms of its level of output, assuming input prices are held constant. We derive the long run total cost function from a firm's expansion path, as the cost and output values pertaining to a long run total cost function are determined via the constrained cost minimization problem of the firm.

- A firm's long run average cost function measures the per unit cost of a firm's output when it can vary all of its inputs. We compute long run average cost by dividing a firm's long run total cost by its level of output, hence LRAC = $\frac{LRTC}{Q}$.
- The slope of a firm's long run average cost curve will vary depending on the type of returns to scale it is experiencing. If the firm's production process is characterized by increasing returns to scale then its per unit costs of production will decline as the firm expands its scale of production and accordingly, its long run average cost function is negatively sloped. Conversely, if a firm is experiencing decreasing returns to scale, its per unit costs of production increase as it increases its scale of production, resulting in a positively sloped long run average cost curve. Finally, if a firm is characterized by constant returns to scale, its per unit costs of production are not affected by its scale of production and its long run average cost function is horizontal.
- A firm experiences economies of scope if it can achieve lower per unit production costs by producing multiple outputs rather than by producing only one good or service.
- A firm's long run marginal cost function measures the change in its long run total cost arising from a change in its level of production, mathematically stated as LRMC = $\frac{dLRTC}{Q}$. Furthermore, long run marginal cost measures the instantaneous slope of the long run total cost curve corresponding to different levels of output.
- Given a cubic long run total cost function, the associated long run average and marginal cost functions will be quadratic or U-shaped.
- The long run average cost and long run marginal cost curves intersect at an output level that corresponds to the minimum value of long run average cost.
- A production externality represents either a negative or beneficial side effect associated with the production of a good or service by a firm that affects at least one other firm's production, thereby constituting an uncompensated cost or benefit to the affected firm(s).
- Social costs measure a firm's private costs associated with the production of a good plus any costs or minus any benefits generated by its production externality.

KEY TERMS

- ❑ cost function
- ❑ diseconomies of scale
- ❑ economies of scale
- ❑ economies of scope
- ❑ explicit cost
- ❑ fixed cost

- implicit cost
- long run average cost
- long run marginal cost
- long run total cost function
- production externality
- social cost
- variable cost

EXERCISES

11.1 Suppose an individual decides to operate her own business. Accordingly, she gives up her current job where she is earning $40,000 per year. Also, she has $100,000 in savings that she invests in the business. The $100,000 had been invested in a mutual fund yielding a return of 5% per year. After one year, she calculates that she has paid out $100,000 for the capital and labor inputs that she hires. What are the total annual costs that an economist would say she is incurring?

11.2 A firm produces output according to the function

$$Q = 4K^{\frac{1}{4}}L^{\frac{1}{4}}$$

where, Q is output, K is capital, and L is labor.

The firm pays input prices $\overline{P}_{K,1} = \$2$ and $\overline{P}_{L,1} = \$8$ for its capital and labor, respectively.

a. Determine the firm's expansion path.

b. Determine the firm's long run total cost function.

11.3 Refer to the information provided in exercise 11.2

a. Determine the firm's long run marginal and average cost curves.

b. Illustrate the curves you derived in part a.

c. Compute the values for LRTC, LRAC, and LRMC, if the firm produces Q = 4 units of output.

11.4 Assume a firm's production process yields the cost function

$$C = 0.05Q^3 - 2Q^2 + 50Q - 2KQ + 2K^2,$$

where C is the firm's cost, Q represents its production of output, and K is the amount of capital it uses.

a. Compute the expression that represents an optimal, or constrained cost minimizing, amount of capital corresponding to any level of output the firm produces.

b. Compute the firm's long run total cost curve in this case.

11.5 Refer to the information provided in exercise 11.4.

a. Determine the firm's corresponding long run marginal cost, LRMC, and long run average cost, LRAC, curves.

b. Without using the LRMC curve, determine the level of output at which LRAC achieves its minimum value. Also, compute the corresponding value of LRAC at this level of output.

c. Determine the amount of capital the firm is using at this point.

d. Interpret the results, you computed in part b. Specifically, what does this level of output represent?

11.6 Refer to the information provided in exercise 11.4 and the results you computed in exercise 11.5.

a. Compute the value of LRMC when LRAC is at its minimum value.

b. Using the relationship you employed in part a, confirm the value of output at which LRAC achieves its minimum value.

c. Sketch the general relationship between the LRMC and LRAC curves.

11.7 Suppose a firm has the production function

$$Q = 8K^{\frac{1}{4}}L^{\frac{3}{4}},$$

where Q is output, and K and L represent the firm's capital and labor inputs, respectively.

a. Determine the degree of homogeneity associated with this production function and interpret your results.

b. What is the shape of the corresponding long run average cost curve?

11.8 There are some situations where a firm's private costs of producing a good may not equal the social, or true, cost of producing the good. Explain how this situation can happen. Define the concept you are using in this case.

CHAPTER 12: COSTS OF PRODUCTION IN THE SHORT RUN

SUMMARY

Our focus in Chapter 12 is on developing various short run cost functions. Throughout this chapter, we make a special point of the fact that short and long run cost curves are related, and thus these costs are not developed independent of one another.

Initially, we fixed a firm's capital input at a particular value, and develop a particular short run total cost curve, noting the decomposition of such a curve into its fixed and variable cost components. Then, we develop a set of short run total cost curves, where each curve in the set is derived for a particular amount of capital, or plant size. At the same time, we establish the relationship between this set of short run total cost curves and the associated long run total cost curve, where this relationship is demonstrated both graphically and mathematically.

Next, we derive the average fixed, variable, and total cost curves from their short run total counterparts. In addition, we derive the short run marginal cost curve. Considerable attention is devoted to discussing the relationships among these short run marginal and average cost curves. In order to emphasize the linkage between short run cost and production theory, we then establish relationships between short run marginal cost and marginal product curves, as well as between average variable and average product curves. Finally, we conclude this chapter by demonstrating the relationship among a set of short run marginal and average total cost curves with the corresponding long run average and marginal cost curves. In summary, the material covered in this chapter, along with that presented in Chapter 11, provide the cost analysis that we will use in subsequent chapters in analyzing firm behavior. The main points presented in this chapter are as follows.

- A short run total cost function expresses a firm's costs as a function of its level of output, holding at least one input and all input prices constant.

- There exists an entire set of short run total cost curves, one for each fixed level of capital, where for each short run total cost cure there will be one level of output at which short run total cost will equal long run total cost. Accordingly, every point on the long run total cost curve corresponds to one point on some short run total cost curve, at which capital has been fixed at a particular level. The input mix used to produce the level of output corresponding to a point of tangency of the short run total cost curve with the long run total cost curve represents an optimal, or cost minimizing, input combination.

- By dividing each of the components in a firm's short run total cost function by its level of output, it is possible to derive short run average costs as $\frac{SRTC}{Q}=\frac{FC}{Q}+\frac{VC}{Q}$, where the term $\frac{SRTC}{Q}$ represents the firm's short run average total cost, or ATC, measuring the short run total cost per unit of output. Moreover, $\frac{FC}{Q}$ represents average fixed cost, denoted AFC, and measures a firm's fixed cost per unit of output, while $\frac{VC}{Q}$ represents average variable cost, AVC, measuring a firm's variable cost per unit of output. Accordingly then, ATC = AFC + AVC.

- A firm's short run marginal cost function measures the change in a firm's short run total cost resulting from a change in its level of production, mathematically stated as $\frac{dSRTC}{dQ}$. Moreover, short run marginal cost measures the instantaneous slope of both the short run total and variable cost curves corresponding to different levels of output. Therefore, SRMC $= \frac{dSRTC}{dQ} = \frac{dVC}{dQ}$.

- If a firm's short run total cost function is cubic, then its associated average total, average variable, and marginal cost curves will be quadratic, or U-shaped. In addition, the short run marginal cost curve intersects the average total and average variable cost curves at their respective minimum values.

- As the amount of labor employed by a firm rises and the marginal product of labor, MP_L, increases, the firm's short run marginal cost decreases, and when MP_L achieves its maximum value, SRMC is minimized. However, as the MP_L decreases as more labor is employed, the firm's short run marginal costs rise. Graphically, MP_L and SRMC will be mirror images of one another when plotted versus the variable input, labor.

- As the amount of labor employed rises and the average product of labor increases, average variable cost will fall, and when AP_L achieves its maximum value, AVC is minimized. After diminishing returns to the variable input set in, and the MP_L falls to where it is less than AP_L, then as more labor is employed, the firm's average variable costs will rise. Graphically, AP_L and AVC will be mirror images of one another when plotted versus the variable input, labor.

- The long run average cost curve is the envelope of the corresponding set of average total cost curves, where each ATC curve is derived for a fixed level of capital. In addition, the long run marginal cost curve intersects the long run average cost curve at its minimum value, and each short run marginal cost curve intersects its corresponding ATC curve at its minimum value. Further, each SRMC curve is equal to LRMC at output levels for which the respective ATC curve is tangent to the LRAC curve.

KEY TERMS

- ❑ average fixed cost
- ❑ average total cost
- ❑ average variable cost
- ❑ short run marginal cost
- ❑ short run total cost function

EXERCISES

12.1 Suppose a firm has the production function

$Q = 4K^{\frac{1}{4}}L^{\frac{1}{4}}$,

where Q is output, K is the firm's capital input, and L represents the labor input. The input prices of capital and labor are $P_K = \$2$ and $P_L = \$8$, respectively.

a. If K is fixed at $\overline{K}_1 = 2$ units, derive the firm's short run total cost, SRTC, curve.

b. Compute the associated average total cost, ATC, and short run marginal cost, SRMC, curves.

12.2 Refer to the information provided in exercise 12.1.

a. If the firm produces Q = 4 units of output, compute the firm's SRTC, ATC, and SRMC values.

b. Compare these short run cost values to their long run counterparts, LRTC, LRAC, and LRMC, which you computed in exercise 11.3 of the previous chapter. What do the results of this comparison indicate about the level at which capital has been fixed, $\overline{K}_1 = 2$ units?

c. Derive the equation for the optimal amount of capital in terms of the level of output produced.

12.3 In capital-labor space, illustrate the derivation of a firm's expansion path using two isoquants, represented as $\overline{Q}_1$ and $\overline{Q}_2$, along with the appropriate isocost equations designated as

$$C_1 = \overline{P}_{K,1}K + \overline{P}_{L,1}L$$

and

$$C_2 = \overline{P}_{K,1}K + \overline{P}_{L,1}L,$$

where $\overline{Q}_1$ is produced at cost, C_1, and $\overline{Q}_2$ at cost, C_2. The input prices of capital, K, and labor L, are represented as $\overline{P}_{K,1}$ and $\overline{P}_{L,1}$ respectively. Next, assume capital is fixed at $\overline{K}_1$ units, that corresponds to optimally producing Q_1 units of output. Illustrate the amount of labor the firm will use, as well as the corresponding cost the firm incurs, if it produces Q_2 units of output. Is this new K - L combination on the firm's expansion path?

12.4 Assume the basis for a firm's set of short run total cost curves is represented by the expression

$C = 0.05\,Q^3 - 2Q^2 + 50Q - 2KQ + 2K^2,$

where C is the firm's cost, Q is its output, and K represents the firm's capital input.

a. If the firm's capital is fixed at $\overline{K}_1 = 12.5$ units, determine its short run total cost curve, SRTC.

b. Identify the fixed cost, FC, and variable cost, VC, components of this curve.

12.5 Refer to the information in exercise 12.4.

a. Derive the average fixed, AFC, average variable, AVC, and average total, ATC, cost curves for the short run total cost curve, SRTC, you derived in exercise 12.4. Also derive the short run marginal, SRMC, cost curve corresponding to this SRTC curve.

b. Compute the values of ATC and SRMC, for the curves you derived in part a, if Q = 25 units.

12.6 Refer to the results you computed in exercise 12.5.

a. How do these results compare to the long run average cost, LRAC, and long run marginal cost, LRMC, values you computed in exercise 11.6 of the previous chapter?

b. Conceptually, what do these results indicate?

c. Will these results hold true for any other level of Q?

12.7 Conceptually, explain the difference between diminishing marginal productivity and decreasing returns to scale.

12.8 Suppose a firm has the short run production function

$$Q = \overline{K}_1^{\frac{3}{4}} L^{\frac{1}{4}},$$

where Q is output, K is capital, and L represents labor. If the price of labor, P_L, is \$9 and the firm is using $\overline{K}_1 = 81$ units of capital and L = 16 units of labor, what is the value of the firm's short run marginal cost?

CHAPTER 13: PERFECT COMPETITON IN THE SHORT RUN

SUMMARY

In Chapter 13 we bring the demand and revenue concepts, developed in Chapters 3-7, together with the production and cost concepts, presented in Chapters 8-12, to analyze firm behavior within the context of a perfectly competitive market structure. Our focus in this chapter is on firm behavior in the short run, where at least one of a firm's inputs is treated as fixed. Initially, we define a market from both product and geographic perspectives. We then describe the general criteria for defining a market structure and discuss how these criteria apply to a perfectly competitive market structure. Specifically, this type of market structure is characterized by a large number of insignificantly small buyers and sellers, homogeneous goods, easy entry and exit to and from the market, and equal access to complete information.

Next, we demonstrate the interaction of market supply and demand curves to show how market prices are determined. Once this is accomplished, we discuss how a perfectly competitive firm reacts to these market prices, thus deriving the firm's demand, marginal revenue, and average revenue curves. After introducing short run cost curves into the model, we analyze a firm's short run profit maximizing behavior both graphically and mathematically. Also demonstrated, is the price at which a firm chooses to shut down production in the short run. Ultimately, this analysis is used to derive the firm's short run supply curve. Next, we demonstrate how to aggregate these individual firms' short run supply curves to generate the short run market supply curve counterpart, where this analysis is conducted for both constant and variable input price cases. The final topic covered in this chapter is that of short run elasticity of supply, which is demonstrated with a simple example. The major topics presented in this chapter are outlined as follows.

- A market for a good or service is defined as an aggregation of actual or potential buyers and sellers who, by their interactions, determine the price at which the good or service is sold. The market for a particular good or service is defined in terms of the attributes of the good, which may be expressed narrowly or broadly, thereby affecting the number of close substitutes comprising the market. We must also define the market for a good or service on a geographical basis.

- A perfectly competitive market is defined by the following structural characteristics: a) a large number of insignificantly small buyers and sellers; b) a homogeneous good or service; c) easy entry and exit of firms to or from the market; and d) buyers and sellers that have equal access to perfect information relevant to the market.

- The interaction of all buyers of a good in the market, represented by the market own-price demand curve, and all producers of the good, represented by the market supply curve, determines the equilibrium price of a good. At the equilibrium price, the market quantity demanded of a good is equal to the market quantity supplied of that good, and thus it represents a stable price that can be maintained indefinitely in the absence of any changes in the underlying determinants of either the market supply or market demand curve.

- A perfectly competitive firm acts as a price-taker in the market because each firm produces such an imperceptibly small portion of total market output that no one firm can exert any influence on the market price by altering its own level of sales.

- A perfectly competitive firm's own-price demand curve is perfectly elastic, and therefore horizontal, at the market determined equilibrium price, since the firm is able to sell any level of output it wishes as long as it sells the good at the market price. The firm's own-price demand curve also represents its marginal and average revenue functions, since $P = MR = AR$ for a perfectly competitive firm.

- The goal of a perfectly competitive firm is that of profit maximization, where its short run profit, $SR\prec$, is the difference between its revenue, TR, and its short run total cost, SRTC, or $SR\prec = TR - SRTC$. The firm's revenue is the product of its predetermined price and its level of sales, or $TR = \overline{P}_1 Q$ and its short run total cost is the summation of its fixed, FC, and variable, VC, costs or, $SRTC = FC + VC(Q\ \overline{K}_1, \overline{P}_{L,1})$. The competitive firm maximizes its profit by producing that level of output for which its $MR = P = SRMC$, where $MR = \frac{dTR}{dQ}$, and $SRMC = \frac{dVC(Q, K_1, P_{L,1})}{dQ}$.

- A firm's short run average, or per unit, profit function, denoted $SR\ AVE\prec$, is defined as $SR\ AVE\pi = \frac{SR\pi}{Q} = \frac{TR}{Q} - \frac{SRTC}{Q}$. Since $\frac{TR}{Q}$ = average revenue, AR, and $\frac{SRTC}{Q}$ = average total cost, ATC, then short run average profit can also be expressed as $SR\ AVE\pi = AR - ATC$.

- The short run supply curve for a perfectly competitive firm is its SRMC curve, provided $P \geq$ average variable cost, AVC, and the portion of the vertical axis, or where $Q = 0$, for $P < AVC$.

- If the price of a variable input varies directly with the quantity of output supplied, then the market supply curve will be steeper, reflecting a weaker response in the quantity supplied of a good due to a change in the price of that good, than for the case when the price of the variable input remains constant.

- The short run elasticity of supply, denoted $E_{Q^S,P}$, is computed as the ratio of the percentage change in the quantity supplied of a good, Q^S, to the percentage change in the price of that good, P, or $E_{Q^S,P} = \frac{\%\Delta Q^S}{\%\Delta P} = \frac{\partial Q^S}{\partial P} \cdot \frac{P}{Q^S}$.

KEY TERMS

- average revenue
- equilibrium condition
- equilibrium price
- market
- market structure
- perfectly competitive market
- short run elasticity of supply
- short run market supply curve

EXERCISES

13.1 The own-price demand curve for a perfectly competitive firm is horizontal, or perfectly price elastic. We say this outcome represents the fact that a perfectly competitive firm is a price taker, reacting to the market determined price of its good.

a. List the structural characteristics that define a market as perfectly competitive.

b. Now, reconcile the fact that a perfectly competitive firm's own-price demand curve is perfectly elastic with these characteristics.

13.2 Suppose the market own-price demand and supply curves for a good are

$$Q^d = 500 - 6P$$

and

$$Q^S = -40 + 3P, \text{ respectively,}$$

where Q^d is the market quantity demanded of the good, Q^S is the market quantity supplied, and P represents the market price.

a. Determine the equilibrium price, as well as the market quantities demanded and supplied of the good.

b. What occurs if P = $80?

c. What occurs if P = $40?

13.3 Illustrate the results you determined in exercise 13.2.

13.4 Suppose a firm has a short run total cost curve of the form

$$SRTC = 0.05Q^3 - 2Q^2 + 25Q + 312.50,$$

where SRTC is the firm's short run total costs and Q represents its production of output.

a. Determine the firm's average total cost, ATC, average variable cost, AVC, average fixed cost, AFC, and short run marginal cost, SRMC, curves.

b. Determine the firm's profit maximizing level of output, if $P = \$18.75$.

c. What is the firm's short run average profit at this level of output?

13.5 Refer to the information provided in exercise 13.4.

a. Suppose the price of the good falls to P = \$5. Now, determine the firm's profit maximizing level of output.

b. Compute the value of its short run average profit at this level of output.

c. What should the firm do at this price?

d. Determine the firm's short run supply curve.

13.6 Illustrate a situation, using short run total cost, SRTC, and total revenue, TR, curves, where a profit maximizing firm is operating at a loss.

13.7 Assume a firm has the short run total cost curve

$$SRTC = 0.025Q^3 - Q^2 + 12.5Q + 156.25,$$

where SRTC is its short run total cost and Q represents its production of output.

a. Determine the firm's profit maximizing level of output, if the price, P, is P = \$9.375.

b. Compute its corresponding short run average profit, SR AVEπ.

13.8 Assume the short run market supply curve for a good is

$$Q^S = -50 + 3P,$$

where Q^S is the market quantity supplied and P is the price of the good. If the market price is P = $50, determine the short run elasticity of supply. Interpret your result.

CHAPTER 14: PERFECT COMPETITION IN THE LONG RUN

SUMMARY

The purpose of this chapter is to extend our discussion of perfectly competitive firm behavior, introduced in Chapter 13, into a long run analysis. This analysis pertains not only to perfectly competitive firm behavior in the long run, but also to the competitive markets within which this type of firm operates. Initially, we develop the conditions for long run perfectly competitive equilibrium both mathematically and graphically. An emphasis is placed on the fact that, in the long run, a firm will adjust its level of capital, as well as labor, so as to produce its output in the most cost efficient manner. Also, by allowing capital to vary, the important characteristic of firm entry and exit, to and from a market, is introduced into the analysis, where we note that the motive for such activity is economic profit. We also demonstrate how the long run results relate to particular short run scenarios pertaining to different levels of capital. Once we have established long run competitive equilibrium, we direct our attention to developing long run industry supply curves. Such curves for constant and increasing cost industries are derived in considerable detail, while a brief discussion is included describing the long run supply curve for a decreasing cost industry. The concept of long run elasticity of supply is also introduced.

We conclude this chapter with an evaluation of perfectly competitive market performance. In order to do so, we establish several criteria for judging market performance, specifically, production efficiency, allocative efficiency, and dynamic efficiency. We also describe a less formal criterion that we simply designate as fairness. By applying these criteria, we draw some generally favorable conclusions regarding the performance of perfectly competitive firms and markets. By so doing, we establish some benchmarks that we will use in subsequent chapters to evaluate the performance associated with other types of market structures. The main topics covered in this chapter are as follows.

- In the long run, a perfectly competitive firm produces its profit maximizing level of output using a constrained cost minimizing combination of inputs.

- As a perfectly competitive firm determines its profit maximizing level of production it is also simultaneously determining its optimal plant size.

- In the long run the existence of profit serves as the incentive for firms to enter or exit a market.

- Entry of new firms into a market results in a rightward shift of the short-run market supply curve. Conversely, exit of firms from a market results in a leftward shift of the short-run market supply curve.

- A long-run perfectly competitive equilibrium is achieved in an industry when all firms produce a level of output that corresponds to its long-run average cost and zero economic profit.

- At a long-run competitive equilibrium in an industry there is no incentive for new firms to enter or existing firms to exit the industry.

- A long-run industry supply curve comprises the set of quantity-price combinations that constitute long-run competitive equilibria in a perfectly competitive market.

- When new firms enter a constant cost industry the firms' cost structures are unaffected due to the fact that the inputs used by these firms are unspecialized and plentiful in supply.

- In the case of a constant cost industry, the long-run industry supply curve is horizontal.

- An industry is characterized as an increasing cost industry if the entry of new firms results in higher cost structures for the firms operating in the industry. This is due to the fact that the inputs used by the firms in this industry are specialized and scarce.

- The long-run industry supply curve for an increasing cost industry is positively sloped.

- Long-run elasticity of supply measures the ratio of the percentage change in the market quantity supplied of a good in the long run to a percentage change in the price of this good.
- The long-run elasticity of supply is denoted mathematically as
$$E_{Q_L^S,P} = \frac{\%\Delta Q_L^S}{\%\Delta P} = \frac{\partial Q_L^S}{\partial P}\frac{P}{Q_L^S}.$$
- Production efficiency refers to producing any given level of output in the least costly manner and producing a level of output that corresponds to a firm's minimum long-run average cost.

- Allocative efficiency refers to the flow of resources to their most highly valued uses.

- Dynamic efficiency refers to the development and adoption of new technology over time.

- X-efficiency refers to the ability of a firm's management to minimize the cost associated with producing each level of output.

- The outcomes associated with a perfectly competitive market structure are generally considered to fulfill the following criteria: production efficiency, allocative efficiency, and dynamic efficiency.

KEY TERMS

- allocative efficiency
- constant cost industry
- dynamic efficiency
- increasing cost industry
- long-run elasticity of supply
- long-run market, or industry, supply curve
- long-run perfectly competitive equilibrium
- production efficiency
- X-efficiency

EXERCISES

14.1 Assume a perfectly competitive firm's long-run total cost function is LRTC = $Q^3 - 4Q^2 + 80Q$.

a. Determine the firm's long-run average cost function.

b. Determine the level of output the perfectly competitive firm produces when it is in long-run equilibrium.

c. What is the value of the firm's long-run average cost when it is in long-run equilibrium?

14.2 Using your responses to exercise 14.1 answer the following questions.

a. When the perfectly competitive firm is in long-run competitive equilibrium, what is the market price of the good it produces and sells?

b. When the perfectly competitive firm is in long-run equilibrium, what is the value of the firm's long-run profit?

c. Plot the perfectly competitive firm's long-run average cost curve and marginal revenue curve. Also indicate the market price level of output corresponding to the firm in long-run equilibrium.

14.3 Assume a perfectly competitive firm's cost curves are based on the function

$$C = \frac{1}{3}Q^3 - 4Q^2 + 20Q - 2KQ + 0.50K^2,$$

where C denotes the firm's total cost, Q represents its level of output, and K designates the firm's capital input.

a. Derive a mathematical equation for determining the optimal amount of capital this firm should use to minimize the cost of producing any level of output when the firm is free to vary its labor input.

b. Determine the firm's long-run total cost curve, where LRTC is a function of Q.

14.4 Using your responses to exercise 14.3, answer the following questions.

a. What is the associated long-run marginal cost curve?

b. If the market price of this good is $9, what is the profit maximizing level of output for this firm and the associated amount of long-run profit earned?

c. Is the profit maximizing level of output produced by this firm, when the market price is $9, a long-run competitive equilibrium level of output? Justify your response.

14.5 Assume a perfectly competitive firm's cost curves are based on the function

$$C = \frac{1}{3}Q^3 - 2Q^2 + 40Q - 2KQ + 0.25K^2,$$

where C denotes the firm's total cost, Q represents its level of output, and K designates the firm's capital input.

a. Develop a mathematical equation for determining the optimal amount of capital this firm should use to minimize the cost of producing any level of output when the firm is able to vary its use of labor.

b. Determine the firm's long-run total cost curve.

c. Determine the firm's associated long-run marginal cost curve.

14.6 Using your responses to exercise 14.5, answer the following questions.

a. What is the associated long-run average cost curve?

b. At what level of output is long-run average cost minimized?

c. At what market price is this firm at a long-run competitive equilibrium?

d. How much capital is the firm using when it is producing its long-run competitive equilibrium level of output?

14.7 Graphically derive the long-run industry supply curve for a perfectly competitive house-sitting service industry, which employs unspecialized inputs. Provide a brief explanation of this process beneath your graphical analysis.

CHAPTER 15: MONOPOLY

SUMMARY

In this chapter, our initial focus is on describing a monopoly within the context of the basic criteria for defining a market structure. These are the number and size distribution of buyers and sellers of a good, the degree of product differentiation, the ease of entry and exit of firms to and from a market, and the amount of market related information available to consumers and producers. Next, we direct our attention to discussing the major sources of monopoly power. These sources are described as barriers to entry that we group into three categories. The first category includes those entry barriers inherent to an industry, where the major examples we discuss are economies of scale over the entire feasible range of market wide output, and high capital requirements. The second category refers to barriers that are created by firm behavior, including activities such as input control, building excess capacity, advertising, and limit pricing. The third category refers to those entry barriers created by government intervention. These include: licensing restrictions, patent protections, zoning laws, government franchises, and trade restrictions.

After discussing the various origins of monopoly, we model and analyze monopoly behavior in the short run both graphically and mathematically. Special emphasis is placed on the fact that, since a monopoly consists of a single seller of a good, the market own-price demand curve and the monopolist's own-price curve are one and the same. We then discuss the implications of this result, specifically, that a monopolist has some discretion over the price it charges and that its marginal revenue is less than the price of its product. Combining these demand and revenue concepts with the cost analysis developed in preceding chapters we complete the monopoly model of short run firm behavior. Particular emphasis is placed on the fact that a monopolist determines its profit maximizing level of output where marginal revenue is equal to marginal cost, and that the corresponding price exceeds both of these values. Finally, we examine monopoly behavior in the long run, stressing the possibilities of a long run profit and a less than cost efficient outcome. The major topics covered in this chapter are as follows.

- Monopoly is a market structure comprised of a single seller of a good, where the good is substantially differentiated from those produced by all other firms. Further, the firm is able to remain the sole producer and seller of the good due to the existence of barriers to entry, which prevent other firms from entering the industry.

- A monopolist, unlike a perfectly competitive firm, possesses some influence over the price of the good it sells, since it is the sole producer. As a result, it can affect the price of the good by altering the amount it sells.

- The structure-conduct-performance school of thought believes the major barriers to entry that cause monopoly are either inherent to the structure of an industry or the result of firm conduct.

- Those barriers that are inherent to an industry are large economies of scale and high capital requirements.
- Those barriers resulting from firm conduct are the building of excess capacity, limit pricing, advertising, and input control.

- The Chicago school of thought believes the main sources of monopoly are barriers to entry erected by the government, such as licenses, patents, zoning restrictions, franchises, tariffs, and import quotas.

- The price charged by a monopolist is inversely related to its sales of output. As a result, the marginal revenue for a non-price discriminating monopolist is less than the price it charges.

- A monopolist determines its profit maximizing level of output, in the short run, where its marginal revenue, MR, is equal to its short run marginal cost, SRMC. Further, the firm determines its price, P, at this level of output, where P > MR = SRMC.

- A monopolist determines its profit maximizing levels output and price, in the long run, where marginal revenue is equal to its long run marginal cost, LRMC.

- A monopolist will not operate on the inelastic portion of its own-price demand curve because its corresponding marginal revenue is negative over this range of output.

- Due to the existence of barriers to entry, a monopolist will not be pressured by competitive forces to be cost efficient and produce a level of output that corresponds to its minimum long run average cost. In addition, due to the lack of entry, the monopolist is able to sustain a positive economic profit in the long run.

KEY TERMS

- barrier to entry
- monopoly
- monopoly power

EXERCISES

15.1 For any positive level of output sold, a monopolists' marginal revenue, MR, is less than the price of its product. Intuitively, explain why this result is true.

15.2 Give the reasoning behind what the Chicago school of economic thought believes to be the main cause of monopoly. Also, list some examples of what they are talking about.

15.3 The structure - conduct - performance school differs from the Chicago school in their reasons for the existence of monopoly. Explain their reasoning and give some examples.

15.4 Assume a monopolist has the own-price demand curve

$$Q = 200 - 0.2P,$$

where Q is the firm's output and P is the price of its product. Suppose its short run total cost, SRTC, curve is

$$SRTC = 1000 + 5Q^2.$$

a. Determine the firm's profit maximizing levels of output and price.

b. Compute the corresponding short run profit.

15.5 Assume a monopolist has the own-price demand curve

$$Q = 44 - \frac{1}{2}P,$$

where Q is the firm's output sold and P is the price of its output. Assume the firm has the long run total cost, LRTC, curve

$$LRTC = \frac{2}{3}Q^3 - 12Q^2 + 120Q,$$

where LRTC is the firm's long run total cost.

a. Determine the firm's inverse own-price demand curve.

b. Determine the firm's marginal revenue, MR, and long run marginal cost, LRMC, curves.

15.6 Refer to the information provided, as well as the results you computed, in exercise 15.5. Determine the firm's long run profit maximizing levels of output, price, and profit.

15.7 Every long run result corresponds to a particular short run situation. The basis for the LRTC curve used in exercises 15.5 and 15.6 is

$$C = \frac{2}{3}Q^3 - 10Q^2 + 120Q - 2KQ + 0.50K^2,$$

where C is the firm's cost, Q represents its output, and K is its capital input. Assume the firm's own-price demand curve is

$$Q = 44 - \frac{1}{2}P,$$

where P is the price of the good.

a. How much capital is the firm using to optimally produce Q = 8 units of output?

b. Derive the firm's corresponding short run total cost curve, SRTC.

c. Compute the firm's average total cost, ATC, and short run marginal cost, SRMC, curves.

d. Demonstrate that the short run profit, SR$\prec$ is equal to the long run profit, LR$\prec$, you computed in exercise 15.6.

15.8 Illustrate a positive long run profit situation, using average and marginal cost curves. Also, illustrate the corresponding short run results in the same figure.

CHAPTER 16: ADDITIONAL TOPICS RELATED TO MONOPOLY

SUMMARY

In this chapter, we expand our discussion of monopoly to include several topics associated with this type of market structure. At the outset, we make a general comparison of the performance results attributed to monopoly to those generated by perfect competition. This is done within the criteria of production efficiency, allocative efficiency, dynamic efficiency, and fairness that we presented in Chapter 14. Next, in order to make more detailed comparisons between monopoly and perfectly competitive outcomes, we introduce the concepts of consumer and producer surplus, as well as the related concept of deadweight loss. After doing so, we then use an example to demonstrate the loss of consumer and producer surplus, or deadweight loss, attributed to monopoly. In addition, we demonstrate the transfer of consumer surplus to a monopolist's revenue and profit that also takes place.

The next topic discussed is that of price discrimination. We analyze this type of behavior in terms of first, second, and third degree price discrimination, providing both mathematical, as well as graphical, examples of each type. The final topic presented in this chapter is that of a multiplant monopoly. After introducing this topic, we use a specific mathematical example to demonstrate the behavior of a profit maximizing multiplant monopolist. Specifically, we show, not only how such a firm determines its profit maximizing levels of output and price, but also how it allocates the production of this output across more than one of its plants. The main topics covered in this chapter are presented below.

- Consumer surplus is measured as the difference between the value consumers' place on each unit of a good and the price they actually pay for that unit, summed over all units sold.

- Producer surplus is measured as the difference between the price a producer receives from selling each unit of a good and the marginal cost associated with producing each respective unit, summed over all units sold.

- Compared to a perfectly competitive market, a monopolist will restrict its output in order to sell its product at a higher price, and as a result, there will be a transfer of part of the consumer surplus generated under a perfectly competitive market structure to the monopolist's profit. Moreover, under monopoly there will also be a loss of both consumer and producer surplus which will be received by no one, known as the deadweight loss associated with monopoly.

- Firms possessing some degree of monopoly power may engage in price discrimination. This activity occurs when a firm charges different price to marginal cost ratios for different units of a good that are the same grade and quality, once an equilibrium price has been established. It should be noted that any price differentials that are cost justified do not constitute price discrimination.

- There are three categories of price discrimination, separated on the degree to which firms are able to discern the values consumers place on different amounts of a good being sold. Specifically, first degree price discrimination entails the charging of a different price for each unit of a good that is equal to the maximum value consumers place on each unit. In the case of second degree price discrimination, a firm groups together several units of the good into specific blocks for which it can determine consumer value and then prices the blocks accordingly. Finally, there is third degree price discrimination, where a firm is able to identify and separate two or more distinct categories, or submarkets, of consumers purchasing its good. In this case, the firm will price its output differently in each submarket, based on the different associated own-price elasticities of demand reflected in each submarket.

- A multiplant monopoly arises when a monopolist allocates its production of output over more than one plant in an effort to take advantage of differing cost conditions across its plants.

- When evaluating the outcomes of monopoly, we generally find that the monopoly output is less, its price is higher, and its costs are higher, than the respective outcomes for a perfectly competitive market.

KEY TERMS

- consumer surplus
- deadweight loss
- price discrimination
- producer surplus

EXERCISES

16.1 Define the concept of a deadweight welfare loss that is attributed to a monopoly outcome. Who receives it? Illustrate a deadweight loss using a positively sloped supply curve.

16.2 Assume the market own-price demand curve for a good is

$$Q = 200 - \frac{1}{4}P,$$

where Q is the quantity demanded of the good and P is its price. Suppose the long run total cost, LRTC, curve associated with producing this good is

$$LRTC = 80Q.$$

a. Assuming the market is perfectly competitive, determine the equilibrium values of output and price.

b. Compute the corresponding long run profit, $LR\pi_C$.

c. Compute the consumer surplus, CS_C.

16.3 Refer to the information provided in exercise 16.2. However, now assume the market is monopolized.

a. Determine the monopolist's profit maximizing levels of output and price.

b. Compute the monopolist's profit.

c. Compute the consumer surplus in this case.

d. Compute the deadweight welfare loss, DWL, attributed to the monopoly.

16.4 Again, refer to the information in exercise 16.2, and assume the market is monopolized. However, now suppose the monopolist engages in first degree price discrimination.

a. Compute the profit maximizing level of output. Compare this result to the perfectly competitive level of output.

b. What can you say about the price in this case?

c. Compute the monopolists' profit for this case involving first degree price discrimination.

16.5 Suppose a monopolist is able to separate the demand for its product into two distinct submarkets. The own-price demand curves for submarkets 1 and 2 are

$$Q_1 = 50 - \frac{1}{2} P_1$$

and

$$Q_2 = 36 - \frac{1}{5} P_2, \text{ respectively.}$$

The terms Q_1 and Q_2 represent the quantities demanded in submarkets 1 and 2, respectively, where P_1 and P_2 are the prices of the good in submarkets 1 and 2, respectively. Assume the marginal cost, MC, and average cost, AC, curves for the firm are

$$MC = AC = \$40.$$

a. Determine the inverse own-price demand curves for each submarket.

b. Assuming the firm engages in third degree price discrimination, determine the profit maximizing levels of output sold and price charged, in each submarket.

c. Compute the firm's profit.

16.6 Refer to the own-price demand curves provided in exercise 16.5. Select either a price or a quantity demanded that is common to both demand curves and compute the corresponding own-price elasticities of demand. How do your results comply with your knowledge of third degree price discrimination?

16.7 One of the criteria that we use when comparing the outcomes associated with monopoly to those for perfect competition is allocative efficiency.

a. Define this criteria.

b. Compare the monopoly and perfectly competitive outcomes using this criterion.

16.8 Suppose a monopolist has the inverse own-price demand curve

$$P = 1000 - 10Q,$$

where Q is output and P is the price of the good. The firm has the marginal, MC, and average, AC, cost curves.

$$MC = AC = \$400.$$

a. If the monopolist does not price discriminate, determine its profit maximizing levels of output and price.

b. Compute the firm's profit, π.

c. Now, suppose the firm engages in second degree price discrimination, where it is able to group the units of the good it sells into two blocks of equal amounts. How much output will the firm sell?

d. Compute the prices for the two blocks of units.

e. Compute the firm's profit, π, in this case.

CHAPTER 17: OLIGOPOLY

SUMMARY

The focus of this chapter is on oligopoly, or a market structure consisting of a few firms selling either homogeneous or slightly differentiated products. Initially, our attention is on providing a general description of oligopoly, emphasizing that the central characteristic is interdependence among the few firms comprising such a market. We note that this interdependence may be manifested through collusive behavior that can be described as either overt or covert, depending on the particular activity the firms choose to undertake.

The first formal oligopoly model discussed is the cartel, where firms agree to jointly determine the values of such strategic variables as price and output. We note that the basis for this model is the multiplant monopoly model presented in Chapter 16. Next, we present the Cournot model, where firms covertly collude by taking each other's output decisions into account when determining their own profit maximizing levels of output. Within this context, we discuss the concepts of conjectural variations and reaction functions, deriving the latter both graphically and mathematically. The next model presented is the Stackelberg model, where unlike the Cournot model, the possibility of nonzero conjectural variations are included. Within this framework, we discuss the different outcomes associated with follower - follower, leader - follower, follower - leader, and leader - leader assumptions.

The last two models analyzed are the dominant firm model and the Sweezy kinked demand curve model. For the dominant firm model, we emphasize the fact that a large firm seeks to maximize its profit subject to the condition of allowing a group of small firm to remain in the market. Once the Sweezy model is presented, we discuss the belief held by many critics of this model, that it consists more of a rationalization of outcomes rather than a model that produces results. Finally, we include an appendix to this chapter that contains a comparison of the Cartel, Cournot, Stackelberg, and perfectly competitive outcomes, where this comparison is accomplished with a specific mathematical example. The major topics covered in this chapter are outlined below.

- An oligopoly is a market structure consisting of a few sellers of a good, where each seller accounts for a significant portion of market-wide sales of the good.

- Since there are so few firms comprising an oligopoly, the behavior of individual firms is interdependent, reflecting the fact that each firm can perceptibly influence market output and price, thereby affecting other firms' profits.

- Collusion by firms occurs when they collectively set their production levels so as to directly affect market price. Firms that execute an explicit agreement to jointly determine the values of output and price that will maximize the combined profits of the firms entered into the agreement are said to be engaging in overt collusion. However, if no explicit agreement exists and the firms merely react to each other's behavior, then these actions are labeled as tacit, or covert, collusion.

- A cartel is a group of firms which, through some type of explicit agreement, collude to jointly determine the price and level of output of the product they sell. From a theoretical perspective, the behavior of firms comprising a cartel can be modeled as a multiplant monopoly.

- In the Cournot model of oligopoly behavior, it is assumed that, while each firm reacts to changes in the output of other firms, it does not expect the other firms to respond to changes in its own output.

- A conjectural variation measures how one firm thinks another firm will react to its own adjustments in some strategic variable. In the case of the Cournot model, it is assumed that the conjectural variations for each firm are set equal to zero. In the Stackelberg model of oligopoly behavior, we assume that some or all of the firms comprising an oligopoly may employ conjectural variations that are not necessarily equal to zero.

- A reaction function expresses one firm's profit maximizing level of output as a function of the output sold by another firm.

- The dominant firm model is a type of oligopoly containing one large firm that accounts for a significantly large portion of the sales in a market, and a large number of small firms each of which sell an insignificantly small portion of the market-wide sales. The one large firm is assumed to have the ability to influence the price of the good, while each small firm has an imperceptible effect on market sales or price, and thus acts as a price taker.

- The Sweezy kinked demand curve model was designed to rationalize price rigidities that are observed in some oligopolistic markets.

- In the Sweezy kinked demand curve model it is assumed that the typical oligopolistic firm faces two potential own-price demand curves for its product, each with a different degree of own-price elasticity of demand, depending upon whether its rivals respond to a change in the price it charges for its good. The Sweezy assumptions are that, if a firm lowers its price, its rivals will respond and lower their prices, and if it raises its price, the rivals will not respond and raise their prices.

KEY TERMS

- cartel
- conjectural variation
- oligopoly
- reaction function

EXERCISES

17.1 Define an oligopoly and give the essential characteristic that is central to virtually all models of this type of market structure. What is the reason underlying the existence of this characteristic?

17.2 Define the concepts of reaction functions and conjectural variations. Why are these concepts relevant to oligopoly, but not to other market structures such as perfect competition and monopoly? How do the Cournot and Stackelberg models utilize reaction functions and conjectural variations?

17.3 Assume a cartel contains two firms, where the market own-price demand curve is

$$Q_T = 800 - 2P.$$

The term Q_T is the total, or market, quantity demanded and P is the price of the good. Since the market consists of two firms the market quantity demanded is equal to the summation of the quantities demanded of firm one, Q_1, and firm two, Q_2, respectively, or

$$Q_T = Q_1 + Q_2.$$

The total cost curves for firms one and two are

$$TC_1 = 200 + 10\,Q_1$$

and

$$TC_2 = 400 + \frac{1}{2}\,Q_2^2, \text{ respectively.}$$

a. Determine the profit maximizing levels of output that will be sold by each of the two firms comprising the cartel. Also, determine the total output sold by the cartel.

b. Compute the price that the cartel will charge and the level of its profit.

17.4 Use the same market own-price demand and total cost curves provided in exercise 17.3. However, now assume the cartel is dissolved and the two firms behave according to the Cournot oligopoly model.

a. Determine the reaction functions for the two firms.

b. Determine the level of output sold by each firm, as well as the market amount of output.

c. Compute the price of the product and the profit levels for the two firms. Compare these results to those you computed for the cartel model in exercise 17.3.

17.5 Refer to the results you computed in exercise 17.4, along with the information provided in exercise 17.3. Now, assume a Stackelberg possibility where firm one behaves as a leader and firm two as a follower.

a. Determine the equilibrium quantities sold by the two firms.

b. Compute the price of the product and the profit levels for the two firms.

17.6 Illustrate linear reactions for two firms. Explain the significance of the vertical and horizontal intercepts of the two reaction functions. Also, demonstrate the equilibrium results regarding the quantities sold by both firms and describe what this equilibrium represents.

17.7 Illustrate two potential own-price demand curves for a firm's product, where the two curves intersect at some quantity-price combination. Now, assume the initial price is at this point of intersection and employ the Sweezy assumptions about how rival firms respond to price changes. Demonstrate the quantity demanded of the firm's product if it decreases its price. Then, demonstrate the quantity demanded of the firm's product if it increases its price. Explain your results.

17.8 Refer to your results demonstrated in exercise 17.1. Now, complete the Sweezy model, introducing the necessary marginal revenue and marginal cost curves. Illustrate your results and explain their significance.

CHAPTER 18: APPLICATIONS OF GAME THEORY TO OLIGOPOLISTIC FIRM BEHAVIOR

SUMMARY

In this chapter we extend our study of oligopolistic firm behavior by applying game theory analysis to this market structure. Throughout this chapter we emphasize the interdependent nature of oligopolistic firms' decision-making processes. While it is true that game theory can be used to model strategic decision-making by players in games of chance, government organizations, or consumers and producers of goods, we focus our analysis on the application of game theory models to firm behavior. Accordingly, the examples used in this chapter largely involve strategy choices made by firms operating in a duopoly. Specifically, we emphasize the applicability of game theory to real world business decisions regarding pricing, production, and advertising.

We begin our analysis by defining the concept of game theory and key terms that are used throughout the chapter. The well-known Prisoner's Dilemma game is described as well as several other types of games. Specifically, we develop the concept of sequential games and apply it to a Stackelberg duopoly model. In addition, we develop the concept of a repeated game and apply it to a cartel production model. We also define and apply the concepts of dominant, maximin, minimax, and tit-for-tat strategies, as well as a Nash equilibrium in a game. In an appendix to this chapter we also demonstrate the method of mixed strategies and apply it to a duopoly production choice game. The main topics presented in this chapter are as follows.

- Game theory is a framework for analyzing choices made by firms, consumers, nations, or any players engaged in strategic decision-making.
- The participants in a game are generally referred to as players.
- The choices available to players in a game are known as the strategies.
- All players in a game are assumed to act rationally by selecting strategies that maximize their payoffs, while taking into consideration the alternative strategies the other players may choose.
- Game theory is useful in modeling the interdependent nature of oligopolistic firms' behavior.
- A dominant strategy is one that consistently optimizes a player's payoff in a game, regardless of the strategies chosen by the other players in the game.
- A Nash equilibrium exists in a game when each player selects the strategy that optimizes its payoff, given the strategies chosen by the other players.
- Some games do not possess a Nash equilibrium.

- A maximin strategy is a strategy that maximizes the minimum gain a player can receive in a game.
- In a constant sum game, the sum of the payoffs received by all of the players in the game is a constant value. Therefore, in a two-person constant sum game the payoff received by one player represents the payoff lost by the other player.
- A minimax strategy is a strategy that minimizes the maximum loss a player can receive in a game.
- A saddle point is an equilibrium solution to a game in which the players follow maximin and minimax strategies and no player has an incentive to change its strategy, given the strategies chosen by the other players in the game.
- A saddle point in a game represents a Nash equilibrium.
- A repeated game is one that is played over and over again, where each player has perfect information regarding the strategies previously chosen by the other players in the game.
- In a repeated game, players can use a strategy known as tit-for-tat where they reward their rivals for cooperative behavior or penalize them for uncooperative behavior.
- A sequential game is one in which the order of the players' participation is decided before the start of the game.
- The Stackelberg oligopoly model, where firms choose to either be leaders or followers, can be formulated as a sequential game.

KEY TERMS

- constant sum game
- dominant strategy
- expected value
- game
- game theory
- maximin strategy
- minimax strategy
- mixed strategies
- Nash equilibrium
- payoff
- players
- repeated game
- risk
- saddle point
- sequential game
- strategies

- tit-for-tat
- uncertainty

EXERCISES

18.1 What type of game would be most appropriate for analyzing the long-term production behavior of the Organization of Petroleum Exporting Countries, OPEC? Justify your response.

18.2 Firm X and firm Y, two chewing gum producers, have two alternative advertising strategies for their respective products. Each firm can choose to follow an extensive advertising strategy or follow a limited advertising strategy. If both firms follow limited advertising strategies, then firm X will earn $5 million in profit and firm Y will earn $4 million in profit. If both firms follow extensive advertising strategies then firm X will earn $6 million and firm Y will earn $6 million. If firm X follows an extensive advertising strategy while firm Y follows a limited advertising strategy, firm X will earn $100,000 in profit and firm Y will earn $7 million in profit. If firm X follows a limited advertising strategy while firm Y follows an extensive advertising strategy, firm X will earn $8 million in profit and firm Y will earn $1 million in losses. Construct the payoff matrix for this game.

18.3 Refer to the payoff matrix you constructed for the game in exercise 18.2.

a. Does firm X possess a dominant strategy in this game? If so, what is its dominant strategy and why is this its dominant strategy?

b. Does firm Y possess a dominant strategy? If so, what is its dominant strategy and why is this its dominant strategy?

18.4 Does the game described in exercise 18.2 possess a Nash equilibrium? Explain your answer.

18.5 Firms S and P act collusively in deciding how much output to produce. If both firms abide by their production agreement, each firm will earn $400,000 in profit. If both firms cheat on their production agreement, each firm will earn $75,000 in profit. If one firm cheats while the other abides by the production agreement, the firm that cheats will earn $750,000 in profit while the firm that abides by the production agreement will earn $5,000 in profit. Construct the payoff matrix for this game.

18.6 Refer to the payoff matrix you constructed for exercise 18.5. Assume this game lasts for four rounds and firm S selects its strategy first. Determine the strategies selected by each firm if they perceive the threat of retaliation for cheating on the production agreement to be a credible threat. Also determine the amount of profit earned by each firm.

18.7 Assume there are only two automobile manufactures comprising the market, firm M and firm L. These firms have two alternative strategies with respect to their product lines. Specifically, they must choose between adding a high-priced sports car to their product line or adding a high-priced S.U.V. to their product line. The payoff matrix below indicates the percentage of market share firm L will claim if it chooses the strategy listed to the left, given the strategy chosen by firm M.

Firm M's Strategies

Firm L's Strategies	Add Sports Car to Product Line	Add SUV to Product Line
Add Sports Car to Product Line	50	80
Add SUV to Product Line	20	60

a. What type of game is depicted in this case? Justify your response.

b. Determine the strategy firm L will choose if it follows a maximin strategy and the value of its associated payoff.

c. Determine the strategy firm M will choose if it follows a minimax strategy and the value of its associated payoff.

CHAPTER 19: MONOPOLISTIC COMPETITION

SUMMARY

In this chapter, we discuss the market structure, or in this case, product group, known as monopolistic competition. Initially, we describe the various characteristics associated with this type of market structure, emphasizing the fact that the firms' products are only slightly differentiated. In order to understand the final model of monopolistic competition, developed by Edward Chamberlin, we define both proportional and perceived own-price demand curves for a typical firm comprising such a market structure. Next, we present the formal model, demonstrating short run equilibrium for a monopolistically competitive firm, where this is accomplished by starting from a disequilibrium situation. By so doing, we show not only a short run equilibrium result, but also describe the process by which it is achieved. Then, we allow for firms to adjust their capital, leading to entry and exit, thus enabling us to construct a long run equilibrium result. We emphasize that this result reflects, not only the coinciding of a firm's perception and reality regarding its demand curve, but also a zero profit, due to the condition of free entry and exit. Finally, we provide an evaluation of the outcomes associated with monopolistic competition, ultimately comparing these results to those generated by perfect competition. Special attention is given to the excess capacity result attributed to monopolistic competition, where we provide both the arguments for and against this outcome. Specifically, that excess capacity leads to higher costs and prices, but also that it reflects having a variety of products.

The main topics covered in this chapter are summarized below.

- A product group is a set of heterogeneous, but closely related goods.
- Monopolistic competition is characterized by: a large number of firms, slightly differentiated products, and no barriers to entry.
- In a monopolistically competitive product group, each firm believes it possesses more price setting discretion than actually exists.
- A proportional own-price demand curve indicates the proportion of the total product group sales, demanded at each price, attributed to a single firm in the group.
- A monopolistically competitive firm bases its decisions, in part, on its perceived own-price demand curve.
- A firm's perceived own-price demand curve is more elastic than the proportional own-price demand curve because the firm believes its actions will go unnoticed by its rivals.
- Short run equilibrium occurs at an output level for which a firm's marginal revenue equals its marginal cost and simultaneously, where its perceived own-price demand equals the proportional own-price demand for its product.

- Long run equilibrium occurs at an output level for which a firm's marginal revenue equals its long and short run marginal costs, as well as where its perceived own-price demand equals the proportional own-price demand for its product.

- In long run equilibrium, a monopolistically competitive firm's long run profits are equal to zero. This result follows because of the absence of barriers to entry.

- Due to the restriction of output, long run equilibrium for a monopolistically competitive firm is characterized by excess capacity. Specifically, the firm does not produce enough output to realize all economies of scale advantages.

KEY TERMS

- excess capacity
- monopolistic competition
- product group
- proportional own-price demand curve

EXERCISES

19.1 In the model of monopolistic competition we use two different types of own-price demand curves for a typical firm.

a. Name and define these two different types of curves.

b. Why do we use them in the model and how do they compare?

19.2 Illustrate the two types of curves mentioned in exercise 19.1, making sure they intersect. Then, decrease the price from the point of intersection and compare the quantities demanded pertaining to the two curves.

19.3 Suppose the own-price demand curve for an entire product group is

$$Q^{D,G} = 10{,}000 - 20P,$$

where $Q^{D,G}$ is the quantity demanded of the goods in the product group and P represents the price of these goods.

a. Compute the proportional own-price demand curve for a typical firm, assuming there are 400 firms comprising the product group.

b. Does the firm use this proportional own-price demand curve in making its decision regarding output and price?

19.4 What conditions must be satisfied for a monopolistically competitive firm to be in short run equilibrium? Illustrate such a result assuming the firm is earning a short run profit. Also, demonstrate these profits.

19.5 What conditions must be satisfied for a monopolistically competitive firm to be in long run equilibrium? Illustrate this result and explain why the profit result must occur.

19.6 What is meant by the concept of excess capacity as applied to a monopolistically competitive firm? Refer to the figure you illustrated in Exercise 19.5. In this figure, illustrate the resulting excess capacity. Evaluate this result from a broad social perspective.

CHAPTER 20: DEMAND FOR LABOR

SUMMARY

In this chapter we demonstrate, under varying conditions, how a profit-maximizing firm determines the amount of labor that it hires and uses in its production process. By doing so, we can ultimately derive both demand for labor curves for a firm and for the industry in which it operates. We emphasize that determining a firm's profit maximizing level of output and the level(s) of the inputs it uses are part of the same process.

The first labor demand curve we derive is for the case of only one variable input. We also assume a firm operates as a perfect competitor in both its output and input markets. Accordingly, we define and discuss the concepts of the value of the marginal product of an input and the marginal expense of an input. Next, we direct our attention toward the more complex case where a firm uses more than one variable input. For this scenario, we develop demand curves for both labor and capital, although our major focus is on the demand for labor curve. Imbedded in this process is a discussion of the substitution and output effects associated with a change in the price of labor. In order to mathematically demonstrate these effects, we derive a firm's constant demand for an input curve. The related topics of elasticity of substitution and relative input shares are also discussed.

Once individual firm demand for labor curves have been derived, we direct our attention toward aggregating these curves to construct their industry and market-wide counterparts. Finally, we relax our earlier assumption that a firm behaves as a perfect competitor in its output market. As a result, we introduce the concept of marginal revenue product, where the firm possesses some discretion over the output price it charges. We conclude this chapter by making a comparison between the amount of labor employed when the output market is perfectly competitive, and the amount employed in the same market, assuming that it is a monopoly.

The key topics covered in this chapter are briefly outlined below.

- The value of the marginal product of an input, or VMP, is the change in a firm's total revenue due to a change in the amount of that input used by the firm in its production process, holding the price of its output and other inputs constant.

- The marginal expense of an input, MEI, is the change in a firm's total cost due to a change in the amount of that input employed by the firm, holding other inputs constant.

- If a firm uses only one variable input in its production process, it will maximize its profit by employing that input, say labor, to the point where $VMP_L = MEI_L$, and as a result, the VMP_L curve represents a firm's demand for labor curve in this case.

- If a firm uses more than one variable input, say two inputs, capital and labor, it will determine its profit maximizing quantities of these inputs where the conditions $VMP_K = MEI_K$ and $VMP_L = MEI_L$ are satisfied simultaneously.

- With more than one variable input, when the price of an input changes, the effect on the quantity demanded of that input depends on the associated substitution and output effects, where the output effect is due strictly to the change in a firm's profit maximizing level of output resulting from a change in the price of that input.

- A constant demand for an input curve expresses the quantity demanded of an input, say labor, as a function of its own price, with output and other determinants of that input held constant.

- For the case of more than one variable input, a firm's demand for an input curve is not simply the associated VMP curve, because the quantity demanded of that input depends on the amount of the other variable input used in the firm's production process.

- The elasticity of substitution, $\leftrightarrow$, for the inputs, capital and labor, is the ratio of the percentage change in the capital-labor ratio to the percentage change in the marginal rate of technical substitution between the two inputs, or the percentage change in the input price ratio, holding output constant.

- The elasticity of substitution is useful in determining the impact of a change in relative input prices on the ratio of the relative share of one input, in terms of its contribution to the value of a firm's output, to the relative share of the other input.

- The labor demand curve for a particular market is the summation of individual firm's demand for labor curves. It should be noted that this summation process incorporates the additional complication that the output price received by all such firms declines with increases in their labor usage, thus causing individual firm demand curves to shift.

- The marginal revenue product of an input, MRP, is the change in a firm's total revenue due to a change in the amount of that input it uses, holding other inputs constant. This concept is applicable to a firm which behaves as a monopolist in its output market, and since a monopolist maximizes its profit where $MR < P$, then $MRP < VMP$, indicating that a monopolist will employ a lower maximizing level of an input than will a group of perfectly competitive firms.

KEY TERMS

- ❑ constant output demand for an input curve
- ❑ elasticity of substitution
- ❑ marginal expense of an input
- ❑ marginal revenue product of an input
- ❑ output effect
- ❑ substitution effect
- ❑ value of the marginal product of an input

EXERCISES

20.1 Suppose a firm has the production function

$$Q = 8\,\overline{K}_1^{\frac{1}{4}}\,L^{\frac{1}{4}}$$

where Q is output, K represents the capital input that is fixed at K_1 = 16 units, and L represents the labor input. Also, the firm pays input prices of $\overline{P}_{K,1}$ = \$2 and $\overline{P}_{L,1}$ = \$4, for its capital and labor inputs, respectively. Assume the firm operates in perfectly competitive markets for both its output and its inputs. The price of the firm's capital is P = \$2.

a. Derive the firm's value of the marginal product of labor curve, VMP_L.

b. Derive the firm's marginal expense of the labor input curve, MEI_L.

20.2 Refer to the information given and computed in exercise 20.1.

a. Derive the firm's demand for labor curve, using the VMP_L and MEI_L curves you developed in exercise 20.1.

b. What is the firm's profit maximizing levels of labor and output assuming $P_L = \$8$?

20.3 Refer to the same information in exercises 20.1 and 20.2.

a. Prove that this firm is determining its profit maximizing level of output according to the price equals short run marginal cost, SRMC, rule.

b. Now, derive the firm's demand for labor curve using the P = SRMC rule.

20.4 A firm produces its output according to the function

$$Q = 4K^{\frac{1}{4}} L^{\frac{1}{4}} \overline{Z}_1^{\frac{1}{2}},$$

where Q represents output, K is the capital input, L is the labor input, and Z represents land, that is fixed at $\overline{Z}_1 = 1$ unit. Assume the firm operates in perfectly competitive markets for both its output and its inputs. Thus, it takes the price of its output, P, as well as the prices of its capital, labor, and land inputs, P_K, P_L, and P_Z, respectively, as given. Assume the price of its output is P = \$512.

a. If P_K = \$4, derive the firm's demand for labor curve.

b. If P_L = \$64 derive the firm's demand for capital curve.

20.5 Refer to the information in exercise 20.4.

a. Determine the firm's profit maximizing levels of capital, labor, and output.

b. Derive the firm's short run supply curve.

20.6 Illustrate a firm's value of the marginal product of labor curve, VMP_L. Suppose the price of labor decreases, say from $P_{L,1}$ to $P_{L,2}$, assuming capital is fixed. Show the firm's profit maximizing levels of labor. Now assume that the capital input is also variable. In the same figure demonstrate the substitution effect on labor when the price of labor decreases from $P_{L,1}$ to $P_{L,2}$. Explain your reasoning. Finally, introduce the associated output effect, assuming that it exceeds the substitution effect and then derive the firm's demand for labor curve.

20.7 Explain both the similarity, as well as the difference, between the concepts of the value of the marginal product of an input, VMP, and the marginal revenue product, MRP, of an input. Also, explain the situations to which each of these concepts are relevant.

CHAPTER 21: SUPPLY OF LABOR

SUMMARY

In this chapter, we complete our analysis of labor markets by developing supply of labor curves. To do so, we return to an individual's constrained utility maximization process, where the goods included in the consumer's utility function are leisure time and real income. First, we develop an indifference curve map and a budget constraint for these two goods. Once this is accomplished, we demonstrate, both graphically and mathematically, how to determine the amounts of leisure, labor, and real income that solve this optimization problem. We solve the problem using a constraint containing only labor income and then using a constraint including non-labor income.

Next, we allow the price of labor, or leisure, to vary, thus developing both demand for leisure and supply of labor curves. Imbedded in this analysis, is a discussion of the income and substitution effects associated with a change in the price of leisure time. An analysis is provided for the case where the substitution effect exceeds the income effect and for the converse situation. Also included, is a discussion of a backward bending supply of labor curve. After a brief summary of the aggregation process necessary to derive a market supply of labor curve, we devote the remainder of this chapter to analyzing monopsony. Special attention is focused on how, in this case, the marginal expense of an input exceeds the price of labor, and thus how a monopsonist is able to drive down the price that it pays for its labor input. We conclude the chapter with a graphical comparison between the price of labor and the amount hired by a monoposonist, to the values of these same variables pertaining to a perfectly competitive labor market.

The main topics covered in this chapter are summarized below.

- An individual derives utility, U, from consuming leisure time, Le, and real income, y, according to a utility function, expressed as U = U (Le, y).

- Economists define leisure time as time not supplied to a labor market. Thus, total time, T, is divided between leisure and labor, L, or $\overline{T} = Le + L$.

- An individual's budget constraint regarding leisure and real income is that real income must equal the price of labor multiplied by the amount of labor that individual supplies, plus any non-labor income, N. Thus, $y = \overline{P}_{L,1}L + N = P_L(\overline{T} - Le) + N$.

- An individual solves this constrained utility maximization problem by consuming leisure and real income at a combination where the marginal rate of substitution, MRS, between leisure and real income, is equal to the ratio of their prices, $\frac{P_{L,1}}{1}$.

- An individual's demand for leisure and supply of labor curves are determined by the constrained utility maximization process for an individual consumer regarding the choice between income and leisure time.

- The slope of a consumer's demand for leisure curve and subsequent supply of labor curve is dependent on the magnitudes of the substitution and income effects associated with a change in the price of leisure time, or labor, on the optimal amounts of these variables selected by a consumer.

- If the substitution effect exceeds the income effect, an individual's supply of labor curve possesses a positive slope. Conversely, if the income effect exceeds the substitution effect, then the supply of labor curve possesses a negative slope.

- A monopsony is a market structure consisting of a single buyer of an input. In this case, a firm will employ an input, say labor, where $VMP_L = MEI_L$, but for which the MEI_L exceeds the price of labor. Accordingly, a monopsonist will employ less labor than will a group of firms behaving as perfect competitors in their input markets.

KEY TERMS

- ❑ labor supply curve
- ❑ monopsony

EXERCISES

21.1 Since economists define leisure time, Le, as time not supplied by an individual to a labor market, all of the individual's time, T, is divided between leisure and labor, L. Use the week as your time period, measured in hours, and assume all of the person's real income, y, is derived from supplying labor.

a. Construct the individual's budget constraint regarding leisure and income if the price of labor, P_L, is \$2/hour.

b. Determine and interpret the y and Le intercepts, as well as the slope, of this budget constraint.

21.2 Again using a week as your time period, assume the price of labor, or leisure, increases to $P_L = \$3$.

a. Construct the individual's budget constraint in this case.

b. Determine the y and Le intercepts, along with the slope of this budget constraint.

c. Illustrate this new constraint, along with the one developed in exercise 21.1, in the same figure. What has appeared to happen to this constraint?

21.3 Use the week as the time period and assume the price of labor, or leisure, is $P_L = \$2$. However, now assume the individual receives some non-labor income, $\overline{N}$, equal to $12/week.

a. Develop the budget constraint in this case, noting the y and Le intercepts, as well as the slope.

b. Illustrate this budget constraint.

21.4 Suppose an individual has the utility function

$$U = 20\,Le^{\frac{1}{2}} + 10\,y^{\frac{1}{2}},$$

where U is some index of utility.

a. Use the budget constraint you developed in exercise 21.1, to derive the individual's demand for leisure and supply of labor curves.

b. Determine the optimal levels of leisure, labor, and real income for this person.

21.5 Use the utility function given in exercise 21.4 along with the budget constraint you developed in exercise 21.3. Recall, this budget constraint contains some non-labor income.

a. Determine the individual's optimal levels of leisure, labor, and real income earned from supplying labor, and total real income.

b. Intuitively, explain why the values computed in part a differ from those computed in exercise 21.4.

21.6 Assume an individual receives income only from supplying labor. Illustrate the substitution effect regarding leisure time due to an increase in the price of leisure from $P_{L,1}$ to $P_{L,2}$. Now, assuming leisure is a normal good, demonstrate the total effect on leisure time, provided the associated income effect exceeds the substitution effect.

21.7 Explain why the marginal expense of the labor input, MEI_L, for a monopolist exceeds the price, or wage, that the firm pays for its labor.

CHAPTER 22: CAPITAL MARKETS

SUMMARY

In this chapter we focus on the market for capital, the other input, besides labor, included in most production functions. We begin this chapter by noting some of the rather unique properties associated with the capital input, where generally, these relate to introducing the dimension of time into the analysis. Since capital usually generates services for more than just the time period in which it is purchased, we note how such factors as depreciation and the changing price of capital over time must be taken into account.

Due to the time dimension, we provide a discussion regarding the concepts of interest rates and the process of discounting. We also establish the difference between real and nominal interest rates and demonstrate their relationship with the Fisher equation.

Next, we focus our attention on developing a supply of capital function. In order to do so, we again return to a consumer's constrained utility maximization process, where now the goods included in the utility functions are the individual's consumption levels of goods in two different time periods. We also develop an intertemporal budget constraint, demonstrating how a consumer can transfer consumption between these two time periods. Once this constrained utility maximization problem is solved to determine the optimal levels of the consumption levels in the two time periods, we allow the interest rate to vary, thus rotating the intertemporal budget constraint. By so doing, we develop an individual's demand for consumption and savings curves, where our analysis includes a discussion of the substitution and income effects associated with the change in interest rates. We should note that the analysis is conducted both for individuals designated as net borrowers and for those described as net savers.

Finally, we conclude this chapter by developing a demand for capital function, where this process involves the maximization of a firm's discounted stream of present and future profits, subject to a capital constraint. By solving this problem we are able to express a firm's demand for capital in terms of the interest rate. The key topics presented in this chapter are outlined as follows.

- An interest rate is the ratio of a per annum payment generated by an asset to the value of that asset, or alternatively, it can be interpreted as the per annum growth rate in the value of an asset.

- A real interest rate is a per annum percentage which expresses a payment in terms of the goods and services that can be purchased with that payment in the current time period. A nominal interest rate is a per annum percentage which expresses a payment in current dollar terms. The nominal interest rate is equal to the real interest rate plus the expected inflation rate.

- The future value of an asset is the value of a present asset in terms of what it is worth in some future time period.

- The present value of an asset or payment is the value of a future asset or payment in terms of what it is worth in the present time period. The process of converting a future value into a present value is known as discounting.

- The supply of funds for the accumulation of capital is provided by those consumers who choose to defer some of their consumption from the present time period to future time periods.

- The optimal levels of an individual's consumption in the present and future time periods can be determined by solving a constrained utility maximization model which embodies an intertemporal utility function along with an intertemporal budget constraint containing these consumption levels as decision variables.

- An individual solves the constrained optimization problem involving her consumption levels in two time periods by selecting a combination of these levels at which the marginal rate of substitution, MRS, between the consumption levels is equal to rate at which the individual is able to exchange them, or $1 + r$.

- An individual who spends more than his present income on consumption in the present time period is designated as a net borrower, whereas an individual who spends less than his present income on consumption in the present time period is designated as a net saver and hence ultimately a lender.

- The impact of a change in the interest rate on an individual's constrained utility maximization solution pertaining to present and future consumption levels depends on the associated substitution and income effects and also on whether the individual is a net borrower or net saver.

- For a net borrower, an increase in the interest rate results in the individual decreasing his present consumption and thus increasing his saving in that time period. This outcome is due to the fact that both the substitution and income effects associated with an increase in the interest rate on present consumption are both inverse for this type of individual.

- For a net saver, an increase in the interest rate produces an income effect that runs counter to the substitution effect. Thus, if the substitution effect is greater than the income effect, an increase in the interest rate will result in a decrease in present consumption and an increase in saving. Conversely, if the income effect exceeds the substitution effect, then an increase in the interest rate will lead to an increase in present consumption and a decrease in saving.

- Ultimately a saving curve, which represents the supply of funds for capital accumulation, can be constructed that expresses savings in terms of the interest rate.

- The optimal amount of capital purchased by a firm can be determined by constructing a constrained profit maximization model that embodies the firm's discounted future profit stream as the objective function and an intertemporal capital formation equation as the constraint.

- Investment is the change in a firm's level of capital for a given time period.

- A firm will determine its optimal level of capital in a particular time period by using capital to the point where the value of the marginal product of capital in that time period is equal to the marginal expense of capital for the same time period.

- A demand for capital curve can be generated from the optimization process expressing the quantity of capital demanded in terms of either the interest rate or the rental rate of capital.

KEY TERMS

- discounting
- future value of an asset or payment
- interest rate
- investment
- nominal interest rate
- present value of an asset or payment
- real interest rate

EXERCISES

22.1 In the process of deriving a firm's input demand functions, we find that it is considerably more complicated to derive its demand for capital than its demand for labor. Conceptually, why is this the case? Specifically, name some of the factors that complicate a firm's demand for capital function.

22.2 Suppose your rich aunt promises you $200,000, to be paid three years from now. Further, she signs a contract, making the promise legally binding. Now suppose you don't really need the money now, but you would prefer to have it in the present time period. Ignoring tax considerations and assuming interest rates are currently 20%, suppose someone offers you $120,000 for the contract. Should you take the offer?

22.3 A bond has the face value of $20,000 and pays an annual coupon worth $2,000. Assume the bond has three years left until it matures, at which time it can be redeemed for the face value.

a. If the current interest rate is 5%, what is the current price of the bond? Specifically, for how much could it be sold?

b. Compute the price of the bond if the current interest rate is 10%.

22.4 A new bond is issued that has a face value of $10,000 and annual coupon payments worth $500. Suppose the bond has a maturity of three years, and the interest rate is presently 5%.

a. Assume you purchase and hold the bond for one year, after which you decide to sell it. If interest rates have remained at 5%, at what price can you sell the bond?

b. Again, assume you hold the bond for one year, but now suppose interest rates have risen to 10% after that year. Now, at what price would you be able to sell the bond?

22.5 Assume the price level in 1999 was 1.50 and for 2000 it increased to 1.75.

a. Compute the inflation rate, $\dot{P}$, for the year 2000.

b. Assuming expected inflation, $\dot{P}^*$, is equal to actual inflation and the real interest rate for year 2000 was 4%, compute the nominal interest rate for that year, using the simplified Fisher equation.

22.6 Use the same information given in exercise 22.5. Again, compute the nominal interest rate for year 2000, but now use the more complex version of the Fisher equation.

22.7 Assume an individual receives fixed levels of income, $\bar{I}_1$ and $\bar{I}_2$ for time periods one and two, respectively. If the price levels for these periods are $P_1 = P_2 = 1.0$, and the interest rate, r, is determined to be $\bar{r}_1$, construct the intertemporal budget constraint that defines the person's ability to transfer her consumption levels C_1 and C_2 in periods one and two, respectively, between the two periods. Then, determine the C_1 and C_2 intercepts, as well as the slope, of this constraint and illustrate your results. Also, interpret these results.

22.8 Refer to the information given in exercise 22.7. Determine the numerical values for the C_1 and C_2 intercepts, as well as the slope, of the intertemporal budget constraint, if the interest rate is 5% and $\bar{I}_1 = \bar{I}_2 = \$40,000$. Now assume the interest rate increases to 10%. Compute the new values for the intercepts and slope of the intertemporal budget constraint. Plot this new constraint, along with the original, in the same figure. Compare the two constraints and explain how they differ.

CHAPTER 23: GENERAL EQUILIBRIUM ANALYSIS IN AN EXCHANGE ECONOMY

SUMMARY

This chapter represents a distinct departure in our previous method of analysis. In the preceding chapters we used partial equilibrium analysis when investigating the attainment of equilibrium by individual consumers or firms, or in product or input markets. In this chapter we develop the concept of general equilibrium analysis. In doing so we use key concepts concerning consumer theory, which we developed in earlier chapters, in a general equilibrium framework.

We begin our discussion of the general equilibrium exchange model by defining this concept and carefully demonstrating the manner in which a two consumer, two good Edgeworth box is constructed. After defining the notion of an initial endowment, we use indifference curve analysis to illustrate the concept of a Pareto optimal endowment. We also demonstrate the manner in which a Pareto optimal allocation may be achieved via exchange between the consumers. Afterward we define the concept of a contract curve and illustrate it in the Edgeworth box.

We extend our analysis of general equilibrium by introducing competitively determined goods prices into our model. Within the confines of the Edgeworth box, we demonstrate that when consumers exchange goods in accordance with their competitively determined relative prices, a Pareto optimal distribution of goods is achieved. This outcome provides the economic intuition underlying our discussion of the First and Second Theorems of Welfare Economics. We conclude our analysis of general equilibrium in an exchange economy by deriving the utility possibilities frontier from a set of Pareto optimal goods allocations lying on a contract curve in an Edgeworth box. The main topics covered in this chapter are as follows.

- Partial equilibrium analysis focuses upon the attainment of equilibrium in individual output and input markets, or for an individual consumer or firm.

- General equilibrium analysis examines the process by which simultaneous equilibrium is attained in all output and input markets, and for all consumers and firms comprising these markets.

- An Edgeworth box is a rectangle, which contains all of the feasible combinations of two goods, say X and Y, available in the economy that can be distributed between two consumers. The length of the Edgeworth box measures the total amount of good X available in the economy, and the height of the box measures the total amount of good Y available.

- A change in the amounts of the two goods available in the economy results in a change in the dimensions of the Edgeworth box.

- The initial endowment is a point lying in the Edgeworth box or on its perimeter, which indicates the amounts of two goods, each consumer in the economy initially possesses before any trade takes place between the consumers.

- A Pareto optimal allocation of goods is one for which no one consumer can be made better off without making another consumer worse off.

- At any Pareto optimal allocation of goods, the consumers' marginal rates of substitution for the goods being traded are equal, and therefore, the consumers' indifference curves are tangent at these combinations of goods.

- The contract curve is the set of Pareto optimal allocations of goods within an Edgeworth box.

- If consumer A and B exchange goods X and Y in accordance with the competitively determined relative prices of the goods, specifically $\frac{P_X}{P_Y}$, then a Pareto optimal distribution of these goods can be attained.

- At a competitively determined Pareto optimal allocation of goods $MRS^A = MRS^B = \frac{P_X}{P_Y}$.

- At a competitively determined Pareto optimal allocation of goods, all goods markets are in equilibrium, therefore general equilibrium in the economy is attained.

- The First Theorem of Welfare Economics states that an allocation of goods that is a competitive equilibrium must also be a Pareto optimal allocation of goods.

- The Second Theorem of Welfare Economics states that there exists a set of goods prices such that each Pareto optimal goods allocation lying on the contract curve is also a competitive equilibrium.

- The utility possibilities frontier is a set of points measuring the combinations of utility levels attainable by two consumers corresponding to allocations of goods that lie on the contract curve.

KEY TERMS

- contract curve
- Edgeworth box
- First Theorem of Welfare Economics
- general equilibrium analysis
- initial endowment
- Pareto optimal, or efficient
- partial equilibrium analysis

- ❑ Second Theorem of Welfare Economics
- ❑ utility possibilities frontier

EXERCISES

23.1 In what way is general equilibrium analysis of consumer exchange behavior different from partial equilibrium analysis of consumer behavior?

23.2 In what way is general equilibrium analysis of consumer exchange behavior similar to partial equilibrium analysis of consumer behavior?

23.3 Assume in a two consumer, two good, exchange economy consumer A's initial endowment contains six units of good X and two units of good Y, and consumer B's initial endowment contains one unit of good X and eight units of good Y. Draw the Edgeworth box for this economy, indicate the initial endowment and label it point E. Also plot each consumer's indifference curve assuming the initial endowment is not Pareto optimal.

23.4 Refer to the Edgeworth box you drew in exercise 23.3. Assume that at a Pareto optimal goods allocation in this economy consumer B receives four units of good X and six units of good Y. Also assume that consumer B is a better negotiator in this economy than consumer A when they engage in exchange.

a. In the Edgeworth box you drew in exercise 23.3, indicate the Pareto optimal goods combination and label it point K. Also indicate each consumer's corresponding indifference curve.

b. Describe the specific exchange that takes place between consumer A and consumer B in achieving this Pareto optimal outcome in the economy.

23.5 Assume there are two consumers in an exchange economy, Samantha and Matt, and two goods, chicken wings and steak. The unit price of chicken wings is $2.00 and the unit price of steak is $8.00. Samantha's initial endowment contains five chicken wings and one steak. Matt's initial endowment contains two chicken wings and nine steaks. At their respective initial endowments, Samantha's marginal rate of substitution of chicken wings for steak is 0.10 and Matt's marginal rate of substitution of chicken wings for steak is 0.50.

a. Does the initial endowment of goods in the economy represent a competitive equilibrium? Justify your response mathematically.

b. Can Matt and Samantha engage in exchange to increase at least one person's utility? If so, explain this exchange process.

23.6 Derive the utility possibilities frontier corresponding to the Edgeworth box illustrated below.

Figure 23.1

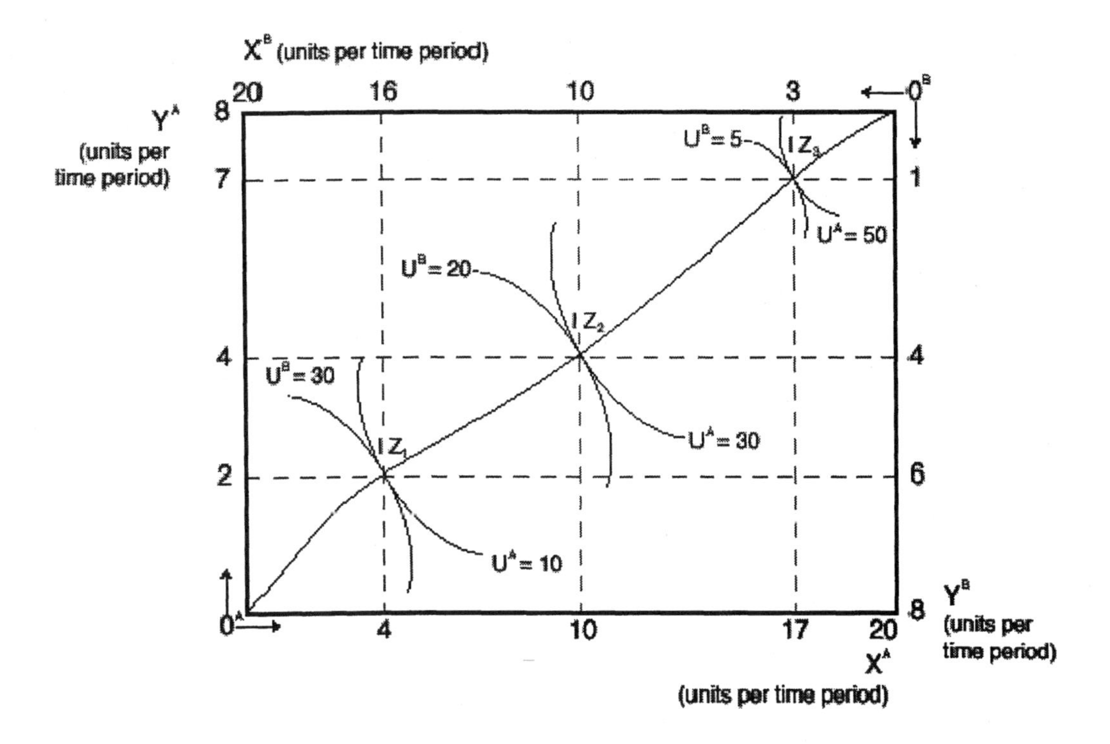

CHAPTER 24: GENERAL EQUILIBRIUM ANALYSIS IN AN ECONOMY WITH PRODUCTION AND EXCHANGE

SUMMARY

In this chapter we extend our analysis of general equilibrium in a two good, two consumer, exchange economy that we introduced in Chapter 23. Specifically, the exchange model is modified so as to include the production of the two goods exchanged in the economy. We derive the Edgeworth production box using graphs of isoquants for two different goods. The concept of technical efficiency is defined and used to establish the notion of a production contract curve. Afterward, we demonstrate that an efficient allocation of inputs used in the production of these goods can be attained when the inputs are traded on the basis of their competitively determined relative prices.

Our discussion of the Edgeworth production box and the concept of technically efficient input combinations provide the basis for deriving the familiar production possibilities frontier. We show that the marginal rate of transformation is measured as the negative of the slope of the production possibilities frontier. In addition, we interpret the slope of the production possibilities frontier as measuring the rate at which the production of one good must be reduced in order to release enough inputs to produce an additional unit of another good, as well as measuring the ratio of the marginal cost of producing an additional unit of each good. Using a production possibilities frontier along with an Edgeworth box we demonstrate the efficiency of perfect competition with the general equilibrium model. Specifically, we derive the efficiency outcome

$$\text{MRT} = \frac{MC_X}{MC_Y} = \frac{P_X}{P_Y} = MRS^A = MRS^B.$$

We conclude our analysis by using the general equilibrium model to demonstrate the economic inefficiencies resulting from monopoly power in output and input markets. The main topics covered in this chapter are as follows.

- An Edgeworth production box is a rectangle that contains all of the feasible combinations of two inputs, labor and capital, available in the economy that can be used in the production of two goods. The length of the Edgeworth production box measures the total amount of labor available in the economy, and the height of the box measures the total amount of capital available.

- A change in the amounts of capital and labor available in the economy will change the dimensions of the Edgeworth production box.

- At a technically efficient input combination, the marginal rates of technical substitution between labor and capital used in the production of each good are equal.

- At a technically efficient input combination, the isoquants for the two goods produced in an economy are tangent.

- A production contract curve is the set of input combinations in an economy that are technically efficient.

- If capital and labor are allocated for the production of goods X and Y in an economy in accordance with the inputs' competitively determined relative prices, $\frac{P_L}{P_K}$, then an efficient distribution of inputs can be attained where $MRTS^X = MRTS^Y = \frac{P_L}{P_K}$.

- At a technically efficient input allocation, where $MRTS^X = MRTS^Y = \frac{P_L}{P_K}$, all input markets in the economy are in equilibrium.

- The production possibilities frontier is a set of points measuring the combinations of two goods that can be produced simultaneously, corresponding to allocations of labor and capital that lie on the production contract curve.

- The marginal rate of transformation measures the rate at which the production of one good in the economy must be reduced in order to release enough labor and capital to product an additional unit of the other good.

- In an economy where two goods, X and Y, are produced using two inputs, labor and capital, and these goods are consumed by individuals A and B, then general equilibrium in production and exchange is attained when $MRS^A = MRS^B$, $MRTS^X = MRTS^Y$, and $MRS^A = MRS^B = MRT$.

- When general equilibrium is attained in production and exchange in an economy, the slope of the consumers' indifference curves is equal to the slope of the production possibilities frontier.

- If all input and output markets are perfectly competitive, then general equilibrium in production and exchange can be attained in an economy.

- Monopoly power in input or output markets distorts the prices of inputs or goods, respectively, so that these inputs and outputs are not efficiently allocated, and general equilibrium is not achieved in an economy.

KEY TERMS

- Edgeworth production box
- marginal rate of transformation
- production contract curve
- production possibilities frontier
- technically efficient

EXERCISES

24.1 Demonstrate the effect of doubling the amounts of capital and labor available in an economy, used to produce goods X and Y, on the Edgeworth production box and the production contract curve.

24.2 Demonstrate the effect of doubling the amounts of capital and labor available in the economy, used in the production of goods X and Y, on the associated production possibilities frontier.

24.3 Ella consumes goods X and Y and her utility function is

$$U^E = 20X^{.5}\,Y^{.5}.$$

Lisa also consumes goods X and Y and her utility function is

$$U^L = 15X^{.5}\,Y^{.5}.$$

The unit price of good X is $75 and the unit price of good Y is $150. Ella consumes twenty units of good X and ten units of good Y. Lisa consumes two units of good X and one unit of good Y. Is the combination of goods consumed by Ella and Lisa a competitive equilibrium in this economy? Justify your response mathematically.

24.4 What must the marginal rate of transformation between goods X and Y equal in order for the combination of goods consumed by Ella and Lisa in exercise 24.3 to represent general equilibrium in production and exchange in this economy?

24.5 Assume two goods are produced in an economy, bread and cheese, using two inputs, labor and capital. A total of 120 units of labor and 60 units of capital are available in the economy. The unit price of labor is \$15 and the unit price of capital is \$30. The production function for bread is

$$Q^B = 2K^{.5} L^{.5},$$

and the production function for cheese is

$$Q^C = 8K^{.5} L^{.5}.$$

If 50 units of labor and 26 units of capital are used to produce bread, and 70 units of labor and 34 units of capital are used to produce cheese, is this allocation of inputs technically efficient? Justify your response mathematically.

24.6 Using the production functions for bread and cheese and the unit prices of labor and capital provided in exercise 24.5, determine an allocation of capital and labor that lies on the production contract curve when these inputs are exchanged on the basis of their competitively determined prices. Also determine the associated amounts of bread and cheese produced in the economy.

CHAPTER 3AW: UNCERTAINTY, RISK, AND EXPECTED UTILITY

SUMMARY

In this chapter we extend our analysis of rational consumer behavior by incorporating the idea of imperfect information into our standard model of consumer choice. This is a natural extension in the sense that in the real world consumers rarely possess perfect information concerning all of the choices they make. Our goal in this chapter is to demonstrate the techniques that can be used to model consumer behavior given the risks inherent in the individual's choices.

We begin our analysis by defining the three states of nature within which individuals make their consumption decisions, specifically certainly, uncertainty, and risk. In an effort to enhance students' understanding of the notion of risk, we briefly review the fundamental statistical concepts of probabilities and expected values.

The idea of an expected value is directly incorporated into an expected, or vonNeumann-Morgenstern, utility function. Using this type of utility function we model the economic behavior of risk averse, risk neutral, and risk preferring consumers. We have included several real-world examples in this chapter to demonstrate the applicability of expected utility analysis. One examines a consumer's investment portfolio choices based on his preferences regarding risk. Other examples deal with an individual's choice between an unreliable used sports car, and a reliable, boring sedan, as well as purchases of insurance, and lottery tickets. The main topics covered in this chapter are as follows.

- The environment in which a consumer makes decisions can be characterized into one of three states: certainty, uncertainty, or risk.
- A state of certainty exists when an individual has access to perfect information regarding the outcome of his consumption choice.
- Uncertainty is a situation in which a consumer does not possess perfect information nor any of the probabilities associated with the occurrence of a specific outcome.
- Risk is a situation that exists when a consumer does not have perfect information, however, he does know the probabilities associated with all of the possible outcomes.
- The expected, or mean, value of a variable, X, that has the ability to take on a number of values, such as $X_1, X_2, \ldots, X_n$, equals the summation of the products of each value of X multiplied by the probability of its occurrence.

- The expected, or mean, value of the variable X is expressed mathematically as

$$E(X) = Pr_1X_1 + Pr_2X_2 + \ldots + Pr_nX_n = \sum_{i=1}^{n} Pr_iX_i,$$

where $Pr_1, Pr_2, \ldots, Pr_n$, represent the probabilities associated with the variable X assuming the values of $X_1, X_2, \ldots, X_n$, respectively.

- A fair game is one for which the cost of playing the game is equal to the expected value of the game.

- An expected utility function, also known as a von Neumann-Morgenstern utility function, measures the expected utility of a set of n possible outcomes as the sum of the products of the utility received from each outcome multiplied by its respective probability of occurrence.

- Mathematically, an expected utility function is generally expressed as

$$E\left[U\left(Pr_i, X_i\right)\right] = Pr_1U\left(X_1\right) + Pr_2U\left(X_2\right) + \ldots + Pr_nU\left(X_n\right) = \sum_{i=1}^{n} Pr_iU\left(X_i\right).$$

- If we assume that a consumer does not have perfect information, then we can model the behavior of a rational consumer using an expected utility function.

- An individual is risk averse if the expected utility she receives from an outcome associated with a risky choice is less than the utility she receives from an outcome with certainty, which is equal to the expected, or mean, outcome associated with the risky choice.

- If an individual is risk averse, his utility function will be concave, such as $U(X) = 4X^{.5}$.

- An individual is risk neutral if the expected utility he receives from an outcome associated with a risky choice is equal to the utility he receives from an outcome with certainty, which is equal to the expected, or mean, outcome associated with a risky choice.

- If an individual is risk neutral his utility function will be linear, such as $U(X) = 3X$.

- An individual is risk preferring if the expected utility she receives from an outcome associated with a risky choice is greater than the utility she receives from an outcome with certainty, which is equal to the expected, or mean, outcome associated with a risky choice.
- If an individual is risk preferring her utility function is convex, such as $U(X) = 12X^2$.

- A risk premium measures the amount of money an individual is willing to forgo in order to make him indifferent between a risky investment and one with a certain return.

- Expected utility analysis can be applied to consumer choice regarding investments, insurance, games of chance, and risky goods.

KEY TERMS

- certainty
- expected utility function
- expected value
- fair game
- risk
- risk-averse
- risk-neutral
- risk-preferring
- risk-premium
- uncertainty
- variance

EXERCISES

3AW.1 Clifford's preferences toward the risk associated with lottery tickets varies as the value of the lottery jackpot changes. Specifically, Clifford is risk-averse when the value of the jackpot is less than $5 million. However, when the jackpot is greater than $5 million, he is risk preferring. Sketch Clifford's utility function for lottery tickets.

3AW.2 Refer to the graph of Clifford's utility function you drew in exercise 3AW.1.

a. What is the effect on Clifford's marginal utility as the value of the jackpot increases from $1 million to $2 million? Explain your response.

b. What is the effect on Clifford's marginal utility as the value of the jackpot increases from $6 million to $7 million? Explain your response.

3AW.3 John and George both receive utility from the value of their respective coin collections. John's utility function is

$$U^J = 20X_J^{.5},$$

where U^J denotes John's level of utility and X^J denotes the value of his coin collection. George's utility function is

$$U^G = 10X_G^{2},$$

where U^G denotes George's level of utility and X^G denotes the value of his coin collection. Plot each person's utility function.

3AW.4 Refer to the information contained in exercise 3AW.3. Which person is more likely to insure his coin collection? Explain your response.

3AW.5 Refer to the data in the table below.

Stock	Bull Market Probability	Bull Market Return	Bear Market Probability	Bear Market Return
J	$Pr_G^J = 0.45$	$X_G^J = \$6,900$	$P_B^J = 0.55$	$X_B^J = \$4,900$
V	$Pr_G^V = 0.30$ \$10,000	$X_G^V =$	$Pr_B^V = 0.70$ \$4,000	$X_B^V =$

a. **Determine the expected value of stock J.**

b. Determine the expected value of stock V.

3AW.6 Olga derives utility from her wealth, denoted X. Her utility function is

$$U = 8X^{.5}.$$

Refer to the information regarding stocks J and V in the table in exercise 3AW.5, along with Olga's utility function to answer the following questions.

a. Determine the expected utility Olga would receive from investing in stock J.

b. Determine the expected utility Olga would receive from investing in stock V.

c. If Olga makes a rational investment decision, which stock will she choose? Justify your response.

3AW.7 a. Explain the economic concept of a risk premium.

b. Using the data in the table in exercise 3AW.5, along with your response to exercise 3AW.6, determine the value of the risk premium and interpret its meaning as it specifically applies to Olga.

SOLUTIONS TO ALL EXERCISES

SOLUTIONS

Chapter 1

1.1 a. $y = 6x^0$

Since a variable raised to the zero power is equal to 1, then $y = 6x^0 = 6\ (1) = 6$.

$$\frac{dy}{dx} = \frac{d6}{dx} = 0$$

b. $y = 12x^3 - 9x^2 + 15x + 40$

$$\frac{dy}{dx} = \frac{d12x^3}{dx} - \frac{d9x^2}{dx} + \frac{d15x}{dx} + \frac{d40}{dx}$$

$= 3\ (12x^{3-1}) - 2\ (9x^{2-1}) + 1\ (15x^{1-1}) + 0$

$= 36x^2 - 18x + 15$

c. $y = 330x^{-3} + 20x^{-2} + 15x^{-1} + 2x + 75$

$$\frac{dy}{dx} = \frac{d330x^{-3}}{dx} + \frac{d20x^{-2}}{dx} + \frac{d15x^{-1}}{dx} + \frac{d2x}{dx} + \frac{d75}{dx}$$

$= -3\ (330x^{-3-1}) + -2\ (20x^{-2-1}) + -1\ (15x^{-1-1}) + 1\ (2x^{1-1}) + 0$

$= -\ 990x^{-4} - 40x^{-3} - 15x^{-2} + 2$

d. $y = (8x^2 - 4)\ (9x^3 - x^2 + 12x)$

$$\frac{dy}{dx} = \frac{d\left[\left(8x^2-4\right)\left(9x^3-x^2+12x\right)\right]}{dx}$$

$$= (8x^2 - 4) \cdot \frac{d\left(9x^3-x^2+12x\right)}{dx} + (9x^3-x^2+12x) \cdot \frac{d\left(8x^2-4\right)}{dx}$$

$= (8x^2 - 4)\ (27x^2 - 2x + 12) + (9x^3 - x^2 + 12x)\ (16x)$

e. $y = (18x^2 + 5x) / (3x - 14)$

$$\frac{dy}{dx} = \frac{d\left[\left(18x^2+5x\right)/(3x-14)\right]}{dx}$$

$$= \frac{(3x-14)\dfrac{d\left(18x^2+5x\right)}{dx} - (18x^2+5x)\dfrac{d(3x-14)}{dx}}{(3x-14)^2}$$

$$= \frac{(3x-14)(36x+5)-\left(18x^2+5x\right)(3)}{(3x-14)^2}$$

1.2 a. $y = 1800x + 500$

$$\frac{dy}{dx} = \frac{d1800x}{dx} + \frac{d500}{dx}$$

$= 1800 + 0$

$= 1800$

$$\frac{d^2y}{dx^2} = \frac{d\left(\frac{dy}{dx}\right)}{dx} = \frac{d1800}{dx} = 0$$

b. $y = \frac{12}{x^3}$

$$\frac{dy}{dx} = \frac{d\left(\frac{12}{x^3}\right)}{dx} = \frac{x^3\left(\frac{d12}{dx}\right) - 12\left(\frac{dx^3}{dx}\right)}{\left(x^3\right)^2}$$

$$= \frac{x^3(0) - 12\left(3x^2\right)}{x^6}$$

$$= \frac{-36x^2}{x^6}$$

$$= \frac{-36}{x^4}$$

$$\frac{d^2y}{dx^2} = \frac{d\left(\frac{dy}{dx}\right)}{dx} = \frac{d\left(\frac{-36}{x^4}\right)}{dx}$$

$$= \frac{x^4\left(\frac{d(-36)}{dx}\right) + 36\left(\frac{dx^4}{dx}\right)}{\left(x^4\right)^2}$$

$$= \frac{x^4(0) + 36\left(4x^3\right)}{x^8}$$

$$= \frac{144x^3}{x^8}$$

$$= \frac{144}{x^5}$$

c. $y = (7x^2 + 20) / 8x^3$

$$\frac{dy}{dx} = \frac{8x^3\frac{d\left(7x^2+20\right)}{dx} - \left(7x^2+20\right)\frac{d8x^3}{dx}}{\left(8x^3\right)^2}$$

$$= \frac{8x^3(14x) - \left(7x^2+20\right)\left(24x^2\right)}{64x^6}$$

$$= \frac{112x^4 - 168x^4 - 480x^2}{64x^6}$$

$$= \frac{-56x^4 - 480x^2}{64x^6}$$

$$= \frac{8x^2(-7x^2-60)}{64x^6}$$

$$= \frac{-7x^2-60}{8x^4}$$

$$\frac{d^2y}{dx^2} = \frac{d\left(\frac{dy}{dx}\right)}{dx^2} = \frac{d\left(\frac{-7x^2-60}{8x^4}\right)}{dx}$$

$$= \frac{8x^4\left(\frac{d(-7x^2-60)}{dx}\right) - (-7x^2-60)\left(\frac{d8x^4}{dx}\right)}{(8x^4)^2}.$$

$$= \frac{8x^4(-14x)+(7x^2+60)(32x^3)}{64x^8}$$

$$= \frac{-112x^5+224x^5+1920x^3}{64x^8}$$

$$= \frac{112x^5+1920x^3}{64x^8}$$

$$= \frac{16x^3(7x^2+120)}{64x^8}$$

$$= \frac{7x^2+120}{4x^5}$$

d. $y = (20x)(5x^3 + 14x^2)$

$$\frac{dy}{dx} = (20x)\frac{d(5x^3+14x^2)}{dx} + (5x^3+14x^2)\frac{d20x}{dx}$$

$= 20x(15x^2 + 28x) + (5x^3 + 14x^2)(20)$

$= 300x^3 + 560x^2 + 100x^3 + 280x^2$

$= 400x^3 + 840x^2$

$$\frac{d^2y}{dx^2} = \frac{d\left(\frac{dy}{dx}\right)}{dx} = \frac{d(400x^3+840x^2)}{dx}$$

$= 1200x^2 + 1680x$

1.3 a. $y = 4000x - 10x^2$

To determine the value of x that optimizes this function take the first derivative of y with respect to x and set this equation equal to zero to formulate the first-order condition as follows.

$$\frac{dy}{dx} = 4000 - 20x = 0$$

Solve the above equation for the value of x that optimizes the value of the function $y = 4000x - 10x^2$.

$4000 - 20x = 0$
$4000 = 20x$
$$x = \frac{4000}{20} = 200.$$

b. To determine whether the function, $y = 4000x - 10x^2$ is at a maximum, a minimum, or an infection point when x = 200, we must examine the second-order condition as follows.

$$\frac{d^2y}{dx^2} = \frac{d\left(\frac{dy}{dx}\right)}{dx} = \frac{d(4000-20x)}{dx} = -20 < 0.$$

Since the second-order condition is a negative value this indicates that the function, $y = 4000x - 10x^2$, is at a maximum when x = 200.

c. To determine the optimal value of y, substitute x = 200 into the original function as follows.

$y = 4000x - 10x^2$
$= 4000\,(200) - 10\,(200)^2$
$= 800{,}000 - 400{,}000$
$= 400{,}000$

1.4 a. The marginal revenue function is determined by taking the first derivation of the total revenue function with respect to q is as follows.

$TR = 400q - 5q^2$
$$MR = \frac{dTR}{dq} = \frac{d(400q - 5q^2)}{dq} = 400 - 10q$$

b. To determine the level of output, q, that maximizes the firm's total revenue, we must set $MR = \frac{dTR}{dq}$ equal to zero, as a first-order condition, and solve for the value of q as follows.

$$\frac{dTR}{dq} = MR = 400 - 10q = 0$$
$400 = 10q$

$$q = \frac{400}{10} = 40 \text{ units.}$$

To ensure that this value of q maximizes the value of TR we must examine the second-order condition as follows.

$$\frac{d\left(\frac{dTR}{dq}\right)}{dq} = \frac{dMR}{dq} = \frac{d(400-10q)}{dq} = -10 < 0$$

Since the second-order derivative is a negative value this indicates that the function, $TR = 400q - 5q^2$, is at a maximum when q = 40 units.

c. We can determine the maximum value of total revenue by substituting q = 40 into the total revenue function.

$$TR = 400q - 5q^2$$
$$= 400\,(40) - 5\,(40)^2$$
$$= 16{,}000 - 8{,}000$$
$$= \$8{,}000.$$

1.5 a. The marginal cost function is determined by taking the first derivative of the total cost function with respect to q as follows.

$$TC = \frac{1}{3}q^3 - 4q^2 + 56q + 20$$

$$MC = \frac{dTC}{dq} = q^2 - 8q + 56.$$

b. To determine the amount of output the firm must produce in order to minimize its marginal cost, we must take the derivative of the marginal cost function with respect to q and set this derivative equal to zero as the first-order condition.

$$\frac{dMC}{dq} = \frac{d\left(q^2 - 8q + 56\right)}{dq} = 2q - 8 = 0.$$

We can now solve the above equation for the value of q that optimizes the marginal cost function as follows.

$$2q - 8 = 0$$
$$2q = 8$$
$$q = \frac{8}{2} = 4 \text{ units.}$$

To ensure that the marginal cost function is minimized when q = 4 units we must examine the second-order derivative of MC with respect to q.

Second-order condition:

$$\frac{d^2MC}{dq^2} = \frac{d\left(\frac{dMC}{dq}\right)}{dq} = \frac{d(2q-8)}{dq} = 2 > 0.$$

Since the second-order derivative of the marginal cost function with respect to q is a positive value, the value of marginal cost is minimized when q = 4 units.

c. We can determine the minimum value of marginal cost by substituting q = 4 units into the marginal cost function as follows.

$MC = q^2 - 8q + 56$
$= (4)^2 - 8(4) + 56$
$= \$40.$

1.6 a. $y = 10x^3 z^2$

$$\frac{\partial y}{\partial x} = 30x^2z^2$$

$$\frac{\partial y}{\partial z} = 20x^3 z$$

b. When x = 2 and z = 3 then,

$$\frac{\partial y}{\partial x} = 30x^2 z^2$$

$= 30\,(2)^2\,(3)^2$
$= 1080$

and

$$\frac{\partial y}{\partial z} = 20x^3 z$$

$= 20\,(2)^3\,(3)$
$= 480.$

c. The total derivate is determined as

$$\frac{dy}{dx} = \frac{\partial y}{\partial x} + \frac{\partial y}{\partial z} \cdot \frac{dz}{dx}.$$

Given that $z = 12x^2$, then

$$\frac{dz}{dx} = \frac{d12x^2}{dx} = 24x.$$

We can substitute $\frac{\partial y}{\partial x} = 30x^2 z^2$ and $\frac{\partial y}{\partial z} = 20x^3 z$ from part a. and

$\frac{dz}{dx} = 24x$ into the formula for the total derivative, $\frac{dy}{dx}$ as follows.

$$\frac{dy}{dx} = \frac{\partial y}{\partial x} + \frac{\partial y}{\partial z} \cdot \frac{dz}{dx}$$
$$= 30x^2 z^2 + 20x^3 z\,(24x)$$
$$= 30x^2 z^2 + 480\, x^4 z.$$

When x = 2 and z = 3 then,

$$\frac{dy}{dx} = 30x^2z^2 + 480\, x^4 z$$
$$= 30\,(2)^2\,(3)^2 + 480\,(2)^4\,(3)$$
$$= 1080 + 23{,}040$$
$$= 24{,}120$$

1.7 a. The marginal product of labor function is determined by taking the partial derivative of the production function with respect to labor as follows.

$$Q = 24K^{\frac{3}{4}}L^{\frac{1}{4}}$$

$$MP_L = \frac{\partial Q}{\partial L} = \frac{\partial 24K^{\frac{3}{4}}L^{\frac{1}{4}}}{\partial L} = 24\left(\frac{1}{4}\right)K^{\frac{3}{4}}L^{-\frac{3}{4}}$$
$$= 6\,K^{\frac{3}{4}}L^{-\frac{3}{4}}$$

The marginal product of capital function is determined by taking the partial derivative of the production function with respect to capital as follows.

$$Q = 24K^{\frac{3}{4}}L^{\frac{1}{4}}$$

$$MP_K = \frac{\partial Q}{\partial K} = \frac{\partial 24K^{\frac{3}{4}}L^{\frac{1}{4}}}{\partial K}$$
$$= 24\left(\frac{3}{4}\right)K^{-\frac{1}{4}}L^{\frac{1}{4}}$$
$$= 18\,K^{-\frac{1}{4}}\,L^{\frac{1}{4}}$$

b. We can determine the value of MP_L and MP_K when the firm uses 81 units of labor and 16 units of capital by substituting these values into the MP_L and MP_K functions we derived in part a. of exercise 1.7.

$$MP_L = 6K^{\frac{3}{4}}L^{-\frac{3}{4}}$$
$$= 6\,(16)^{\frac{3}{4}}\,(81)^{-\frac{3}{4}}$$
$$= 6\,(8)\left(\frac{1}{27}\right)$$

$$= \frac{48}{27}$$

$$= \frac{16}{9}$$

$$= 1.78$$

$$MP_K = 18K^{-\frac{1}{4}} L^{\frac{1}{4}}$$

$$= 18\,(16)^{-\frac{1}{4}}(81)^{\frac{1}{4}}$$

$$= 18\left(\frac{1}{2}\right)(3)$$

$$= \frac{54}{2}$$

$$= 27$$

SOLUTIONS

Chapter 2

2.1 a.

$y = 252x + 6xz - 3x^2 - 6z^2$

$\frac{\partial y}{\partial x} = 252 - 6z - 6x = 0$

$\frac{\partial y}{\partial z} = 6x - 12z = 0$

$6x = 12z$

$x = 2z$

$252 - 6z - 6(2z) = 0$

$252 - 6z - 12z = 0$

$z^* = 14$

$x^* = 2z^* = 2(14) = 28$

b. To determine the optimal value of y, substitute $x^* = 28$ and $z^* = 14$ into the objective function as follows.

$y^* = 252x^* + 6x^*z^* - 3(x^*)^2 - 6(z^*)^2$

$y^* = 252(28) + 6(28)(14) - 3(28)^2 - 6(14)^2$

$= 7056 + 2352 - 2352 - 1176$

$= 5880$

2.2 a.

$\mathcal{L} = 252x + 6xz - 3x^2 - 6z^2 + \lambda(36 - x - z)$

$= 252x + 6xz - 3x^2 - 6z^2 + 36\lambda - \lambda x - \lambda z$

$\frac{\partial \mathcal{L}}{\partial x} = 252 + 6z - 6x - \lambda = 0$

$\frac{\partial \mathcal{L}}{\partial z} = 6x - 12z - \lambda = 0$

$\frac{\partial \mathcal{L}}{\partial \lambda} = 36 - x - z = 0$

$252 + 6z - 6x = 6x - 12z$

$252 + 18z = 12x$

$x = 21 + 1.5z$

$36 - (21 + 1.5z) - z = 0$

$36 - 21 - 1.5z - z = 0$

$2.5z = 15$

$z^* = 6$

$36 - x - z = 0$

$36 - x - 6 = 0$

$x^* = 30$

b. Substitute $x^* = 30$ and $z^* = 6$ into the objective function to determine the optimal value of y.

$$y^* = 252x^* + 6x^*z^* - 3(x^*)^2 - 6(z^*)^2$$
$$= 252(30) + 6(30)(6) - 3(30)^2 - 6(6)^2$$
$$= 7560 + 1080 - 2700 - 216$$
$$= 5724$$

c. The optimal value of y computed in this exercise is smaller than the optimal value of y computed in exercise 2.1. This is due to the fact that there is a binding constraint in this problem which restricts the values that the decision variables, x and z, can assume and this reduces the optimal value of the objective variable, y.

2.3 a. The value of λ^* is determined by substituting $x^* = 30$ and $z^* = 6$ into the equation for either $\frac{\partial \mathcal{L}}{\partial x}$ or $\frac{\partial \mathcal{L}}{\partial z}$.

$$\frac{\partial \mathcal{L}}{\partial z} = 6x - 12z - \lambda = 0$$
$$6(30) - 12(6) = \lambda$$
$$180 - 72 = \lambda$$
$$\lambda^* = 108$$

b. The value of λ^* indicates that if the constraint is relaxed by one unit then the optimal value of the objective function would change by the value of $\lambda^* = 108$.

2.4 a. Minimize $y = 5x^2 + 2xz + 3z^2$
subject to $x + 2z = 380$

$$\mathcal{L} = 5x^2 + 2xz + 3z^2 + \lambda(380 - x - 2z)$$
$$= 5x^2 + 2xz + 3z^2 + 380\lambda - \lambda x - 2\lambda z$$

$$\frac{\partial \mathcal{L}}{\partial x} = 10x + 2z - \lambda = 0$$
$$\frac{\partial \mathcal{L}}{\partial z} = 2x + 6z - 2\lambda = 0$$
$$\frac{\partial \mathcal{L}}{\partial \lambda} = 380 - x - 2z = 0$$
$$2(10x + 2z) = \lambda(2)$$
$$20x + 4z = 2\lambda$$
$$20x + 4z = 2x + 6z$$
$$2z = 18x$$
$$z = 9x$$

$380 - x - 2(9x) = 0$
$380 - x - 18x = 0$
$19x = 380$
$x^* = 20$
$z^* = 9(x^*) = 9(20) = 180$

b. To determine the minimum value of y, substitute $x^* = 20$ and $z^* = 180$ into the objective function as follows.

$y^* = 5(x^*)^2 + 2(x^*)(z^*) + 3(z^*)^2$
$= 5(20)^2 + 2(20)(180) + 3(180)^2$
$= 2000 + 7200 + 97{,}200$
$= 106{,}400$

2.5 a. To determine the value of λ^*, substitute $x^* = 20$ and $z^* = 180$ into the equation for $\frac{\partial \mathcal{L}}{\partial x}$ or $\frac{\partial \mathcal{L}}{\partial z}$ as follows.

$\frac{\partial \mathcal{L}}{\partial x} = 10x + 2z - \lambda = 0$
$10(20) + 2(180) = \lambda$
$200 + 360 = \lambda$
$\lambda^* = 560$

b. The constraint in this problem is binding due to the fact that the value of λ^* is not equal to zero. This indicates that a change in the constraint will affect the optimal value of the objective function. If the value of $\lambda^* = 0$ this would indicate that the constraint was not binding.

c. The value of λ^* indicates that if the constraint is relaxed by one unit to be
$x + 2z = 379$
then the optimal value of the objective function will increase by the value of λ^* to $106{,}400 + 560 = 106{,}960$.

2.6 a. Maximize $y = 200x^{.5}z^{.5}$
subject to $10x + 5z = 1000$

$\mathcal{L} = 200x^{.5}z^{.5} + \lambda(1000 - 10x - 5z)$
$= 200x^{.5}z^{.5} + 1000\lambda - 10\lambda x - 5\lambda z$
$\frac{\partial \mathcal{L}}{\partial x} = 100x^{-.5}z^{.5} - 10\lambda = 0$

$$\frac{\partial \mathcal{L}}{\partial z} = 100\, x^{.5}\, z^{-.5} - 5\,\lambda = 0$$

$$\frac{\partial \mathcal{L}}{\partial \lambda} = 1000 - 10x - 5z = 0$$

$$\frac{100x^{-.5}z^{.5}}{100x^{.5}z^{-.5}} = \frac{10\lambda}{5\lambda}$$

$$\frac{z}{x} = 2$$

$$z = 2x$$

$$1000 - 10x - 5z = 0$$
$$1000 - 10x - 5\,(2x) = 0$$
$$1000 - 10x - 10x = 0$$
$$1000 = 20x$$
$$x^* = 50$$
$$z^* = 2x^* = 2\,(50) = 100$$

b. To determine the maximum value of y, substitute the optimal values of x and z, $x^* = 50$ and $z^* = 100$ into the objective function as follows.

$$y^* = 200\,(x^*)^{.5}\,(z^*)^{.5}$$
$$= 200\,(50)^{.5}\,(100)^{.5}$$
$$= 14{,}142.136$$

c. Substitute $x^* = 50$ and $z^* = 100$ into the equation for either $\frac{\partial \mathcal{L}}{\partial x}$ or $\frac{\partial \mathcal{L}}{\partial z}$ to determine the value of λ^* as follows.

$$\frac{\partial \mathcal{L}}{\partial x} = 100x^{-.5}\, z^{.5} - 10\lambda = 0$$
$$(100)\,(50)^{-.5}\,(100)^{.5} - 10\lambda = 0$$
$$(100)\,(0.1414)\,(10) = 10\lambda$$
$$\lambda^* = 14.142$$

The value of λ^* indicates that if the constraint in this problem was relaxed by one unit to
$10x + 5z = 1001$,
the maximum value of the objective function increases by the value of λ^* from 14,142.136 to 14,142.136 + 14.142 = 14,156.278.

2.7 a. Since the primal problem is a maximization problem, the associated dual is a minimization problem. The objective function in the dual is the constraint in the primal problem in exercise 2.6. The constraint in the dual is the objective function in the primal problem. The constraint in the dual is set equal to the maximized value of the primal objective function determined in exercise 2.6.

Minimize $w = 10x + 5z$
subject to $200x^{.5}z^{.5} = 14{,}142.136$

b. The values of the decision variables that optimize the dual problem are the same as those that optimize the primal problem. Therefore, $x^* = 50$ and $z^* = 100$ for both the primal and the dual problems.

c. The value of λ^{D*}, associated with the dual problem, is equal to the reciprocal of λ^* computed for the primal problem. Therefore, $\lambda^{D*} = \frac{1}{\lambda^*} = \frac{1}{14142} = 0.0707$.

SOLUTIONS

Chapter 3

3.1 a. $U = 160X^{.25}Y^{.75}$

$$MU_X = \frac{\partial U}{\partial X} = 40X^{-.75}Y^{.75} = 40\left(\frac{Y}{X}\right)^{.75}$$

b. $U = 160X^{.25}Y^{.75}$

$$MU_Y = \frac{\partial U}{\partial Y} = 120X^{.25}Y^{-.25} = 120\left(\frac{X}{Y}\right)^{.25}.$$

c. Steve's marginal utility function for good X, soda pop, is

$$MU_X = 40X^{-.75}Y^{.75} = 40\left(\frac{Y}{X}\right)^{.75}$$

Since X is in the denominator of MU_X, if Steve increases his consumption of good X, thereby causing the value of X to increase, this will result in a decrease in the value of MU_X. Thus, Steve's marginal utility from good X, soda pop, decreases as he increases his consumption of this good.

d. Steve's marginal utility for good Y, pizza, is

$$MU_Y = 120X^{.25}Y^{-.25} = 120\left(\frac{X}{Y}\right)^{.25}.$$

Since Y is the denominator of MU_Y, if Steve increases his consumption of good Y, pizza, thereby causing the value of Y to increase, this will result in a decrease in the value of MU_Y. Thus, Steve's marginal utility from good Y, pizza, decreases as he increases his consumption of this good.

3.2 a. Steve's marginal rate of substitution of good X, soda pop, for good Y, pizza, is computed as follows.

$$MRS = \frac{\frac{\partial U}{\partial X}}{\frac{\partial U}{\partial Y}} = \frac{MU_X}{MU_Y} = \frac{40X^{-.75}Y^{.75}}{120X^{.25}Y^{-.25}} = \frac{Y}{3X}.$$

Steve's marginal rate of substitution of soda pop, X, for pizza, Y, is $MRS = \frac{Y}{3X}$.

Since X is in the denominator of the MRS, if Steve increases his consumption of good X, soda pop, then his marginal rate of substitution of good X for good Y diminishes.

b. When Steve consumes 2 units of good X, soda pop, and 12 units of good Y, pizza, his marginal rate of substitution of soda pop for pizza is computed by substituting

X = 2 and Y = 12 into the formula for his marginal rate of substitution found in part a.

$$\text{MRS} = \frac{Y}{3X} = \frac{12}{3(2)} = 2$$

c. Steve's marginal rate of substitution of good X, soda pop, for good Y, pizza, is equal to 3 indicating that when he is consuming 2 units of good X and 12 units of good Y, he is willing to substitute 1 unit of good X for 2 units of good Y, while maintaining the same level of utility.

3.3 a. Donna's marginal rate of substitution of good X, shoes, for good Y, dresses, is computed as

$$\text{MRS} = \frac{\frac{\partial U}{\partial X}}{\frac{\partial U}{\partial Y}} = \frac{MU_X}{MU_Y}.$$

Given that Donna's utility function is

$U = 20X^{.5}\,Y^{.5}$

then

$$MU_X = \frac{\partial U}{\partial X} = 10X^{-.5}\,Y^{.5}$$

$$MU_Y = \frac{\partial U}{\partial Y} = 10X^{.5}\,Y^{-.5}$$

and

$$\text{MRS} = \frac{MU_X}{MU_Y} = \frac{10X^{-.5}Y^{.5}}{10X^{.5}Y^{-.5}} = \frac{Y}{X}.$$

b. Set Donna's utility function equal to 40 and determine for values of X, shoes, and Y, dresses, that solve this equation as follows.

$U = 20X^{.5}\,Y^{.5}$

$40 = 20X^{.5}\,Y^{.5}$

$(40)^2 = (20X^{.5}\,Y^{.5})^2$

$1600 = 400XY$

$4 = XY$

$$Y = \frac{4}{X}$$

Point	Units of Good X	Units of Good Y
A	1	4
B	2	2
C	4	1

Figure 3.1

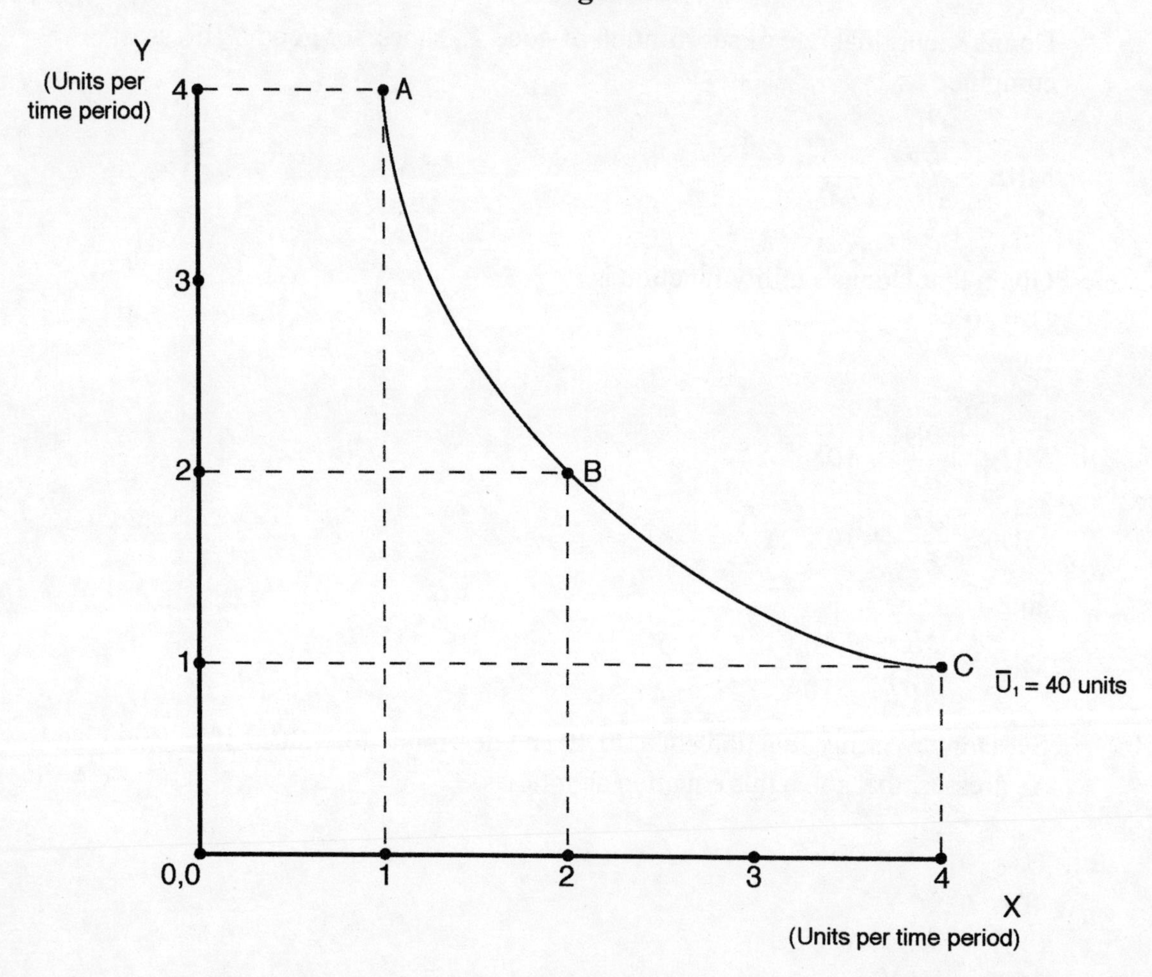

c. To determine the value of Donna's MRS at three points on her U = 40 indifference curve, substitute into the formula for her MRS the values of X and Y corresponding to the three goods combinations you plotted in the graph in part b.

At point A, X = 1 and Y = 4, therefore,

MRS at point A = $\frac{Y}{X} = \frac{4}{1} = 4$.

At point B, X = 2 and Y = 2, therefore,

MRS at point B = $\frac{Y}{X} = \frac{2}{2} = 1$.

At point C, X = 4 and Y = 1, therefore,

MRS at point C = $\frac{Y}{X} = \frac{1}{4}$.

The value of Donna's marginal rate of substitution of good X, shoes, for good Y, dresses, diminishes as she substitutes more units of good X for good Y.

3.4 a. U = 200X + 800Y

$MU_X = \frac{\partial U}{\partial X}$ = 200 which is a constant value, therefore, Samantha's marginal utility from steak does not diminish as she consumes additional units of steak.

b. U = 200X + 800Y

$MU_Y = \frac{\partial U}{\partial Y}$ = 800 which is a constant value, therefore Samantha's marginal utility from lobster does not diminish as she consumes additional units of lobster.

3.5 a. U = 200X + 800Y

$$MRS = \frac{\frac{\partial U}{\partial X}}{\frac{\partial U}{\partial Y}} = \frac{200}{800} = \frac{1}{4}.$$

Samantha's marginal rate of substitution is a constant value equal to $\frac{1}{4}$. This value indicates that Samantha is always willing to substitute 1 unit of good X, steak, for $\frac{1}{4}$ unit of good Y, lobster, while maintaining the same level of utility.

b. Since Samantha's marginal rate of substitution is equal to a constant value of $\frac{1}{4}$ this indicates that her marginal rate of substitution does not diminish as she substitutes additional units of good X, steak, for good Y, lobster.

c. To plot Samantha's indifference curve, set her utility function equal to 2400 and determine values of X, steak, and Y, lobster, that solve this equation as follows.

U = 200X + 800Y

$$2400 = 200X + 800Y$$
$$800Y = -200X + 2400$$
$$Y = -\frac{1}{4}X + 3$$

Units of Good X	Units of Good Y
0	3
4	2
12	0

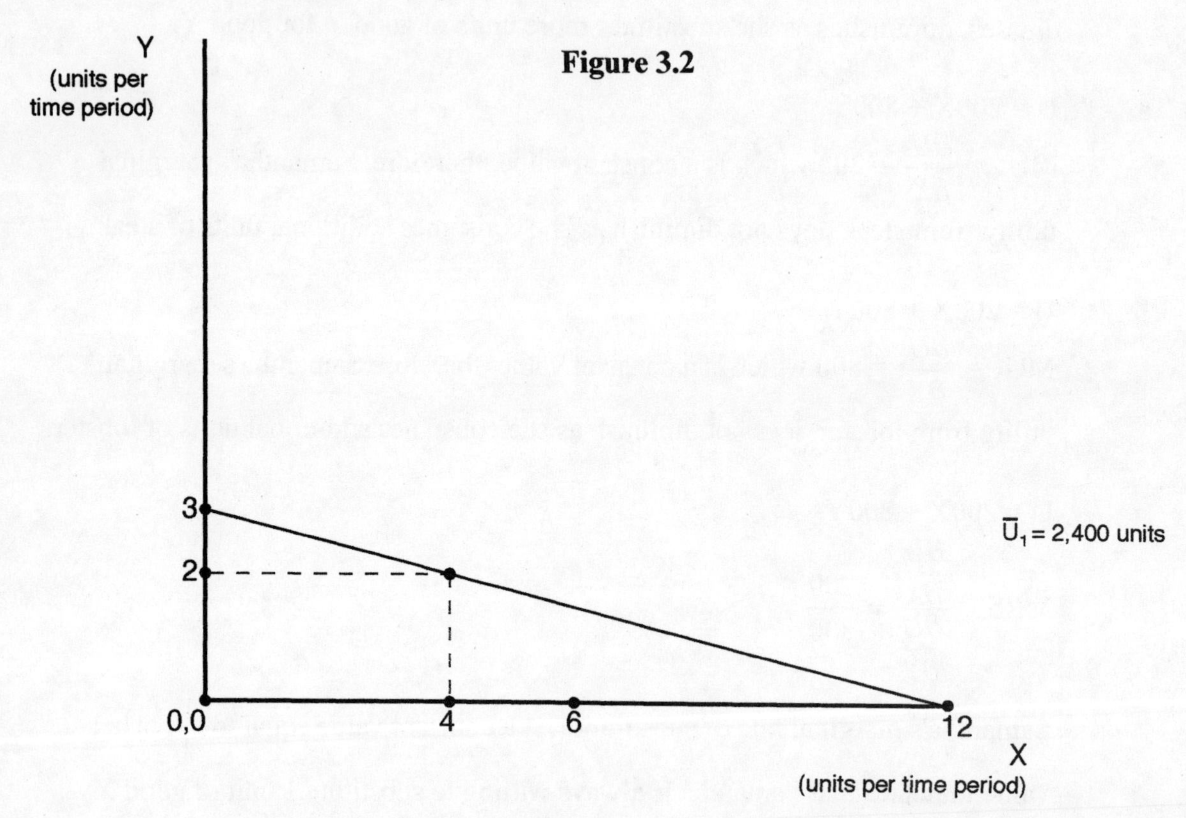

Figure 3.2

3.6 a. Since Olga only receives utility from consuming soft pretzels, X, and packs of mustard, Y, in a one to two proportion, her utility function is

$$U = \text{minimum}\left(\frac{X}{1}, \frac{Y}{2}\right).$$

b. Olga perceives soft pretzels and packs of mustard as perfect complements since she only derives utility from these goods when she consumes them in fixed proportions.

c. Since Olga perceives the goods to be perfect complements, her indifference curve is L-shaped. To plot Olga's indifference curve corresponding to her receiving 16 units of utility, set her utility function equal to 16 and determine values of X and Y that solve the equation as follows.

$$U = \text{minimum}\left(\frac{X}{1}, \frac{Y}{2}\right)$$

$$16 = \text{minimum}\left(\frac{X}{1}, \frac{Y}{2}\right)$$

Units of Good X	Units of Good Y
16	32
16	40
40	32

Figure 3.3

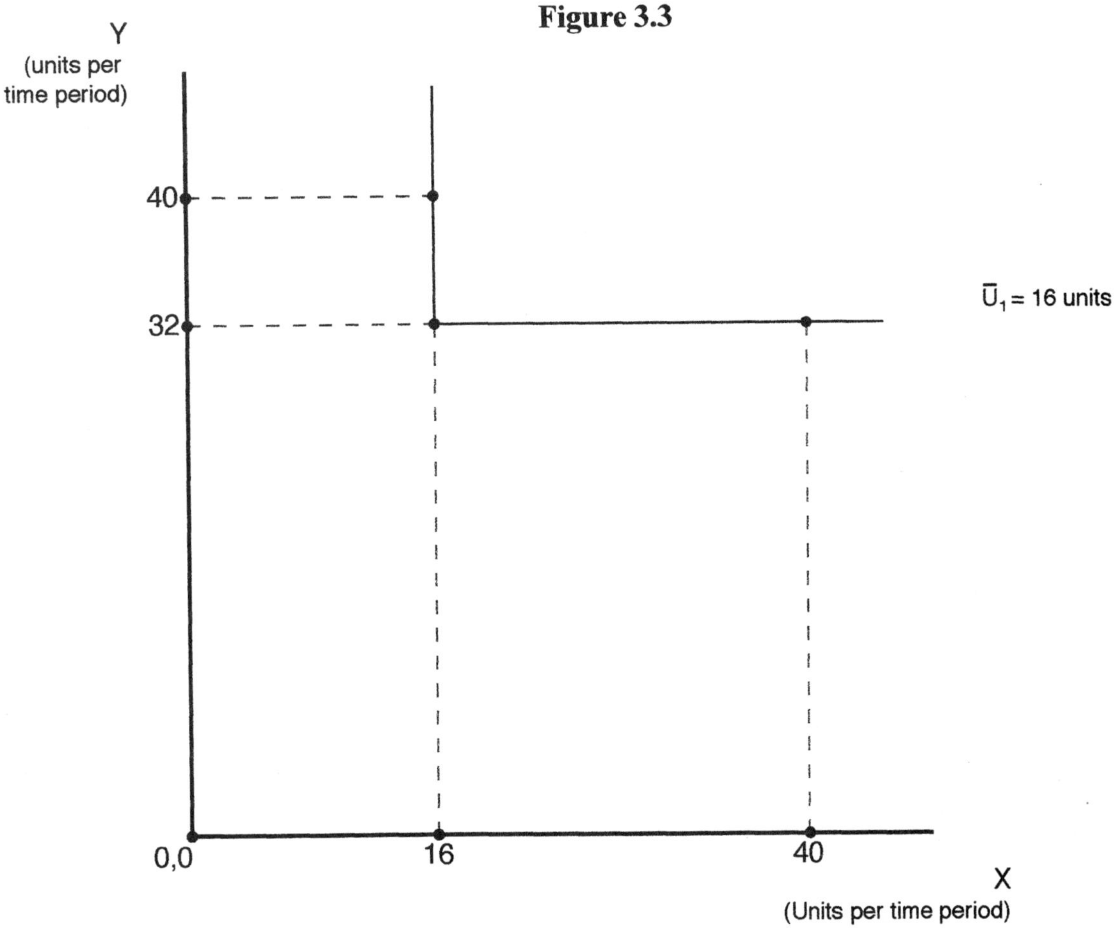

Y (units per time period)

40

32

0,0

16

40

X (Units per time period)

$\bar{U}_1$ = 16 units

d. $U = \text{minimum}\left(\frac{X}{1}, \frac{Y}{2}\right)$

If X= 3 and Y = 8 then Olga's utility is computed as

$U = \text{minimum}\left(\frac{3}{1}, \frac{8}{2}\right) = \text{minimum } (3, 4) = 3.$

If X = 3 and Y = 6 then Olga's utility is computed as

$U = \text{minimum}\left(\frac{3}{1}, \frac{6}{2}\right) = \text{minimum } (3, 3) = 3.$

Therefore, Olga does not receive more utility from the goods combination with more units of good Y, mustard, since the two goods must be consumed in fixed proportions according to a 1 to 2 ratio of good X, soft pretzels, to good Y, mustard. The two additional packs of mustard, good Y, will not yield any additional utility to the consumer when she is also consuming three pretzels.

3.7 a. U = 5X - 15Y

$MU_X = \frac{\partial U}{\partial X} = 5$

George's marginal utility from consuming additional units of cheese does not diminish since it is a constant value equal to 5. Each additional unit of cheese George consumes gives him 5 additional units of utility.

b. U = 5X - 15Y

$MU_Y = \frac{\partial U}{\partial Y} = -15.$

George's marginal utility from consuming broccoli does not diminish since it is a constant value equal to -15. Each additional unit of broccoli George consumes reduces his utility by 15 units.

c. Since the marginal utility George receives from consuming additional units of cheese is a positive, constant value, George regards cheese as an economic "good". However, since the marginal utility George receives from consuming additional units of broccoli is a negative, constant value. George regards broccoli as an economic "bad".

d. To determine the level of utility George receives when he consumes 6 units of cheddar cheese, good X, and 1 units of broccoli, good Y, substitute these values into George's utility function as follows

$$U = 5X - 15Y$$
$$= 5(6) - 15(1)$$
$$= 15.$$

To plot George's indifference curve which contains 6 units of cheddar cheese, good X, and 1 unit of broccoli, good Y, set his utility function equal to 15 and determine other values of X and Y that solve this equation.

$$U = 5X - 15Y$$
$$15 = 5X - 15Y$$
$$15Y = 5X - 15$$
$$Y = \frac{1}{3}X - 1.$$

Units of Good X	**Units of Good Y**
3	0
6	1
9	2

Figure 3.4

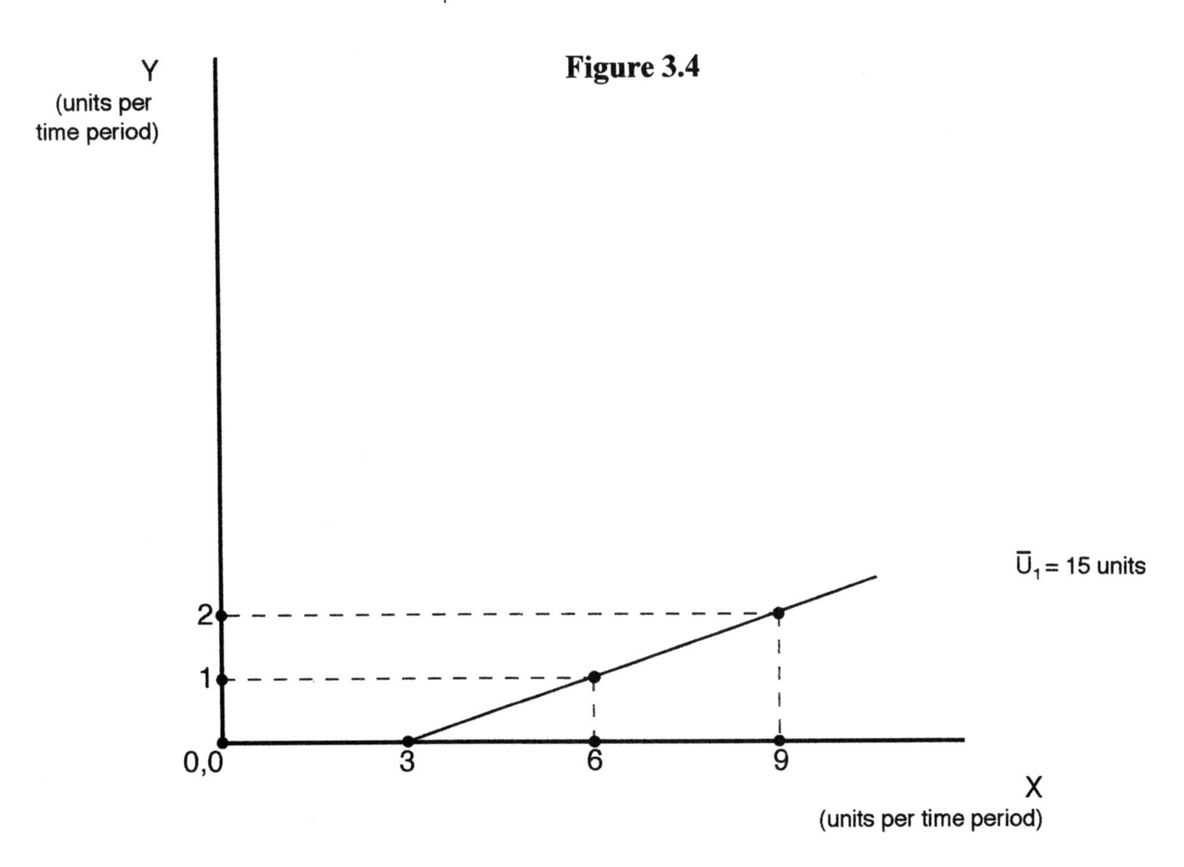

3.8 Economists typically use strictly convex indifference curves in their analysis of consumer behavior because the marginal rate of substitution between the goods in the consumer's utility function diminishes. This is consistent with the behavior of many consumers who, as they gain additional units of one good, are willing to reduce their consumption of the other good, which is becoming increasingly scarce, by fewer and fewer units, while remaining at the same level of utility.

SOLUTIONS

Chapter 4

4.1 a. Given $\overline{P}_{X,1} = \$1.00, \overline{P}_{Y,1} = \$1.50$ *and* $\overline{I}_1 = \$12.00$, Dave's budget equation is

$$1.00X + 1.50Y = 12.00$$

To plot Dave's budget equation, first determine its slope and intercept values as follows.

$$\text{slope of budget constraint} = \frac{-\overline{P}_{X,1}}{\overline{P}_{Y,1}} = \frac{-\$1.00}{\$1.50} = \frac{-1}{1.5}$$

$$\text{X-intercept of budget constraint} = \frac{\overline{I}_1}{\overline{P}_{X,1}} = \frac{\$12.00}{\$1.00} = 12$$

$$\text{Y-intercept of budget constraint} = \frac{\overline{I}_1}{\overline{P}_{Y,1}} = \frac{\$12.00}{\$1.50} = 8$$

Insert Figure 4.1

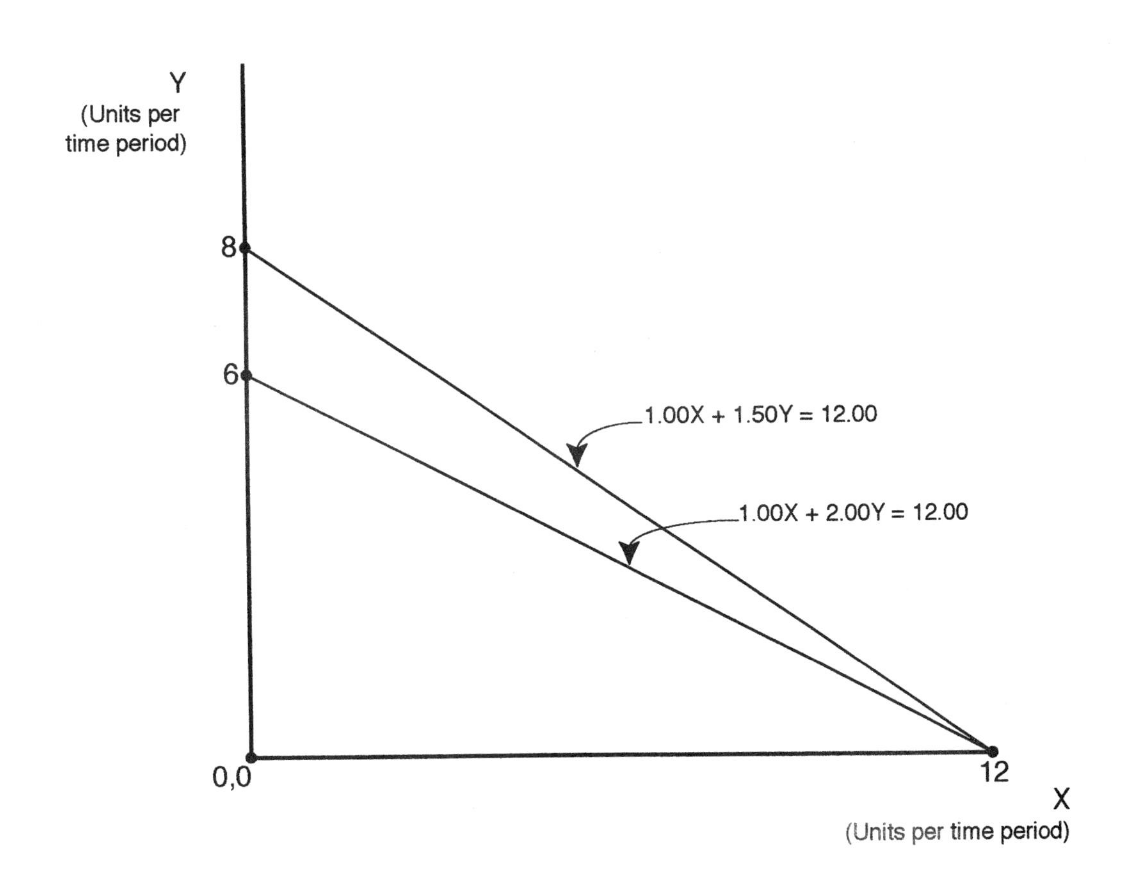

b. When $\overline{P}_{X,1} = \$1.00, \overline{P}_{Y,2} = \$2.00$ *and* $\overline{I}_1 = \$12.00$, Dave's new budget equation is

$$1.00X + 2.00Y = 12.00$$

To plot this new budget constraint, first determine the values of its slope and intercepts as follows.

$$\text{slope of budget constraint} = \frac{-\overline{P}_{X,2}}{\overline{P}_{Y,1}} = \frac{-\$1.00}{\$2.00} = \frac{-1}{2}$$

$$\text{X-intercept of budget constraint} = \frac{\overline{I}_1}{\overline{P}_{X,1}} = \frac{\$12.00}{\$1.00} = 12$$

$$\text{Y-intercept of budget constraint} = \frac{\overline{I}_1}{\overline{P}_{Y,2}} = \frac{\$12.00}{\$2.00} = 6$$

Dave's new budget constraint is steeper than his original budget constraint.

c. When $\overline{P}_{X,1} = \$1.00, \overline{P}_{Y,1} = \$1.50$ *and* $\overline{I}_2 = \$36.00$, Dave's budget constraint is

$$1.00X + 1.50Y = 36.$$

The slope of this new budget constraint is $\frac{-\overline{P}_{X,1}}{\overline{P}_{Y,1}} = \frac{-\$1.00}{\$1.50} = \frac{-1}{1.5}$, which is the same as the slope of budget constraint in part a. The X- and Y-intercepts of the new budget constraint are

$$\text{X- intercept} = \frac{\overline{I}_2}{\overline{P}_{X,1}} = \frac{\$36.00}{\$1.00} = 36$$

and

$$\text{Y- intercept} = \frac{\overline{I}_2}{\overline{P}_{Y,1}} = \frac{\$36.00}{\$1.50} = 24,$$

therefore, both the X- and the Y- intercepts are larger than in the original budget constraint in part a. Since only the consumer's income has increased, this will result in an increase in the consumer's budget set from

$$1.00X + 1.50Y \leq 12$$

to

$$1.00X + 1.50Y \leq 36.$$

Dave's budget constraint has shifted to the right in a parallel fashion as a result of the increase in his income, *ceteris paribus*.

4.2 a. If $\overline{I}_1 = \$80,000, \overline{P}_{X,1} = \$100$ *and* $\overline{P}_{Y,1} = \$500$, then the consumer's budget equation is

$$100X + 500Y = 80{,}000,$$

and the budget set is

$$100X + 500Y \leq 80{,}000.$$

b. If $\bar{I}_1 = \$80{,}000, \bar{P}_{X,1} = \$100 \text{ and } \bar{P}_{Y,1} = \$500$, then

$$\text{slope of the budget constraint} = \frac{-\bar{P}_{X,1}}{\bar{P}_{Y,1}} = \frac{-\$100}{\$500} = \frac{-1}{5}$$

$$\text{X- intercept} = \frac{\bar{I}_1}{\bar{P}_{X,1}} = \frac{\$80{,}000}{\$100} = 800$$

$$\text{Y- intercept} = \frac{\bar{I}_1}{\bar{P}_{Y,1}} = \frac{\$80{,}000}{\$500} = 160$$

c. If $\bar{I}_2 = \$40{,}000, \bar{P}_{X,2} = \$50 \text{ and } \bar{P}_{Y,2} = \$250$ then the consumer's budet equation is

$$50X + 250Y = 40{,}000$$

and the budget set is

$$50X + 250Y \leq 40{,}000.$$

$$\text{slope of budget constraint} = \frac{-\bar{P}_{X,2}}{\bar{P}_{Y,2}} = \frac{-\$50}{\$250} = \frac{-1}{5}$$

$$\text{X- intercept} = \frac{\bar{I}_2}{\bar{P}_{X,2}} = \frac{\$40{,}000}{\$50} = 800$$

$$\text{Y- intercept} = \frac{\bar{I}_2}{\bar{P}_{Y,2}} = \frac{\$40{,}000}{\$250} = 160$$

The above slope and intercept values are the same as those computed in part b., when $\bar{P}_{X,1} = \$100, \bar{P}_{Y,1} = \$500, \text{ and } \bar{I}_1 = \$80{,}000$. Therefore, the consumer's budget constraint and budget set are unchanged when his income and the prices of goods X and Y are simultaneously reduced by one-half.

4.3 a. Maximize $U = 7200\, X^{.75}\, Y^{.25}$
subject to $\bar{P}_{X,1}X + \bar{P}_{Y,1}Y = \bar{I}_1$

$$\mathcal{L} = 7200X^{.75}\, Y^{.25} + \lambda\left(\bar{I}_1 - \bar{P}_{X,1}X - \bar{P}_{Y,1}Y\right)$$

$$= 7200X^{.75}\, Y^{.25} + \lambda\bar{I}_1 - \bar{P}_{X,1}\lambda X - \bar{P}_{Y,1}\lambda Y$$

$$\frac{\partial\mathcal{L}}{\partial X} = 5400X^{-.25}\, Y^{.25} - \bar{P}_{X,1}\lambda = 0$$

$$\frac{\partial\mathcal{L}}{\partial Y} = 1800X^{.75}\, Y^{-.75} - \bar{P}_{Y,1}\lambda = 0$$

$$\frac{\partial\mathcal{L}}{\partial \lambda} = \bar{I}_1 - \bar{P}_{X,1}X - \bar{P}_{Y,1}Y = 0$$

$$5400X^{-.25}Y^{.25} = \overline{P}_{X,1}\lambda$$

$$1800X^{.75}Y^{-.75} = \overline{P}_{Y,1}\lambda$$

$$\frac{5400X^{-.25}Y^{.25}}{1800X^{.75}Y^{-.75}} = \frac{\overline{P}_{X,1}\lambda}{\overline{P}_{Y,1}\lambda}$$

$$\frac{3Y}{X} = \frac{\overline{P}_{X,1}}{\overline{P}_{Y,1}}$$

$$Y = \frac{\overline{P}_{X,1}X}{3\overline{P}_{Y,1}}$$

$$\overline{I}_1 - \overline{P}_{X,1}X - \overline{P}_{Y,1}\left(\frac{\overline{P}_{X,1}X}{3\overline{P}_{Y,1}}\right) = 0$$

$$\overline{I}_1 - \overline{P}_{X,1}X - \frac{1}{3}\overline{P}_{X,1}X = 0$$

$$\overline{I}_1 - \frac{4}{3}\overline{P}_{X,1}X = 0$$

$$X = \frac{3\overline{I}_1}{4\overline{P}_{X,1}}$$

To determine the optimal value of X, substitute $\overline{P}_{X,1} = \$90$ and $\overline{I}_1 = \$1200$ into the above equation as follows.

$$X^* = \frac{3(1200)}{4(90)} = 10 \text{ units}$$

To determine the optimal value of Y, substitute $\overline{P}_{X,1} = \$90,\ \overline{P}_{Y,1} = \$30$ and $X^* = 10$ into the equation

$$Y^* = \frac{\overline{P}_{X,1}X^*}{3\overline{P}_{Y,1}} = \frac{(90)(10)}{3(30)} = 10 \text{ units.}$$

b. To determine the maximum amount of utility Jan can receive, substitute $X^* = 10$ and $Y^* = 10$ into the objective function as follows.

$$U^* = 7200\,(X^*)^{.75}\,(Y^*)^{.25}$$
$$= 7200\,(10)^{.75}\,(10)^{.25}$$
$$= 72{,}000$$

To determine the optimal value of λ, substitute $X^* = 10$, $Y^* = 10$, $\overline{P}_{X,1} = \$90$ and $\overline{P}_{Y,1} = \$30$ into the equation for $\frac{\partial \mathcal{L}}{\partial X}$ or $\frac{\partial \mathcal{L}}{\partial Y}$ as follows.

$$\frac{\partial \mathcal{L}}{\partial X} = 5400X^{-.25}\,Y^{.25} - \overline{P}_{X,1}\lambda = 0$$

$$= 5400X^{-.25}\,Y^{.25} = \overline{P}_{X,1}\lambda$$

$$\lambda^* = \frac{5400(X^*)^{-.25}(Y^*)^{.25}}{\overline{P}_{X,1}}$$

$$= \frac{5400(10)^{-.25}(10)^{.25}}{90} = 60$$

d. The value of $\lambda^* = 60$ indicates that if Jan's income increases by one dollar, from \$1200 to \$1201, her utility will increase by the value of $\lambda^* = 60$, from 72,000 to 72,000 + 60 = 72,060. Conversely, if Jan's income decreases by one dollar from \$1200 to \$1199 her utility will decrease by the value of $\lambda^* = 60$, from 72,000 to 72,000 - 60 = 71,940.

4.4 a. Minimize $E = \overline{P}_{X,1}X + \overline{P}_{Y,1}Y$

subject to $\overline{U}_1 = 7200X^{.75}Y^{.25}$

$$\mathcal{L}^D = \overline{P}_{X,1}X + \overline{P}_{Y,1}Y + \lambda^D\left(\overline{U}_1 - 7200X^{.75}Y^{.25}\right)$$

$$= \overline{P}_{X,1}X + \overline{P}_{Y,1}Y + \overline{U}_1\lambda^D - 7200\lambda^D X^{.75}Y^{.25}$$

$$\frac{\partial \mathcal{L}}{\partial X} = \overline{P}_{X,1} - 5400\lambda^D X^{-.25}Y^{.25} = 0$$

$$\frac{\partial \mathcal{L}}{\partial Y} = \overline{P}_{Y,1} - 1800\lambda^D X^{.75}Y^{-.75} = 0$$

$$\frac{\partial \mathcal{L}}{\partial \lambda^D} = \overline{U}_1 - 7200X^{.75}Y^{.25} = 0$$

$$\frac{\overline{P}_{X,1}}{\overline{P}_{Y,1}} = \frac{5400\lambda^D X^{-.25}Y^{.25}}{1800\lambda^D X^{.75}Y^{-.75}}$$

$$\frac{\overline{P}_{X,1}}{\overline{P}_{Y,1}} = \frac{3Y}{X}$$

$$Y = \frac{X\overline{P}_{X,1}}{3\overline{P}_{Y,1}}$$

$$\overline{U}_1 - 7200X^{.75}\left(\frac{X\overline{P}_{X,1}}{3\overline{P}_{Y,1}}\right)^{.25} = 0$$

$$\overline{U}_1 = 7200X\left(\frac{\overline{P}_{X,1}}{3\overline{P}_{Y,1}}\right)^{.25}$$

$$X = \frac{\overline{U}_1}{7200}\left(\frac{\overline{P}_{X,1}}{3\overline{P}_{Y,1}}\right)^{-.25}$$

From the corresponding primal problem in exercise 4.3, we determined that $\overline{U}_1 = 72{,}000$. Also $\overline{P}_{X,1} = \$90$ and $\overline{P}_{Y,1} = \$30$. Substitute these values into the above equation for X as follows.

$$X^* = \frac{72{,}000}{7200}\left(\frac{90}{3(30)}\right)^{-.25} = 10(1)^{-.25} = 10 \text{ units.}$$

To determine the optimal value of Y^*, substitute $X^* = 10$, $\overline{P}_{X,1} = \$90$, and $\overline{P}_{Y,1} = \$30$ into the equation for Y as follows.

$$Y^* = \frac{X^*\overline{P}_{X,1}}{3\overline{P}_{Y,1}} = \frac{10(90)}{3(30)} = \frac{900}{90} = 10 \text{ units.}$$

b. Substitute $X^* = 10$ and $Y^* = 10$ into the objective function to determine the minimum expenditure necessary to purchase the optimal combination of goods as follows.

$$\begin{aligned} E^* &= \overline{P}_{X,1}X^* + \overline{P}_{Y,1}Y^* \\ &= (\$90)\,(10) + (\$30)\,(10) \\ &= \$900 + \$300 \\ &= \$1200 \end{aligned}$$

c. To determine the optimal value of λ^D, substitute $\overline{P}_{X,1} = \$90$, $\overline{P}_{Y,1} = \$30$, $X^* = 10$, and $Y^* = 10$ into the equations for either $\frac{\partial \mathcal{L}^D}{\partial X}$ or $\frac{\partial \mathcal{L}^D}{\partial Y}$ as follows.

$$\frac{\partial \mathcal{L}^D}{\partial X} = \overline{P}_{X,1} - 5400\lambda^D X^{-.25}Y^{.25} = 0$$

$$\lambda^D = \frac{\overline{P}_{X,1}X^{.25}Y^{-.25}}{5400}$$

$$\lambda^D = \frac{\overline{P}_{X,1}\left(X^*\right)^{.25}\left(Y^*\right)^{-.25}}{5400}$$

$$\lambda^D = \frac{90(10)^{.25}(10)^{-.25}}{5400} = \frac{1}{60} = 0.0167.$$

The value of $\lambda^D = \frac{1}{60} = 0.0167$ indicates that if the predetermined value of Jan's utility increases by one unit from 7200 to 7201 then the minimum expenditure necessary to achieve this higher level of utility will increase by \$0.0167 from \$1200 to \$1200 + \$0.0167 = \$1200.0167.

d. The optimal values of X and Y computed for the primal problem in exercise 4.3 are the same as those computed in the dual problem in exercise 4.4. The value of λ^* determined for the primal problem in exercise 4.3 is equal to the reciprocal of the value of λ^{D*} determined for the dual problem. Specifically, $\lambda^* = 60$ and $\lambda^{D*} = \frac{1}{60}$.

4.5 a. Maximize $U = \text{minimum}\left(\frac{X}{4}, \frac{Y}{1}\right)$

subject to $\overline{P}_{X,1}X + \overline{P}_{Y,1} = \overline{I}_1$

In order for Matt to receive utility from these goods he must consume goods X and Y in a ratio of

$$\frac{X}{Y} = \frac{4}{1},$$

or X = 4Y.

In addition, when Matt maximizes his utility, he must choose a combination of goods that exhausts his income. Therefore, given Matt's budget constraint is

$$\overline{P}_{X,1}X + \overline{P}_{Y,1} = \overline{I}_1,$$

substituting X = 4Y into Matt's budget constraint we obtain

$$\overline{P}_{X,1}(4Y) + \overline{P}_{Y,1}Y = \overline{I}_1.$$

Solve the above equation for Y as follows.

$$4\overline{P}_{X,1}Y + \overline{P}_{Y,1}Y = \overline{I}_1$$

$$Y\left(4\overline{P}_{X,1} + \overline{P}_{Y,1}\right) = \overline{I}_1$$

$$Y = \frac{\overline{I}_1}{4\overline{P}_{X,1} + \overline{P}_{Y,1}}.$$

To determine the optimal value of Y, substitute $\overline{P}_{X,1} = \$1,00, \overline{P}_{Y,1} = \$0.50,$ $\textit{and } \overline{I}_1 = \$360$ into the above equation for Y.

$$Y^* = \frac{360}{4(1.00) + (0.50)} = \frac{360}{4.50} = 80 \text{ units.}$$

To determine the optimal value of X, substitute Y* = 80 into the equation for X as follows.

$X^* = 4Y^* = 4(80) = 320$ units.

b. To determine the maximum amount of utility Matt can receive, substitute $X^* = 320$ and $Y^* = 80$ into his utility function as follows.

$$U^* = \text{minimum}\left(\frac{X^*}{4}, \frac{Y^*}{1}\right) = \text{minimum}\left(\frac{320}{4}, \frac{80}{1}\right) = \text{minimum } (80, 80) = 80.$$

4.6 a. Stewart's utility function is linear. This indicates that he perceives the two goods, mozzarella cheese and cheddar cheese, as perfect substitutes. In addition, since $MU_X = \frac{\partial U}{\partial X} = 140 > 0$ and $MU_Y = \frac{\partial U}{\partial Y} = 140 > 0$ he perceives each type of cheese as an economic "good".

b. Maximize $U = 140X + 140Y$
subject to $\overline{P}_{X,1}X + \overline{P}_{Y,1}Y = \overline{I}_1$

Since Stewart's utility function is linear, the corresponding indifference curves must be linear. Also given

$U = 140X + 140Y$
then

$$MU_X = \frac{\partial U}{\partial X} = 140$$

and

$$MU_Y = \frac{\partial U}{\partial Y} = 140$$

indicating that the marginal utility Stewart receives from an additional unit of good X is equal to the marginal utility he receives from an additional unit of good Y. Assuming that Stewart is a rational consumer he will choose to spend all of his \$280 in income on the cheaper of the two goods in order to maximize his utility. In this case since $\overline{P}_{X,1} = \$4$ *and* $\overline{P}_{Y,1} = \$2$ he will spend all of his income on good Y and purchase $\frac{\overline{I}_1}{\overline{P}_{Y,1}} = \frac{\$280}{\$2} = 140$ units of good Y and zero units of good X.

b. To determine the maximum amount of utility Stewart receives, substitute $X^* = 0$ and $Y = 140$ into his utility function as follows.

$$U^* = 140X^* + 140Y^*$$
$$= 140\,(0) + 140\,(140)$$
$$= 19{,}600.$$

4.7 Given $\overline{P}_{X,1} = \$4, \overline{P}_{Y,1} = \$2, \text{ and } \overline{I}_1 = \$280$, then the slope and intercept values of Stewart's budget constraint, 4X + 2Y = 280, are determined as follows.

$$\text{slope of budget constraint} = \frac{-\overline{P}_{X,1}}{\overline{P}_{Y,1}} = \frac{-\$4}{\$2} = -2$$

$$\text{X- intercept} = \frac{\overline{I}_1}{\overline{P}_{X,1}} = \frac{\$280}{\$4} = 70$$

$$\text{Y- intercept} = \frac{\overline{I}_1}{\overline{P}_{Y,1}} = \frac{\$280}{\$2} = 140$$

To plot the indifference curve associated with Stewart's maximum level of utility, recall that his optimal combination of goods contains zero units of good X and 140 units of good Y, which yields 19,600 units of utility. Recall his utility function is U = 140X + 140Y.

Set U = 19,600 units and determine values of X and Y that solve this equation as follows.
19,600 = 140X + 140Y
140Y = 19,600 - 140X
Y = 140 - X

Units of Good X	Units of Good Y
0	140
70	70
140	0

We can plot the goods combination (140, 0), the X-intercept of the U = 19,600 indifference curve, and (0, 140) the Y-intercept of the same indifference curve, in the same graph as Stewart's budget constraint. Recall that the X-intercept of his budget constraint is at the goods combination (70, 0) and the Y-intercept is at (0, 140). The optimal goods combination, $X^* = 0$ units and $Y^* = 140$ units, is a corner solution, as illustrated in the graph on the following page.

Figure 4.2

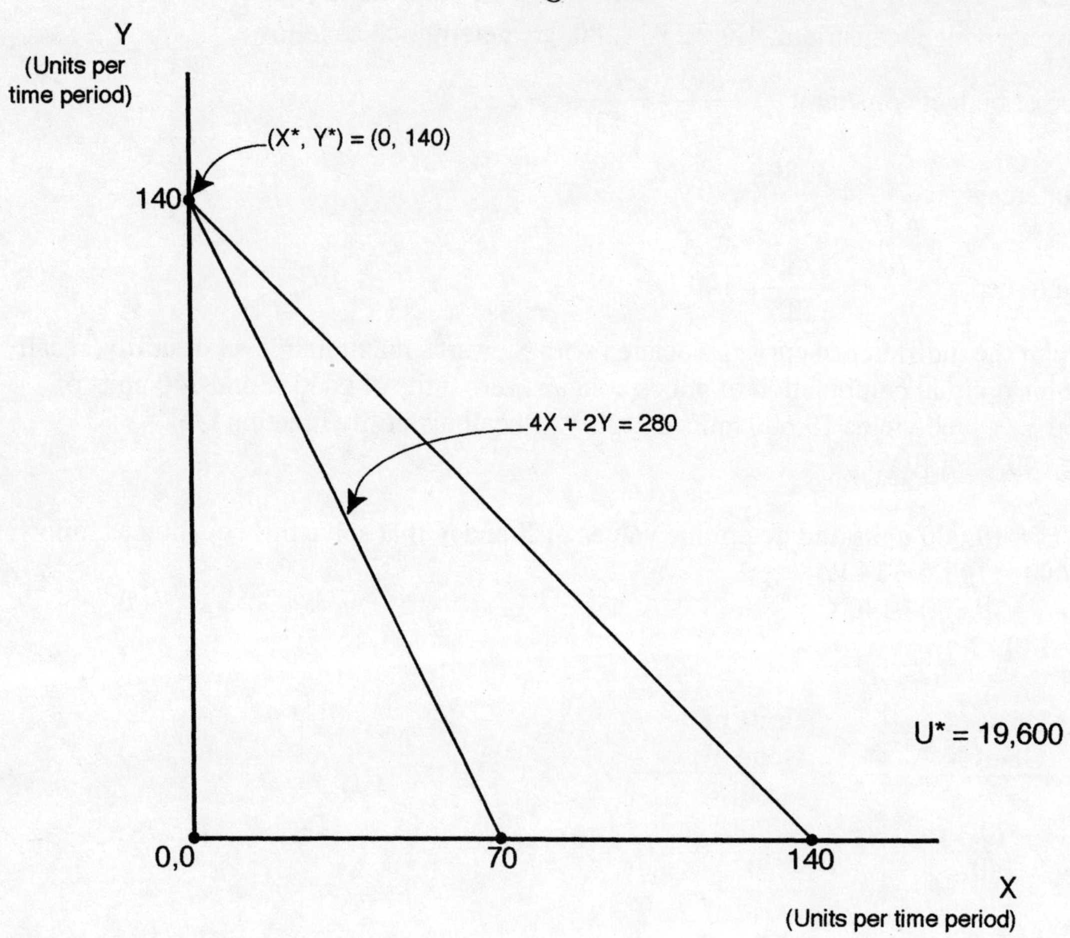
Y
(Units per
time period)
(X*, Y*) = (0, 140)
140
4X + 2Y = 280
U* = 19,600
0,0
70
140
X
(Units per time period)

SOLUTIONS

Chapter 5

5.1 a. Maximize $U = 80X^{.25}Y^{.25}$

subject to $\bar{P}_{X,1}X + \bar{P}_{Y,1}Y = \bar{I}_1$

$$\mathcal{L} = 80X^{.25}Y^{.25} + \lambda(\bar{I}_1 - \bar{P}_{X,1}X - \bar{P}_{Y,1}Y)$$

$$= 80X^{.25}Y^{.25} + \lambda\bar{I}_1 - \lambda\bar{P}_{X,1}X - \lambda\bar{P}_{Y,1}Y$$

$$\frac{\partial\mathcal{L}}{\partial X} = 20X^{-.75}Y^{.25} - \lambda\bar{P}_{X,1} = 0$$

$$\frac{\partial\mathcal{L}}{\partial Y} = 20X^{.25}Y^{-.75} - \lambda\bar{P}_{Y,1} = 0$$

$$\frac{\partial\mathcal{L}}{\partial\lambda} = \bar{I}_1 - \bar{P}_{X,1}X - \bar{P}_{Y,1}Y = 0$$

$$\frac{20X^{-.75}Y^{.25}}{20X^{.25}Y^{-.75}} = \frac{\lambda\bar{P}_{X,1}}{\lambda\bar{P}_{Y,1}}$$

$$\frac{Y}{X} = \frac{\bar{P}_{X,1}}{\bar{P}_{Y,1}}$$

$$Y = \frac{\bar{P}_{X,1}X}{\bar{P}_{Y,1}}$$

$$\bar{I}_1 - \bar{P}_{X,1}X - \bar{P}_{Y,1}\left(\frac{\bar{P}_{X,1}X}{\bar{P}_{Y,1}}\right) = 0$$

$$\bar{I}_1 - \bar{P}_{X,1}X - \bar{P}_{X,1}X = 0$$

$$2\bar{P}_{X,1}X = \bar{I}_1$$

$$X = \frac{\bar{I}_1}{2\bar{P}_{X,1}}$$

Since $\bar{P}_{X,1} = \$100, \bar{P}_{Y,1} = \$100$, and $\bar{I}_1 = \$3200$ then

$$X^* = \frac{\bar{I}_1}{2\bar{P}_{X,1}} = \frac{\$3200}{2(\$100)} = 16 \text{ units}$$

and

$$Y^* = \frac{\bar{P}_{X,1}X^*}{\bar{P}_{Y,1}} = \frac{(\$100)(16)}{\$100} = 16 \text{ units.}$$

b. To determine the maximum amount of utility Raymond receives, substitute $X^* = 16$ and $Y^* = 16$ into his utility function as follows.

$U^* = 8\,(X^*)^{.25}\,(Y^*)^{.25}$

$= 80\,(16)^{.25}\,(16)^{.25}$

$= 80\,(16)^{.5}$

$= 320$

5.2 a. Given the constrained utility maximization problem in part a. of exercise 5.1, recall it was determined that

$$X^* = \frac{\bar{I}_1}{2\bar{P}_{X,1}}.$$

Raymond's own-price demand curve for good X expresses his optimal level of consumption of good X as a function of the own price of good X, while holding the price of good Y and Raymond's income constant. Therefore, since $\bar{I}_1 = \$3200$, his own-price demand curve for good X is

$$X^* = X\left(P_X, \bar{P}_{Y,1}, \bar{I}_1\right) = \frac{\bar{I}_1}{2P_X} = \frac{3200}{2P_X} = \frac{1600}{P_X}.$$

b. Given the constrained utility maximization problem in part a. of exercise 5.1, recall it was determined that

$$Y^* = \frac{\bar{P}_{X,1}X^*}{\bar{P}_{Y,1}},$$

where

$$X^* = \frac{\bar{I}_1}{2\bar{P}_{X,1}}.$$

Therefore, after substituting $X^* = \frac{\bar{I}_1}{2\bar{P}_{X,1}}$, into the equation for Y^*, we obtain

$$Y^* = \frac{\bar{P}_{X,1}\left(\frac{\bar{I}_1}{2\bar{P}_{X,1}}\right)}{\bar{P}_{Y,1}} = \frac{\bar{I}_1}{2\bar{P}_{Y,1}}.$$

Raymond's own-price demand curve for good Y expresses his optimal consumption level of good Y as a function of the own price of good Y, while holding the price of good X and Raymond's income constant. Therefore, since $\bar{I}_1 = \$3200$, his own-price demand curve for good Y is

$$Y^* = Y\left(\bar{P}_{X,1}, P_Y, \bar{I}_1\right) = \frac{\bar{I}_1}{2P_Y} = \frac{3200}{2P_Y} = \frac{1600}{P_Y}.$$

5.3 a. Given the constrained utility maximization problem in part a. of exercise 5.1, recall it was determined that

$$X^* = \frac{\bar{I}_1}{2\bar{P}_{X,1}}.$$

Raymond's Engel curve for good X expresses his optimal consumption level of good X as a function of his income, while holding the prices of all goods constant. Therefore, since $\bar{P}_{X,1} = \$100$ then his Engel curve for good X is

$$X^* = X\left(\bar{P}_{X,1}\bar{P}_{Y,1}I\right) = \frac{I}{2\bar{P}_{X,1}} = \frac{I}{2(\$100)} = \frac{I}{200}.$$

b. To determine whether good X is normal or inferior, take the derivative of Raymond's Engel curve for good X, determined in part a., with respect to I.

$$X^* = X\left(\bar{P}_{X,1}, \bar{P}_{Y,1}, I\right) = \frac{I}{200}$$

$$\frac{\partial X}{\partial I} = \frac{1}{200} > 0$$

Since $\frac{\partial X}{\partial I} > 0$ good X is normal, indicating that as Raymond's income increases his optimal consumption level of good X rises.

c. Given the constrained utility maximization problem in part a of exercise 5.1, recall it was determined that

$$Y^* = \frac{\bar{P}_{X,1}X^*}{\bar{P}_{Y,1}}$$

where

$$X^* = \frac{\bar{I}_1}{2\bar{P}_{X,1}}.$$

Therefore, after substituting $X^* = \frac{\bar{I}_1}{2\bar{P}_{X,1}}$ into the equation for Y^*, we obtain

$$Y^* = \frac{\bar{P}_{X,1}\left(\frac{\bar{I}_1}{2\bar{P}_{X,1}}\right)}{\bar{P}_{Y,1}} = \frac{\bar{I}_1}{2\bar{P}_{Y,1}}.$$

Raymond's Engel curve for good Y expresses his optimal consumption level of good Y as a function of his income, while holding the prices of all goods constant. Therefore, since $\bar{P}_{Y,1} = \$100$, his Engel curve for good Y is

$$Y^* = Y\left(\bar{P}_{X,1}, \bar{P}_{Y,1}, I\right) = \frac{I}{2\bar{P}_{Y,1}} = \frac{I}{2(100)} = \frac{I}{200}.$$

d. To determine whether good Y is normal or inferior, take the derivative of Raymond's Engel curve for good Y, determined in part c., with respect to I.

$$Y^* = Y\left(\bar{P}_{X,1}, \bar{P}_{Y,1}, I\right) = \frac{I}{200}$$

$$\frac{\partial Y}{\partial I} = \frac{1}{200} > 0$$

Since $\frac{\partial Y}{\partial I} > 0$ good Y is normal, indicating that as Raymond's income increases his optimal consumption level of good Y rises.

5.4 a. Substitute $\overline{P}_{X,1} = \$2$ and $\overline{I}_1 = \$40,000$ into the individual's own-price demand function to derive his cross-price demand curve.

$$X = X\,(\overline{P}_{X,1}, P_Y, \overline{I}_1) = 200 - 4\overline{P}_{X,1} - 1.5P_Y + 0.008\overline{I}_1$$
$$X = 200 - 4\,(2) - 1.5\;P_Y + 0.008\;(40{,}000)$$
$$= 200 - 8 - 1.5\;P_Y + 320$$
$$= 512 - 1.5\;P_Y$$

b. To determine whether goods X and Y are gross substitutes of gross complements take the derivative of the cross-price demand curve with respect to P_Y as follows

$$X = 512 - 1.5\;P_Y$$
$$\frac{\partial X}{\partial P_Y} = -1.5$$

Since $\frac{\partial X}{\partial P_Y} < 0$ this indicates that goods X and Y are gross complements meaning that as the price of good Y rises, the quantity demanded of good X decreases.

5.5 Minimize $E = \overline{P}_{X,1}X + \overline{P}_{Y,1}Y$

subject to $\overline{U}_1 = 80X^{.25}Y^{.25}$

$$\mathcal{L} = \overline{P}_{X,1}X + \overline{P}_{Y,1}Y + \lambda\left(\overline{U}_1 - 80X^{.25}Y^{.25}\right)$$
$$= \overline{P}_{X,1}X + \overline{P}_{Y,1}Y + \lambda\overline{U}_1 - 80\lambda X^{.25}Y^{.25}$$
$$\frac{\partial\mathcal{L}}{\partial X} = \overline{P}_{X,1} - 20\lambda X^{-.75}Y^{.25} = 0$$
$$\frac{\partial\mathcal{L}}{\partial Y} = \overline{P}_{Y,1} - 20\lambda X^{.25}Y^{-.75} = 0$$
$$\frac{\partial\mathcal{L}}{\partial \lambda} = \overline{U}_1 - 80X^{.25}Y^{.25} = 0$$
$$\frac{20\lambda X^{-.75}Y^{.25}}{20\lambda X^{.25}Y^{-.75}} = \frac{\overline{P}_{X,1}}{\overline{P}_{Y,1}}$$
$$\frac{Y}{X} = \frac{\overline{P}_{X,1}}{\overline{P}_{Y,1}}$$
$$Y = \frac{\overline{P}_{X,1}X}{\overline{P}_{Y,1}}$$
$$\overline{U}_1 - 80X^{.25}\left(\frac{\overline{P}_{X,1}X}{\overline{P}_{Y,1}}\right)^{.25} = 0$$

$$\overline{U}_1 - 80X^{.50}\left(\frac{\overline{P}_{X,1}}{\overline{P}_{Y,1}}\right)^{.25} = 0$$

$$80X^{.50}\left(\frac{\overline{P}_{X,1}}{\overline{P}_{Y,1}}\right)^{.25} = \overline{U}_1$$

$$X^{.50} = \frac{\overline{U}_1}{80}\left(\frac{\overline{P}_{X,1}}{\overline{P}_{Y,1}}\right)^{-.25}$$

$$\left(X^{.50}\right)^2 = \left[\frac{\overline{U}_1}{80}\left(\frac{\overline{P}_{X,1}}{\overline{P}_{Y,1}}\right)^{-.25}\right]^2$$

$$X = \frac{\overline{U}_1^2}{(80)^2}\left(\frac{\overline{P}_{X,1}}{\overline{P}_{Y,1}}\right)^{-.50}$$

$$X^* = \frac{(320)^2}{(80)^2}\left(\frac{100}{100}\right)^{-.50} = \frac{102{,}400}{6400}(1)^{-.50} = 16 \text{ units}$$

$$Y^* = \frac{\overline{P}_{X,1}X^*}{\overline{P}_{Y,1}} = \frac{(100)(16)}{100} = 16 \text{ units}$$

5.6 a. Given the constrained expenditure minimization problem in exercise 5.5 it was determined that

$$X^* = \frac{\overline{U}_1^2}{(80)^2}\left(\frac{\overline{P}_{X,1}}{\overline{P}_{Y,1}}\right)^{-.50}$$

Raymond's compensated demand curve for good X expresses his optimal consumption level of good X as a function of the own price of good X while holding the price of good Y and Raymond's utility constant. Therefore, since $\overline{U}_1 = 320$ and $\overline{P}_{Y,1} = \$100$, his compensated demand curve for good X is

$$X' = X\left(P_X, \overline{P}_{Y,1}, \overline{U}_1\right) = \frac{\overline{U}_1^2}{(80)^2}\left(\frac{P_X}{\overline{P}_{Y,1}}\right)^{-.50}$$

$$= \frac{(320)^2}{(80)^2}\left(\frac{P_X}{100}\right)^{-.50}$$

$$= \left(\frac{102{,}400}{6400}\right)\left(\frac{10}{P_X^{.50}}\right)$$

$$= \frac{160}{P_X^{.50}}$$

$$= 160\, P_X^{-.50}.$$

b. Given the constrained expenditure minimization problem in exercise 5.5 it was determined that

$$Y^* = \frac{\overline{P}_{X,1}X^*}{\overline{P}_{Y,1}}$$

where

$$X^* = \frac{\overline{U}_1^2}{(80)^2}\left(\frac{\overline{P}_{X,1}}{\overline{P}_{Y,1}}\right)^{-.50}.$$

After substituting $X^* = \frac{\overline{U}_1^2}{(80)^2}\left(\frac{\overline{P}_{X,1}}{\overline{P}_{Y,1}}\right)^{-.50}$ into the equation for Y^* we obtain

$$Y^* = \left(\frac{\overline{P}_{X,1}}{\overline{P}_{Y,1}}\right)\left(\frac{\overline{U}_1^2}{80^2}\right)\left(\frac{\overline{P}_{X,1}}{\overline{P}_{Y,1}}\right)^{-.50}$$

$$= \left(\frac{\overline{P}_{X,1}}{\overline{P}_{Y,1}}\right)^{.50}\left(\frac{\overline{U}_1^2}{(80)^2}\right).$$

Raymond's compensated demand curve for good Y expresses his optimal consumption level of good Y as a function of the own price of good Y while holding the price of good X and Raymond's utility constant. Therefore, since $\overline{U}_1 = 320$ and $\overline{P}_{X,1} = \$100$, his compensated demand curve for good Y is

$$Y' = Y\left(\overline{P}_{X,1}, P_Y, \overline{U}_1\right) = \left(\frac{\overline{P}_{X,1}}{P_Y}\right)^{.50}\left(\frac{\overline{U}_1^2}{(80)^2}\right) = \left(\frac{100}{P_Y}\right)^{.50}\left(\frac{(320)^2}{(80)^2}\right) = \left(\frac{10}{P_Y^{.50}}\right)\left(\frac{102{,}400}{6400}\right)$$

$$= \frac{160}{P_Y^{.50}} = 160P_Y^{-.50}$$

5.7 a.& b. If a good is inferior, but not a Giffen good, an increase in its price will lead to a smaller reduction in the quantity demanded of the good than if the good was a normal good. In panel (A) in the figure below, an increase in the price of good X leads to a substitution effect, which reduces the individual's consumption of good X from X^*_1 to X'_2. The income effect increases the individual's consumption of the good from X'_2 to X^*_4. The total effect of the increase in the price of good X is to reduce the quantity demanded of good X and is shown as movement from X^*_1 to X^*_4. The corresponding, negatively sloped, steep, individual own-price demand curve is shown in panel (B).

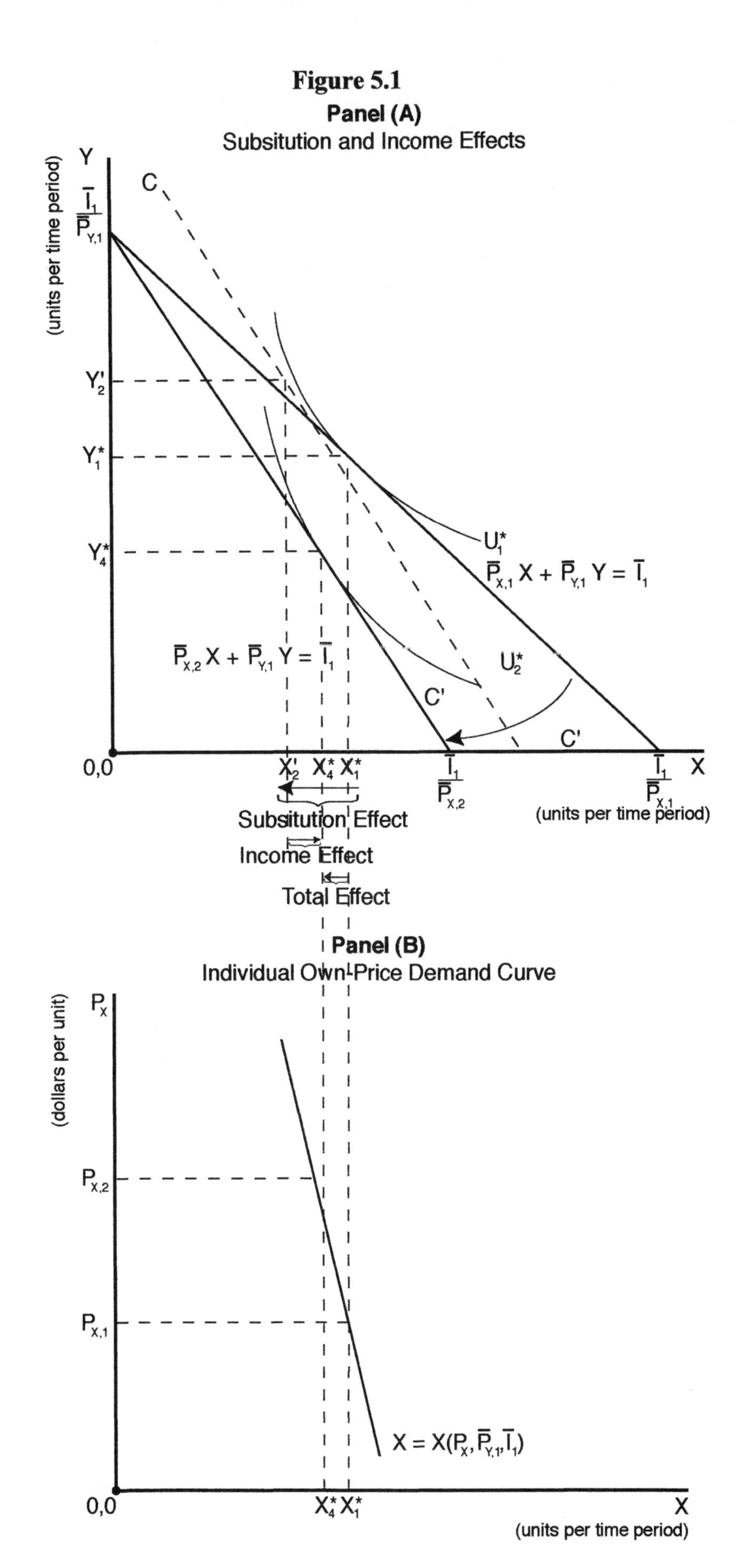
Panel (A)
Subsitution and Income Effects
Y
(units per time period)
C
U*1
U*2
C'
Y'2
Y*1
Y*4
0,0
X'2
X*4
X*1
X
(units per time period)
Subsitution Effect
Income Effect
Total Effect
Panel (B)
Individual Own-Price Demand Curve
Px
(dollars per unit)
Px,2
Px,1
0,0
X*4
X*1
X
(units per time period)

Figure 5.1

5.8 If an individual perceives a good as a Giffen good then the corresponding own-price demand curve is positively sloped, indicating that an increase in the price of this good results in an increase in the quantity demanded of the good. In the case of a Giffen good, the income effect dominates the substitution effect. As you can see in panel (A) in the figure below, an increase in the price of good X, from $\overline{P}_{X,1}$ to $\overline{P}_{X,2}$, results in a total effect of an increase in the quantity demanded of good X from X^*_1 to X^*_5. Specifically, the substitution effect, which reduces the consumer's purchase of good X from X^*_1 to X'_2, is overpowered by the income effect, which increases the quantity demanded of good X from X'_2 to X^*_5. The corresponding, positively sloped, individual own-price demand curve is shown in panel (B).

Figure 5.2

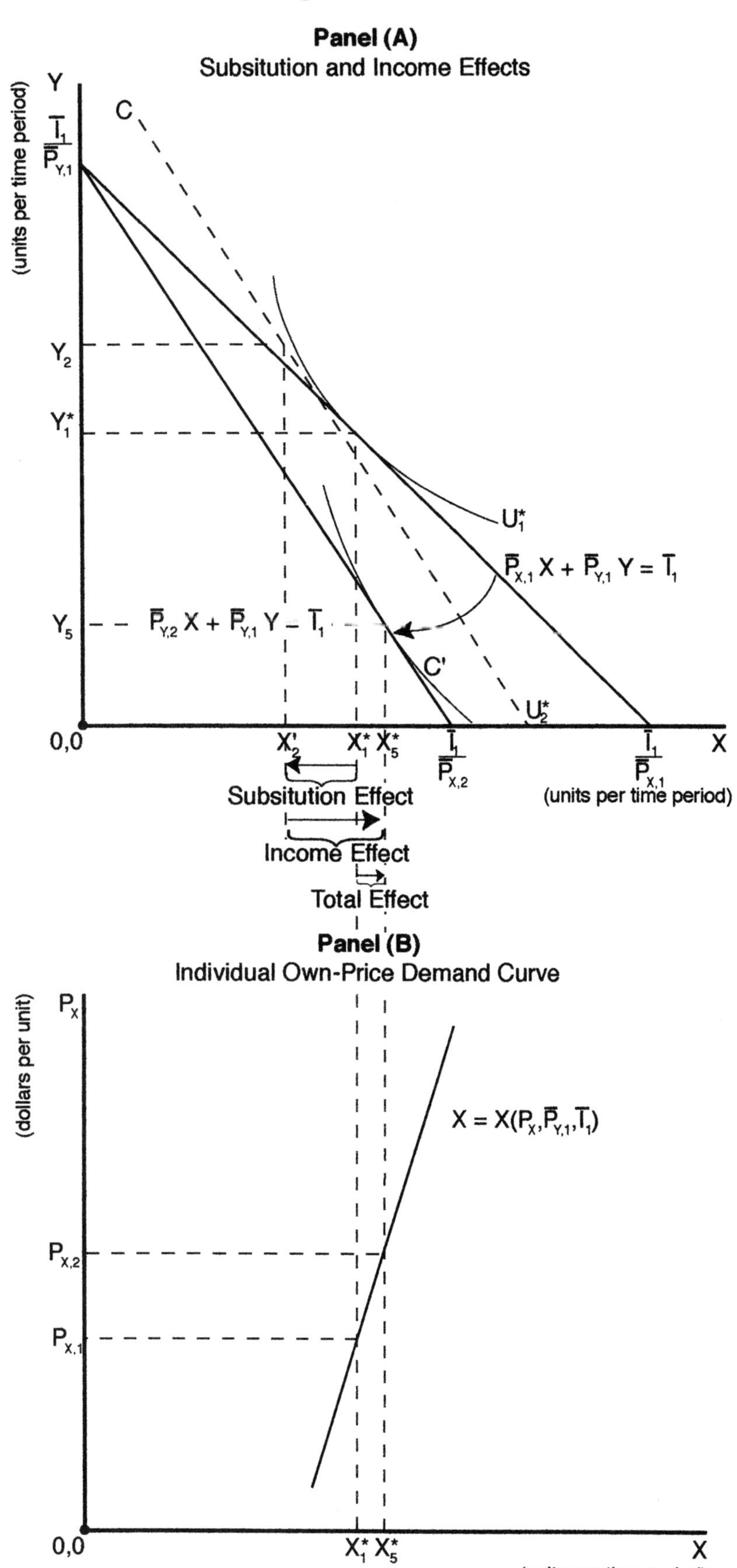

Panel (A)
Subsitution and Income Effects
Y
(units per time period)
C
U1*
PX,1 X + PY,1 Y = T1
PX,2 X + PY,1 Y = T1
C'
U2*
Y2
Y1*
Y5
0,0
X'2
X1*
X5*
T1 / PX,2
T1 / PX,1
X
(units per time period)
Subsitution Effect
Income Effect
Total Effect
Panel (B)
Individual Own-Price Demand Curve
PX
(dollars per unit)
X = X(PX,PY,1,T1)
PX,2
PX,1
0,0
X1*
X5*
X
(units per time period)

SOLUTIONS

Chapter 6

6.1 a. Since the two consumers have different reservation prices for good X, the market own-price demand curve must be derived in segments. For $25 < P_X \leq 100$, consumer 2 does not demand any amount of the good, whereas consumer 1 does. Thus, the market demand for $25 < P_X \leq 100$ is the same as the individual own-price demand curve for consumer 1, or

$$X^{D,M} = X^{D,}{}_1 = 200 - 2P_X.$$

However, if the price falls to $P_X \leq 25$, then both consumers will demand amounts of the good. Thus, for $P_X \leq 25$, the market own-price demand curve is the summation of the two individual curves, or

$$X^{D,M} = X^D{}_1 + X^D{}_2$$

$$= (200 - 2P_X) + (100 - 4P_X)$$

$$= 200 - 2P_X + 100 - 4P_X$$

$$= 300 - 6\,P_X.$$

b. If $P_X = \$20$, then consumer 1 demands the amount

$$X^D{}_1 = 200 - 2(20) = 160$$

and consumer 2 demands the amount

$$X^{D,}{}_2 = 100 - 4(20) = 20.$$

Thus the market amount is

$$X^{D,M} = X^D{}_1 + X^D{}_2 = 160 + 20 = 180.$$

Alternatively, this amount can be computed using the market own-price demand curve derived in part a as

$$X^{D,M} = 300 - 6\,P_X = 300 - 6\,(20)$$

$$= 180.$$

6.2 $X^D{}_1 = 200 - 2\,P_X$ for $P_X \leq 100$

Thus

$2\ P_X = 200 - X^D{}_1$

$P_X = 100 - \frac{1}{2} X^D{}_1$

and

$X^D{}_2 = 100 - 4\ P_X$ for $P_X \leq 25$,

thus

$4\ P_X = 100 - X^D{}_2$

$P_X = 25 - \frac{1}{4}\ X^D{}_2.$

a. The market own-price demand curve, derived in exercise 6.1 is

$X^{D,M} = 200 - 2\ P_X$ for $25 < P_X \leq 100$

and

$X^{D,M} = 300 - 6\ P_X$ for $P_X \leq 25$.

Thus, for $25 < P_X \leq 100$

$2P_X = 200 - X^{D,M}$

$P_X = 100 - \frac{1}{2}\ X^{D,M}$,

and for $P_X \leq 25$

$6\ P_X = 300 - X^{D,M}$

$P_X = 50 - \frac{1}{6}\ X^{D,M}.$

b. The slope of this inverse own-price demand curve is

$$\frac{dP_X}{dX^{D,M}} = -\frac{1}{2} \text{ for } 25 < P_X \leq 100$$

and

$$\frac{dP_X}{dX^{D,M}} = -\frac{1}{6} \text{ for } P_X \leq 25.$$

The $X^{D,M}$ intercept is

$$0 = 50 - \frac{1}{6}X^{D,M}$$

$$\frac{1}{6}X^{D,M} = 50$$

$$X^{D,M} = 300.$$

The P_X intercept is the same as the P_X intercept of the own-price demand curve for consumer 1 since, for any price above $25, only this consumer demands the good, or

$$P_X = 100 - \frac{1}{2}X^{D,M} = 100 - \frac{1}{2}(0)$$
$$= 100.$$

6.3 a. **Figure 6.1**

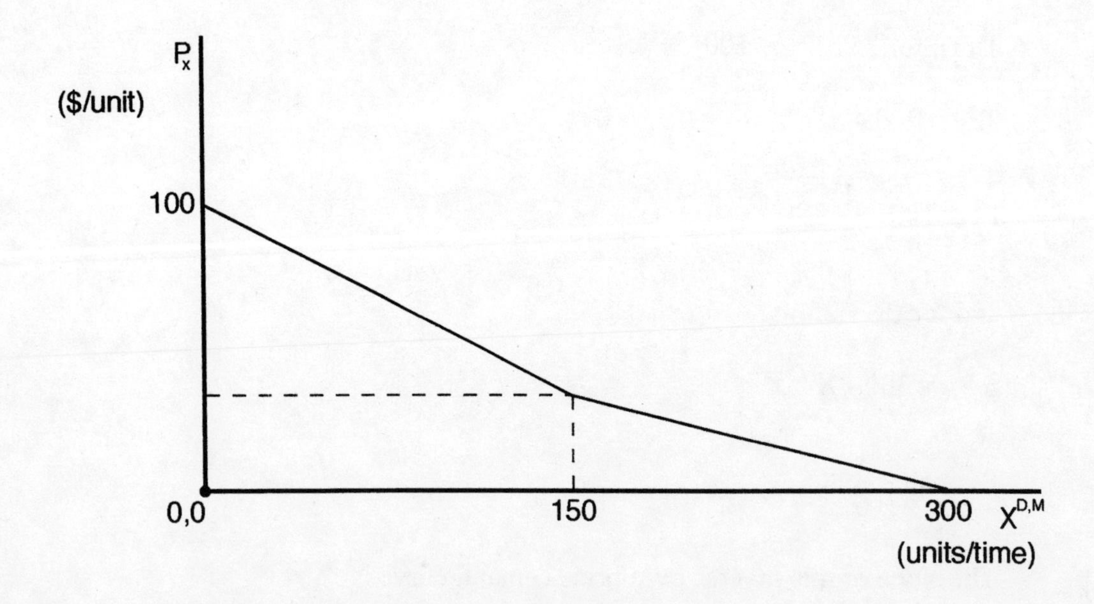

b. This curve has a kink in it, because for any price greater than \$25, consumer 2 does not demand any amount of the good. Thus, the market own-price demand curve above this price is simply the own-price curve for consumer 1. Below P = \$25, both consumers demand the good and thus the market curve is the summation of both consumer's individual own-price demand curves. This kink occurs at P = \$25 and therefore, at this price

$$X^{D,M} = X^{D}_{1} = 200 - 2P_X$$

$$= 200 - 2(25) = 150.$$

6.4 a. The inclusion of X_1, with a positive slope coefficient, in the own-price demand curve for consumer 2, represents a network externality. More specifically, in this case, this represents a bandwagon effect because consumer 2's quantity demanded of good X is, in part, directly related to consumer 1's demand for the good.

b. If the qualifier that consumer 2's own-price demand curve only pertains to the range where $P_X \leq \$25$, then for $P > \$25$ the market own-price demand curve, even with a bandwagon effect, is still just the same as that for consumer 1, or

$$X^{D,M} = X^{D}_{1} = 200 - 2\,P_X.$$

However, for $P < \$25$, the market own-price demand curve is

$$X^{D,M} = X^{D}_{1} + X^{D}_{2}$$

$$= (200 - 2P_X) + (100 - 4P_X + X_1)$$

$$= 200 - 2\,P_X + 100 - 4P_X + (200 - 2P_X)$$

$$= 300 - 6\,P_X + 200 - 2P_X$$

$$= 500 - 8\,P_X.$$

6.5 In this case, when $P_X > 25$, the own-price demand curve for consumer 2 is

$$X^{D}_{2} = X^{D}_{1}.$$

Thus

$$X^{D,M} = X^{D}_{1} + X^{D}_{2} = X^{D}_{1} + X^{D}_{1}$$

$$= (200 - 2P_X) + (200 - 2P_X)$$

$$= 400 - 4P_X \text{ for } 25 < P_X \leq 100.$$

When $P_X \leq \$25$, then

$$X^{D,M} = X^D{}_1 + X^D{}_2$$

$$= (200 - 2P_X) + (100 - 4P_X + X^D{}_1)$$

$$= 300 - 6P_X + X^D{}_1$$

$$= 300 - 6P_X + (200 - 2P_X)$$

$$= 500 - 8\ P_X.$$

6.6 A network externality occurs when some consumers' own-price demand for a good are, in part, related to other consumers' quantities demanded of the good. The concepts of bandwagon and snob effects are types, or sub-cases, of network externalities. In the case of a bandwagon effect, the quantities demanded of a good for some consumers are directly related to the quantities demanded of that good demanded by other consumers. For a snob effect, the quantities demanded of a good by some consumers are inversely related to the quantities of that good demanded by other consumers. Some examples of network externalities are communication devices such as telephones and personal computers where, as the price falls and more people consume the product, the quantities demanded by other consumers increase beyond that simply related to the decrease in the price of the good. Conceptually, the reasoning behind this result is that individuals derive more benefits from communication devices when they have more people with whom to communicate.

SOLUTIONS

Chapter 7

7.1 The airline can increase its revenue if it raises ticket prices in those markets where there is little competition from other airlines or rail services. In such areas, the lack of substitute forms of travel will make demand more inelastic for United's passengers. United airlines should also raise prices for its business travelers, who typically have inelastic demand for air travel, and raise prices for its leisure travelers, who tend to have more elastic demand for air travel. In summary, United Airlines will raise its revenue if it raises prices in those markets and for those passengers with inelastic demand, since this will result in an increase in the company's total revenue. In addition, United will raise its revenue by lowering its prices in those markets and for those passengers with elastic demand.

7.2 a. By substituting $I = 25$ and $P_Y = 12$ into the market own-price demand function we can obtain the market own-price demand curve. Given the market own-price demand function,

$X = 142 - 5.0\ P_X - I - 3.5\ P_Y$

$$\begin{aligned} X &= 142 - 5.0\ P_X - 25 - 3.5\ (12) \\ &= 142 - 5.0\ P_X - 25 - 42 \\ &= 75 - 5.0\ P_X \end{aligned}$$

b. If $P_X = 10$ then the quantity demanded of good X is

$$\begin{aligned} X &= 75 - 5.0\ (10) \\ &= 75 - 50 \\ &= 25. \end{aligned}$$

c. $$E_{X,P_X} = \left|\frac{\partial X}{\partial P_X}\frac{P_X}{X}\right| = \left|(-5.0)\left(\frac{10}{25}\right)\right| = 2$$

d. $E_{X,P_X} = 2$ indicates that a one percent change in the price of good X will result in a two percent change in the quantity demanded of good X in the opposite direction. In addition, since $E_{X,P_X} = 2 > 1$ this indicates that when $P_X = 10$, demand for good X is elastic.

e. Since demand for good X is elastic, any percentage change in the price of this good will cause a greater percentage change in the quantity demanded in the opposite direction. Therefore, the total revenue from good X, computed as $TR_X = P_X X$, must decrease if the price of good X increases.

7.3 a. Given $X = 142 - 5.0\ P_X - I - 3.5\ P_Y$,

if $P_X = 10$, and $I = 25$ then the cross-price demand curve is

$X = 142 - 5.0\,(10) - 25 - 3.5\,P_Y$
$= 142 - 50 - 25 - 3.5\,P_Y$
$= 67 - 3.5\,P_Y$

and if $P_Y = 12$ then
$X = 67 - 3.5\,(12)$
$= 67 - 42$
$= 25$

The cross-price elasticity of demand is computed as follows.

$$E_{X,P_Y} = \frac{\partial X}{\partial P_Y}\frac{P_Y}{X} = (-3.5)\left(\frac{12}{25}\right) = \frac{-42}{25} = -1.68.$$

b. $E_{X,P_Y} = -1.68$ indicates that a one percent change in the price of good Y results in a 1.68 percent change in the quantity demanded of good X in the opposite direction. Since $E_{X,P_y} < 0$ this indicates that goods X and Y are gross complements.

c. A seller of goods X and Y can use the information regarding E_{X,P_Y} to market these goods together, since they are gross complements, such as in nearby floor displays or on the same page in a catalog or website. The seller would also know from the value of E_{X,P_Y} that if he reduced the price of good Y by one percent that his sales of good X would rise by 1.68 percent.

7.4 a. The Engel curve for this good is determined by substituting $P_X = 10$ and $P_Y = 12$ into the market own-price demand function as follows.

$X = 142 - 5.0\,P_X - I - 3.5\,P_Y$
$= 142 - 5.0\,(10) - I - 3.5\,(12)$
$= 142 - 50 - I - 42$
$= 50 - I$

and when $I = 25$

$X = 50 - I = 50 - 25 = 25.$

The income elasticity of good X is computed as

$$E_{X,I} = \frac{\partial X}{\partial I}\frac{I}{X} = (-1)\left(\frac{25}{25}\right) = -1.$$

b. $E_{X,I} = -1$ indicates that if the consumers' income rises by one percent, the quantity demanded of good X falls by one percent. The fact that $E_{X,I} < 0$ indicates that good X is an inferior good.

c. A seller of this good can use this information regarding the income elasticity of good X to develop a effective marketing strategy for the good. Since the income elasticity indicates that good X is an inferior good, a seller of good X would want to advertise this good toward consumers with low incomes.

7.5 a. $Z = 100 - 100P_Z$

$$\frac{\partial Z}{\partial P_Z} = -100$$

Set the own-price elasticity of demand for good Z equal to 1 and solve for the associated value of P_Z as follows.

$$E_{Z,P_Z} = \left| \frac{\partial Z}{\partial P_Z} \frac{P_Z}{Z} \right| = 1$$

Substitute $\frac{\partial Z}{\partial P_Z} = -100$ and $Z = 100 - 100\ P_Z$ into the above equation for the own-price elasticity of good Z.

$$E_{Z,P_Z} = \left| (-100)\left(\frac{P_Z}{100 - 100P_Z}\right) \right| = 1$$

$$\frac{100P_Z}{100 - 100P_Z} = 1$$

$100P_Z = 100 - 100P_Z$
$200\ P_Z = 100$
$P_Z = \$0.50$

To determine the value of Z when $P_Z = \$0.50$, substitute $P_Z = \$0.50$ into the market demand curve for good Z.

$Z = 100 - 100\ P_Z$
$= 100 - 100\ (0.50)$
$= 100 - 50$
$= 50$

Therefore the own-price elasticity of demand for good Z is equal to one when $Z = 50$ and $P_Z = 0.50$.

b. Recall the relationship between the value of marginal revenue and own-price elasticity of demand. Specifically, in this problem,

$$MR_Z = P_Z\left(1 - \frac{1}{E_{Z,P_Z}}\right).$$

Determine the value of MR_Z by substituting $E_{Z,P_Z} = 1$ and $P_Z = 0.50$ into the above equation.

$$MR_Z = (0.50)\left(1 - \frac{1}{1}\right)$$
$$= (0.50)\,(0)$$
$$= 0$$

Therefore, $MR_Z = 0$ when $E_{Z,P_Z} = 1$.

c. Recall that the total revenue from the sale of a good is maximized when MR = 0, and accordingly the value of own-price elasticity of demand for the good is equal to one. In part a. it was determined that $E_{Z,P_Z} = 1$ when Z = 50 and P_Z = 0.50. Therefore, the maximum value of total revenue in this case is

$$TR = P_Z Z$$
$$= (0.50)\,(50)$$
$$= \$25.$$

7.6 a. Given the market own-price demand curve,

$$W = 500\ P_W^{-1},$$

where,

$$E_{W,P_W} = \left|\frac{\partial W}{\partial P_W}\frac{P_W}{W}\right|,$$

substitute $\frac{\partial W}{\partial P_W} = -500P_W^{-2}$ and $W = 500\ P_W^{-1}$ into the formula for the own-price elasticity of demand as follows.

$$E_{W,P_W} = \left|\left(-500P_W^{-2}\right)\left(\frac{P_W}{500P_W^{-1}}\right)\right|$$
$$= \left|\frac{-500P_W^{-1}}{500P_W^{-1}}\right|$$
$$= |-1|$$
$$= 1.$$

b. In part a. E_{W,P_W} was found to equal one, indicating that demand for good W is unit elastic. Therefore, a one percent change in the price of good W results in a one percent change in the quantity demanded of good W in the opposite direction. Also, since E_{W,P_W} is a constant value, this indicates that the value of the own-price elasticity of demand for good W does not change as the price of this good varies.

c. The value of marginal revenue associated with the sale of good W can be computed using the following formula.

$$MR_W = P_W\left(1 - \frac{1}{E_{W,P_W}}\right).$$

Substituting $E_{W,P_W} = 1$ into the above formula we find

$$MR_W = P_W\left(1 - \frac{1}{1}\right).$$
$$= P_W\,(0)$$
$$= 0.$$

d. In part c. we determined that $MR_W = 0$, a constant value, thereby indicating that the value of marginal revenue does not change as the price of good W varies.

7.7 a. Given the cross-price demand curve, $X = 8P_Y^2$, then the cross-price elasticity of demand is computed as follows,

$$E_{X,P_Y} = \frac{\partial X}{\partial P_Y}\frac{P_Y}{X} = (16P_Y)\left(\frac{P_Y}{X}\right).$$

Substituting $X = 8P_Y^2$ into the above equation for E_{X,P_Y} we find

$$E_{X,P_Y} = (16P_Y)\left(\frac{P_Y}{8P_Y^2}\right) = \frac{16P_Y^2}{8P_Y^2} = 2.$$

b. $E_{X,P_Y} = 2$ indicates that if the price of good Y changes by one percent this will result in a two percent change in the quantity demanded of good X in the same direction. Also since E_{X,P_Y} is a constant value then the value of E_{X,P_Y} will not change as the price of good Y varies.

c. Since the value of E_{X,P_Y} was computed to be a positive value, this indicates that goods X and Y are gross substitutes.

7.8 a. Given the Engel curve for good Y,

$$Y = 2 + 2I^{.5},$$

then the income elasticity of good Y is computed as follows,

$$E_{Y,I} = \frac{\partial Y}{\partial I}\frac{I}{Y} = \left(I^{-.5}\right)\left(\frac{I}{Y}\right).$$

Substituting $Y = 2 + 2I^{.5}$ into the above equation for $E_{Y,I}$ we find

$$E_{Y,I} = \left(I^{-.5}\right)\left(\frac{I}{2+2I^{.5}}\right) = \frac{I^{.5}}{2+2I^{.5}}.$$

b. From part b. we know

$$E_{Y,I} = \frac{I^{.5}}{2+2I^{.5}}$$

and if I = 1 (in thousands of dollars) then the value of income elasticity is computed as follows.

$$E_{Y,I} = \frac{(1)^{.5}}{2+2(1)^{.5}} = \frac{1}{2+2} = \frac{1}{4} = 0.25.$$

c. When I = 1, $E_{Y,I} = 0.25$, a positive value, therefore we can categorize good Y as a normal good. In addition, since $0 < E_{Y,I} < 1$, this indicates that good Y is a necessity.

SOLUTIONS

Chapter 8

8.1 a. Once an input is fixed, in this case, capital, the analysis pertains to the short run. By definition, the short run is a time period during which at least one of a firm's inputs is treated as fixed.

b. $$TP_L = Q = f(\overline{K}_1, L)$$
$$= 4\overline{K}_1^{\frac{1}{4}} L^{\frac{3}{4}} = 4(16)^{\frac{1}{4}} L^{\frac{3}{4}}$$
$$= 4(2) L^{\frac{3}{4}} = 8L^{\frac{3}{4}}.$$

8.2 a. $$MP_L = \frac{\partial Q}{\partial L} = \frac{dTP_L}{dL} = \frac{d\left(8L^{\frac{3}{4}}\right)}{dL}$$
$$= 6L^{-\frac{1}{4}} = \frac{6}{L^{\frac{1}{4}}}.$$

b. $$AP_L = \frac{Q}{L}\Big|\overline{K}_1 = \frac{TP_L}{L}$$
$$= \frac{8L^{\frac{3}{4}}}{L} = 8L^{-\frac{1}{4}} = \frac{8}{L^{\frac{1}{4}}}.$$

8.3 If L = 81 units, then

a. $$MP_L = \frac{6}{L^{\frac{1}{4}}} = \frac{6}{(81)^{\frac{1}{4}}} = \frac{6}{3} = 2 \text{ units.}$$
$$AP_L = \frac{8}{L^{\frac{1}{4}}} = \frac{8}{(81)^{\frac{1}{4}}} = \frac{8}{3} = 2\frac{2}{3} \text{ units.}$$

b. If L = 256 units

$$MP_L = \frac{6}{(256)^{\frac{1}{4}}} = \frac{6}{4} = 1\frac{1}{2} \text{ units.}$$
$$AP_L = \frac{8}{(256)^{\frac{1}{4}}} = \frac{8}{4} = 2 \text{ units.}$$

When L = 81 units, $MP_L = 2$ and when L is increased to L = 256 units, $MP_L = 1\frac{1}{2}$. The fact that the MP_L decreases as the amount of labor use increases, holding capital constant at K = 16 units, reflects the law of diminishing marginal productivity of an input, in this case, labor.

8.4 a. $TP_L = Q = 4\overline{K}_1^{\frac{1}{2}} + 8L^{\frac{1}{2}}$

$$= 4(4)^{\frac{1}{2}} + 8L^{\frac{1}{2}}$$

$$= 4(2) + 8L^{\frac{1}{2}}$$

$$= 8 + 8L^{\frac{1}{2}}.$$

b. $$MP_L = \frac{dTP_L}{dL} = \frac{d\left(8 + 8L^{\frac{1}{2}}\right)}{dL}$$

$$= \frac{d(8)}{dL} + \frac{d\left(8L^{\frac{1}{2}}\right)}{dL} = 4L^{-\frac{1}{2}} = \frac{4}{L^{\frac{1}{2}}}.$$

$$AP_L = \frac{TP_L}{L} = \frac{8 + 8L^{\frac{1}{2}}}{L} = \frac{8}{L} + 8L^{-\frac{1}{2}}$$

$$= \frac{8}{L} + \frac{8}{L^{\frac{1}{2}}}.$$

c. If L = 4 units, then

$$MP_L = \frac{4}{L^{\frac{1}{2}}} = \frac{4}{4^{\frac{1}{2}}} = \frac{4}{2} = 2 \text{ units,}$$

and if L = 9 units, then

$$MP_L = \frac{4}{9^{\frac{1}{2}}} = \frac{4}{3} = 1\frac{1}{3} \text{ units.}$$

The MP_L does obey the law of diminishing marginal productivity, as evidenced by the fact that the labor term appears in the denomination of the MP_L curve, as well as by the results computed above.

The capital input does not appear in the MP_L function. Thus, changing its level will not affect the marginal productivity of labor.

8.5 a. $TP_L = Q = \overline{K}_1 L = 2L$

$$MP_L = \frac{\partial Q}{\partial L} = \frac{dTP_L}{dQ} = \frac{d(2L)}{dL} = 2 \text{ units.}$$

b. $TP_L = Q = \overline{K}_2 L = 3L$

$$MP_L = \frac{\partial Q}{\partial L} = \frac{dTP_L}{dQ} = \frac{d(3L)}{dL} = 3 \text{ units.}$$

c. The MP_L does not obey the law of diminishing marginal productivity, as it is equal to a constant, depending on the level at which capital is fixed.

d. As demonstrated above, a change in the amount of capital used, clearly affects the MP_L in a direct manner. Conceptually, this result follows because increasing the amount of capital makes the labor input more productive in this case.

8.6 a. **Figure 8.1**

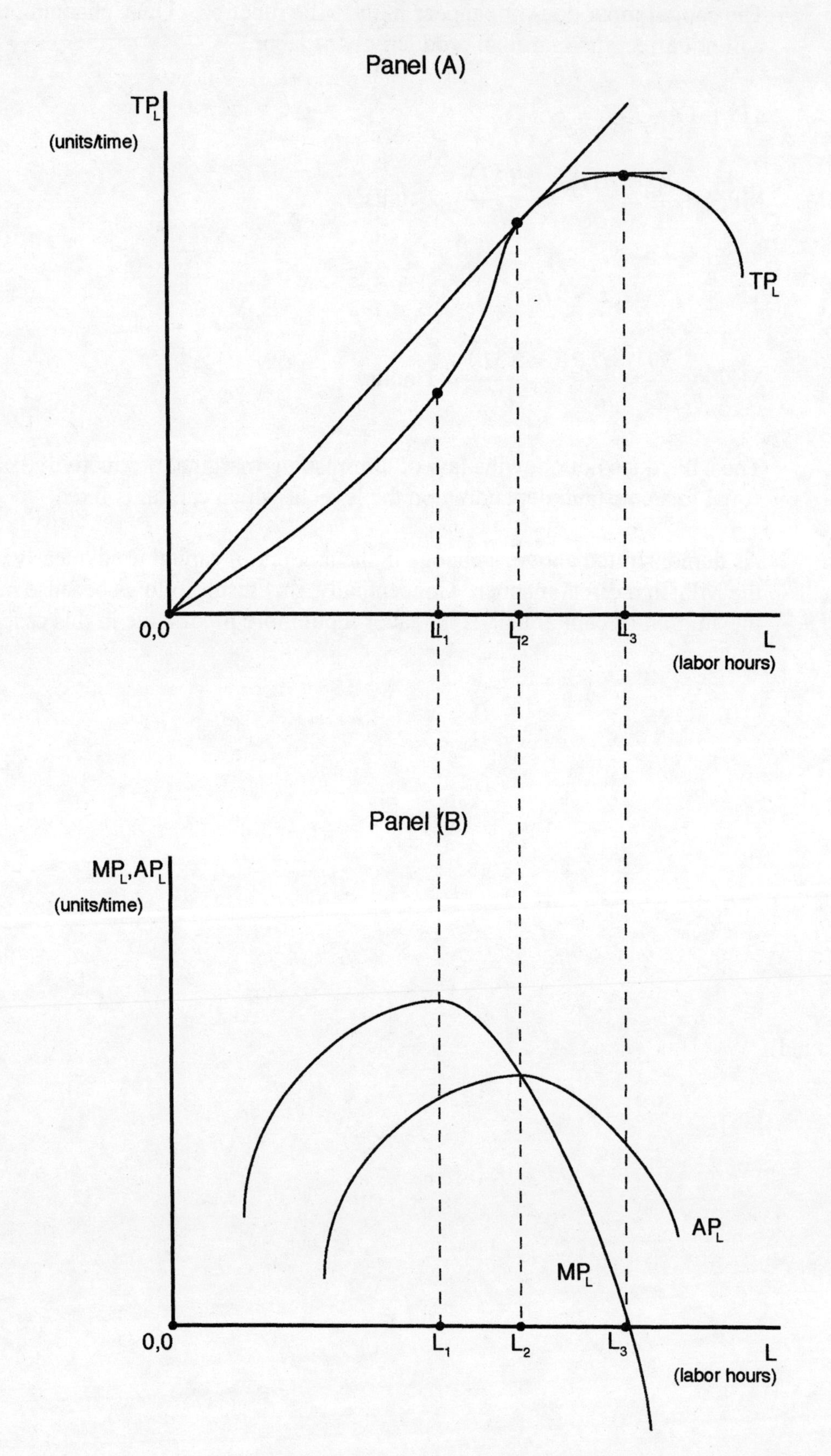

b. $MP_L = AP_L$ at L_3, where AP_L achieves its maximum value. $MP_L = 0$, where Q, or TP_L, achieves its maximum value.

8.7

Figure 8.2

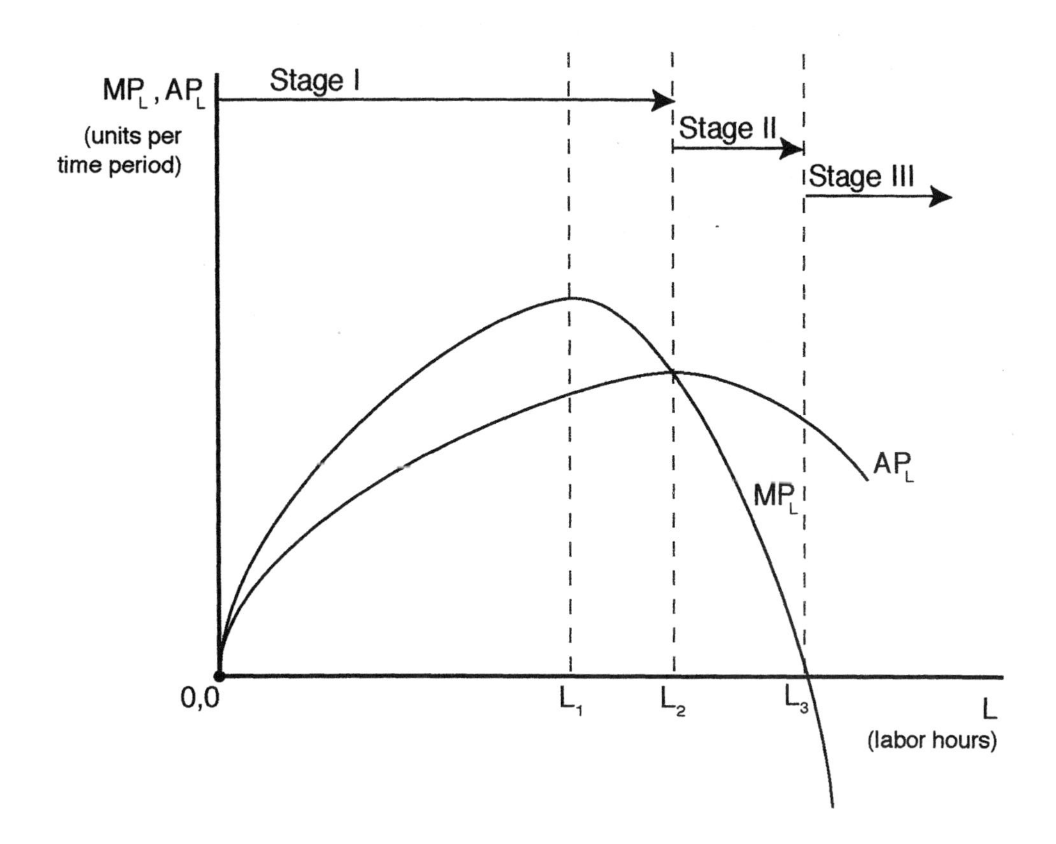

Stage I: refers to the range of labor use, where $MP_L > AP_L$, or alternatively stated, where AP_L rises as labor increases.

Stage II: refers to the range of labor use where $MP_L \leq AP_L$ and $MP_L \geq 0$.

Stage III: refers to the range of labor use where $MP_L < 0$.

The firm will not operate in Stage I because it is using so little labor relative to its fixed amount of capital that $MP_K < 0$. The firm will not operate in Stage III because it is using too much labor relative to its fixed amount of capital and thus, $MP_L < 0$. The stage in which the firm will operate is stage II, where both MP_L and MP_K are nonnegative.

SOLUTIONS

Chapter 9

9.1 a. This production process is based on the condition of fixed proportions, where the inputs must be used according to some specified ratio in order to produce the output.

b. The production function is represented as

$$Q = \text{minimum}\left(\frac{K}{1}, \frac{L}{3}\right).$$

This is a fixed coefficient production function, where the level of output produced is equal to the minimum of the two values in the function.

9.2 a. If L = 6 and K = 2, then

$$Q = \min\left(\frac{2}{1}, \frac{6}{3}\right) = \min(2,2) = 2 \text{ units.}$$

b. If L = 7 and K = 2, then

$$Q = \min\left(\frac{2}{1}, \frac{7}{3}\right) = \min(2, 2\frac{1}{3}) = 2 \text{ units,}$$

or the same level of output as before. With 2 units of capital the 7th unit of labor is useless.

c. $$Q = \min\left(\frac{4}{1}, \frac{L}{3}\right) = \min(4, \frac{L}{3}) = 4$$

$$\frac{L}{3} = 4$$

L = 12 units.

d.

Figure 9.1

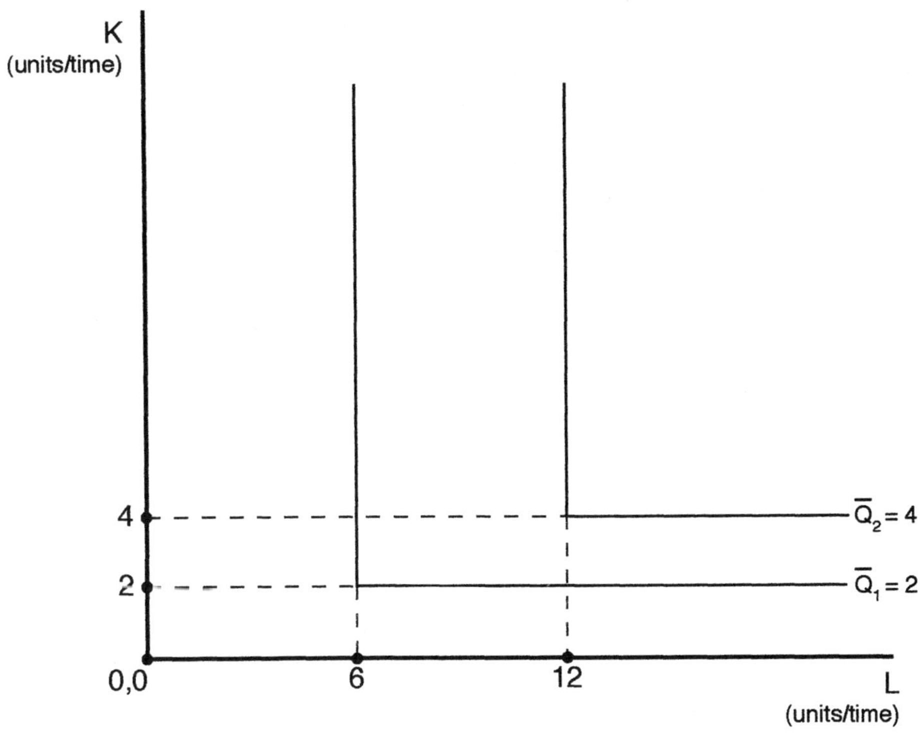

9.3 a. The isoquant for Q = 4 units is

$$\overline{Q}_1 = 4 = 2K^{\frac{1}{4}}L^{\frac{3}{4}},$$

or

$$K^{\frac{1}{4}} = \frac{4}{2L^{\frac{3}{4}}} = \frac{2}{L^{\frac{3}{4}}}$$

$$K = \frac{2^4}{L^3} = \frac{16}{L^3} = 16L^{-3}.$$

b. $$\text{K}^* = \frac{16}{L^3} = \frac{16}{(2)^3} = \frac{16}{8} = 2 \text{ units.}$$

c. $$\text{MRTS} = -\frac{dK}{dL} = -\frac{d(16L^{-3})}{dL}$$

$$= 48L^{-4} = \frac{48}{L^4}.$$

If L = 2 units, then

$$\text{MRTS} = \frac{48}{2^4} = \frac{48}{16} = 3.$$

d. $$\text{MRTS} = \frac{MP_L}{MP_K}$$

$$MP_L = \frac{\partial Q}{\partial L} = \frac{\partial\left(2K^{\frac{1}{4}}L^{\frac{3}{4}}\right)}{\partial L}$$
$$= \frac{3}{2}K^{\frac{1}{4}}L^{-\frac{1}{4}}$$

$$\text{MP}_\text{K} = \frac{\partial Q}{\partial K} = \frac{\partial\left(2K^{\frac{1}{4}}L^{\frac{3}{4}}\right)}{\partial K}$$
$$= \frac{1}{2}K^{-\frac{3}{4}}L^{\frac{3}{4}}.$$

Therefore

$$\text{MRTS} = \frac{\frac{3}{2}K^{\frac{1}{4}}L^{-\frac{1}{4}}}{\frac{1}{2}K^{-\frac{3}{4}}L^{\frac{3}{4}}} = \frac{3K}{L},$$

and if L = K = 2 units, then

$$\text{MRTS} = \frac{3(2)}{2} = 3,$$

or the same value computed earlier.

9.4 a. An isoquant can be established by fixing the level of output at some value, say $\overline{Q}_1$. Thus

$$\overline{Q}_1 = 10K^{\frac{1}{2}} + 20L^{\frac{1}{2}},$$

or

$$10K^{\frac{1}{2}} = 20L^{\frac{1}{2}} - \overline{Q}_1$$

$$K^{\frac{1}{2}} = 2L^{\frac{1}{2}} - \frac{1}{10}\overline{Q}_1$$

$$K = \left(2L^{\frac{1}{2}} - \frac{1}{10}\overline{Q}_1\right).$$

b. Recall

$$\text{MRTS} = \frac{MP_L}{MP_K},$$

where

$$\text{MP}_\text{L} = \frac{\partial Q}{\partial L} = \frac{\partial\left(10K^{\frac{1}{2}} + 20L^{\frac{1}{2}}\right)}{\partial L}$$

$$= 10\text{L}^{-\frac{1}{2}}$$

and

$$\text{MP}_\text{K} = \frac{\partial Q}{\partial K} = \frac{\partial\left(10K^{\frac{1}{2}} + 20L^{\frac{1}{2}}\right)}{\partial K}$$

$$= 5\text{K}^{-\frac{1}{2}}.$$

Thus

$$\text{MRTS} = \frac{MP_L}{MP_K} = \frac{10L^{-\frac{1}{2}}}{5K^{-\frac{1}{2}}} = \frac{\partial K^{\frac{1}{2}}}{L^{\frac{1}{2}}}.$$

Since K is in the numerator and L is in the denominator then, as K decreases and L increases, the value of the MRTS becomes smaller. Thus, the MRTS diminishes as labor is substituted for capital.

9.5 a. Since the production function is linear this indicates that capital and labor are perfectly substitutable. This production function also indicates that the marginal product of each input is constant since,

$$\text{MP}_\text{L} = \frac{\partial Q}{\partial L} = \frac{\partial(10K + 20L)}{\partial L} = 20$$

and

$$\text{MP}_\text{K} = \frac{\partial Q}{\partial K} = \frac{\partial(10K + 20L)}{\partial K} = 10.$$

b. $$\text{MRTS} = \frac{\frac{\partial Q}{\partial L}}{\frac{\partial Q}{\partial K}} = \frac{20}{10} = 2.$$

The marginal rate of technical substitution is equal to a constant value of 2. This means that in this production process the firm can substitute one unit of labor for two units of capital, and maintain the same level of output. Since the MRTS is equal to a constant value, this production process does not exhibit diminishing marginal rate of technical substitution.

c. $Q = 10K + 20L$
If $L = 3$ and $K = 4$ then
$Q = 10\,(4) + 20\,(3) = 100$.

To determine the equation for this isoquant, set
$Q = 100$ and solve the above production function for the value of K as follows.

$100 = 10K + 20L$
$-10K = 20L - 100$
$K = -2L + 10$.

To determine the intercept of the isoquant with the capital axis, set $L = 0$ and solve for the value of K as follows.

$K = -2\,(0) + 10$
$K = 10$.

To determine the intercept of the isoquant with the labor axis, set $K = 0$ and solve for the value of L as follows.

$0 = -2L + 10$
$2L = 10$
$L = 5$.

Figure 9.2

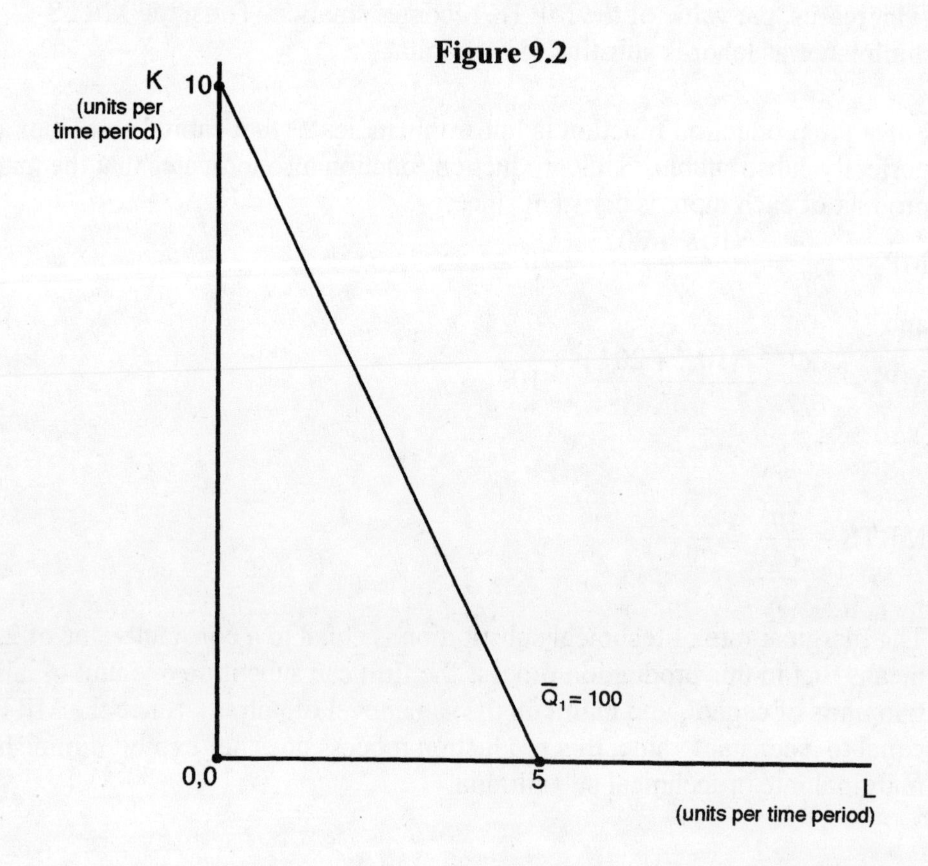

9.6 a. False. Isoquants cannot intersect since each isoquant represents the set of input combinations capable of producing a particular level of output. Therefore, a single input combination cannot simultaneously lie on more than one isoquant since it cannot simultaneously represent more than one level of output. In addition, isoquants that intersect violate the assumption of transitivity.

b. True. When two inputs are used in fixed proportions in a production process, the isoquants are L-shaped.

c. False. When two inputs are perfectly substitutable in a production process, the associated isoquants are linear and downward sloping.

d. True. An input combination that contains a greater amount of inputs produces a greater amount of output than an input combination with lesser amounts of inputs.

9.7 a. This is a description of a fixed proportions production process. The production function in this case, is

$$\text{Q} = \text{minimum}\left(\frac{K}{2}, \frac{L}{1}\right).$$

b. This is a description of a production process where capital and labor are perfectly substitutable. Therefore, the production function is linear and of the form,

$$\text{Q} = 4\text{K} + \text{L}.$$

c. This is a description of a production process where the marginal rate of technical substitution diminishes. The production function can be

$$\text{Q} = \text{K}^{.5}\,\text{L}^{.5}.$$

Given this production function the

$$\text{MRTS} = \frac{MP_L}{MP_K} = \frac{\frac{\partial Q}{\partial L}}{\frac{\partial Q}{\partial K}} = \frac{0.5K^{.5}L^{-.5}}{0.5K^{-.5}L^{.5}} = \frac{K}{L}.$$

As the firm increases its use of labor and decreases its use of capital, the value of the MRTS will diminish since the value of the numerator will become smaller as the value of the denominator becomes larger.

9.8 a.

Figure 9.3

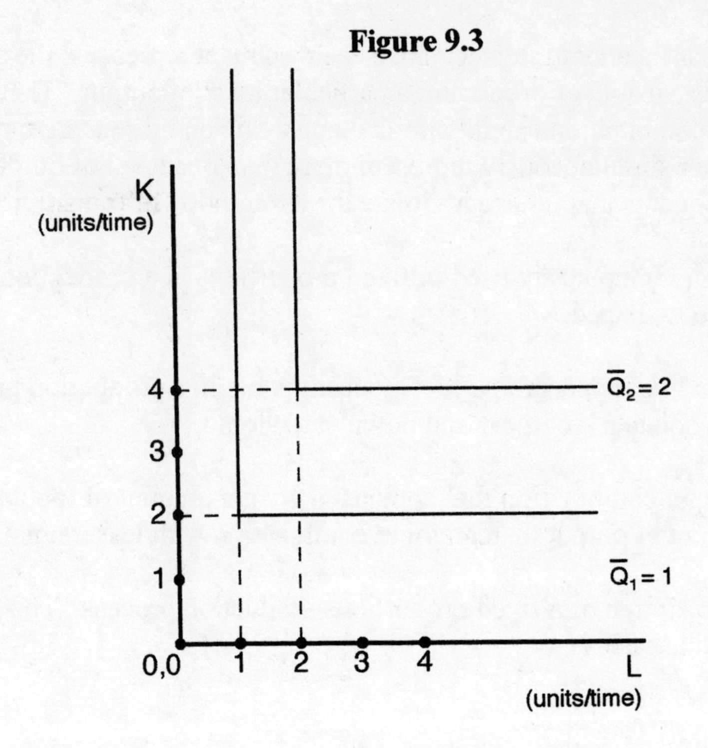

b.

Figure 9.4

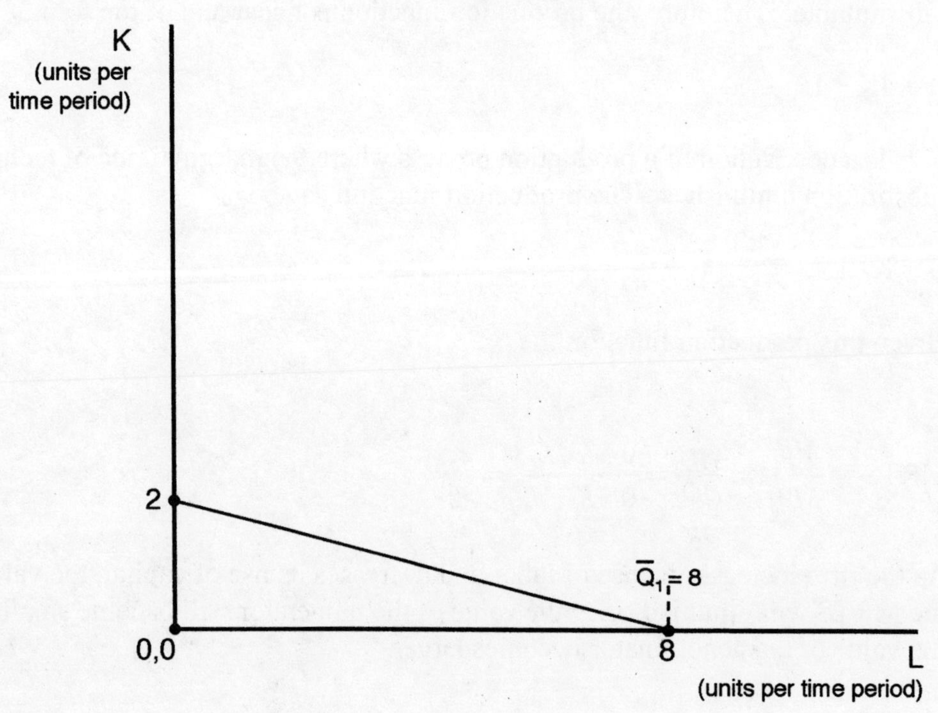

c. **Figure 9.5**

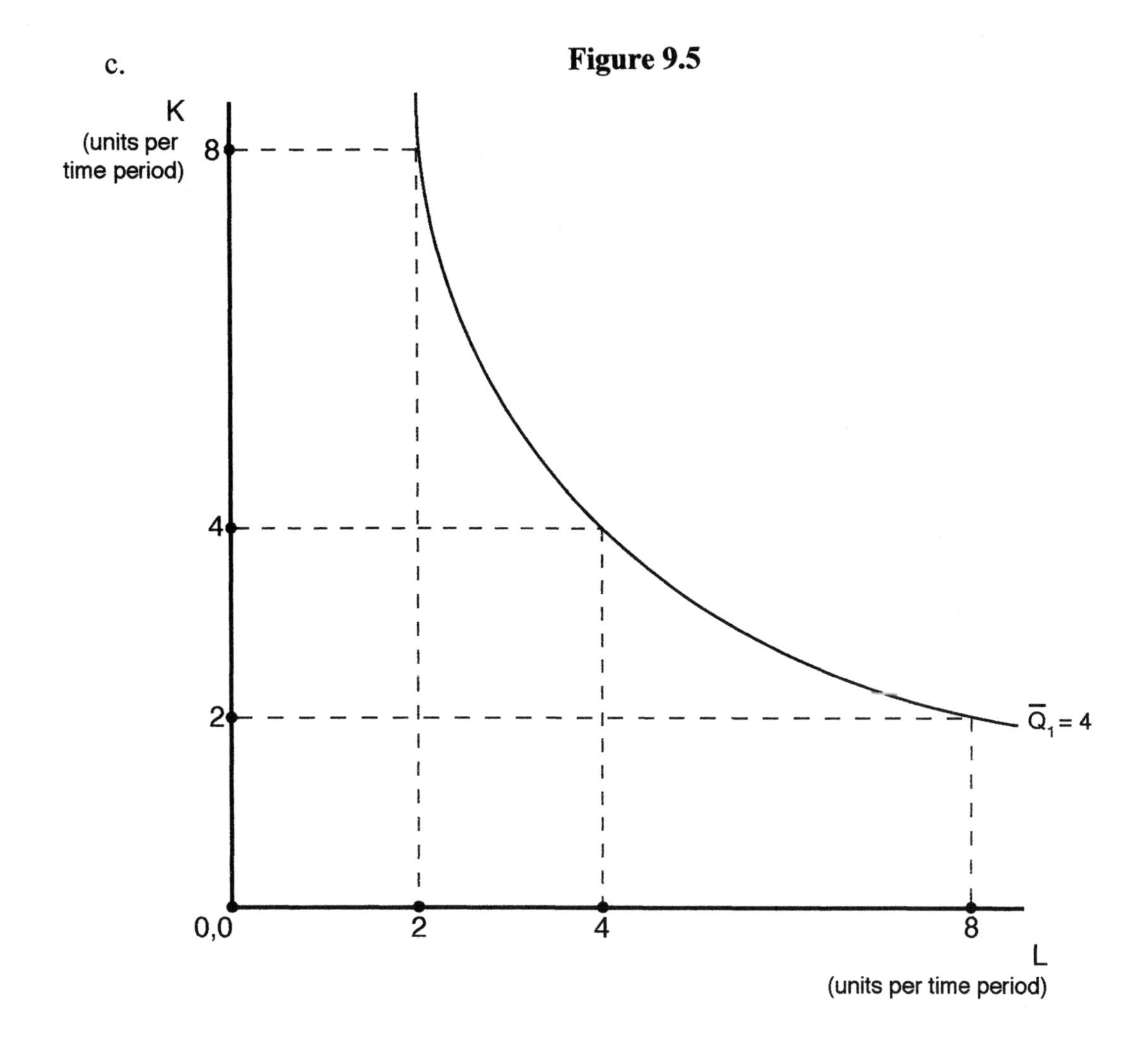
K
(units per
time period)
8
4
2
0,0
2
4
8
L
(units per time period)
$\bar{Q}_1 = 4$

SOLUTIONS

Chapter 10

10.1 a. Given the production function
$Q = 81K^{.70}L^{.35}$,

$$MRTS = \frac{MP_L}{MP_K} = \frac{\frac{\partial Q}{\partial L}}{\frac{\partial Q}{\partial K}} = \frac{28.35K^{.70}L^{-.65}}{56.7K^{-.30}L^{.35}} = \frac{K}{2L}$$

b. If $\overline{P}_{K,1} = \$90$, $\overline{P}_{L,1} = \$30$, and $\overline{C}_1 = \$100{,}000$, then the isocost equation, $\overline{P}_{K,1}K + \overline{P}_{L,1}L = \overline{C}_1$, in this case is
$90K + 30L = 100{,}000$.

c. The necessary condition for a constrained cost minimum is, in general,
$MRTS = \frac{\overline{P}_{L,1}}{\overline{P}_{K,1}}$.
From part a. we know for the production function $Q = 81K^{.70}L^{.35}$,
$MRTS = \frac{K}{2L}$,
and if $\overline{P}_{L,1} = \$30$ and $\overline{P}_{K,1} = \$90$ then the necessary condition for a constrained cost minimum in this case is

$$\frac{K}{2L} = \frac{30}{90},$$
$$\frac{K}{2L} = \frac{1}{3},$$
or
$$\frac{K}{L} = \frac{2}{3}.$$

10.2 a. If $\overline{P}_{L,1} = \$25$, $\overline{P}_{K,1} = \$100$, and $\overline{C}_1 = \$250{,}000$ then the isocost equation is
$100K + 25L = 250{,}000$.

b. Given $\overline{P}_{L,1} = \$25$, $\overline{P}_{K,1} = \$100$ and $\overline{C}_1 = \$250{,}000$ then:

$$\text{slope of the isocost equation} = \frac{-\overline{P}_{L,1}}{\overline{P}_{K,1}} = \frac{-\$25}{\$100} = \frac{-1}{4}$$

$$\text{K-intercept of the isocost equation} = \frac{\overline{C}_1}{\overline{P}_{K,1}} = \frac{\$250{,}000}{\$100} = 2500$$

$$\text{L-intercept of the isocost equation} = \frac{\overline{C}_1}{\overline{P}_{L,1}} = \frac{\$250{,}000}{\$25} = 10{,}000$$

Figure 10.1

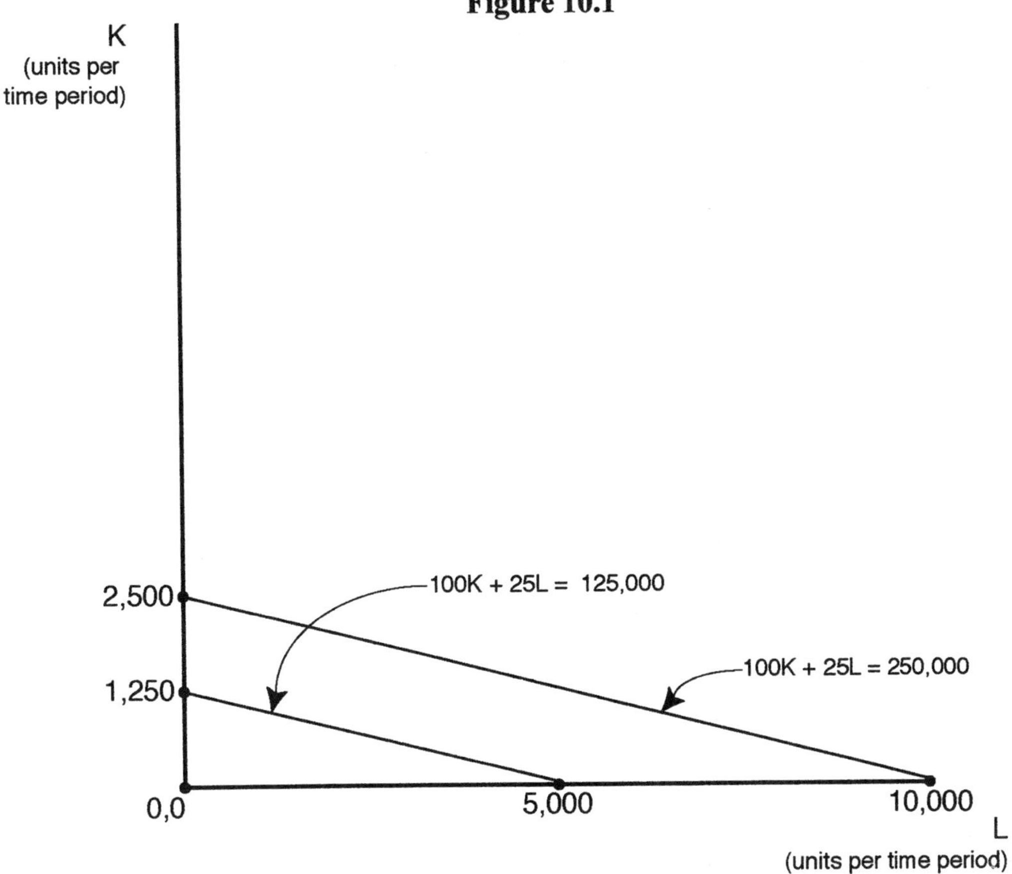

c. If $\overline{P}_{K,1} = \$100$, $\overline{P}_{L,1} = \$25$, and $\overline{C}_2 = \$125{,}000$ then the isocost equation would now be

$$100K + 25L = 125{,}000.$$

d. If $\overline{P}_{K,1} = \$100$, $\overline{P}_{L,1} = \$25$, and $\overline{C}_2 = \$125{,}000$ then

$$\text{slope of the isocost equation} = \frac{-\overline{P}_{L,1}}{\overline{P}_{K,1}} = \frac{-\$25}{\$100} = \frac{-1}{4}$$

$$\text{K-intercept of the isocost equation} = \frac{\overline{C}_2}{\overline{P}_{K,1}} = \frac{\$125{,}000}{\$100} = 1250$$

$$\text{L-intercept of the isocost equation} = \frac{\overline{C}_2}{\overline{P}_{L,1}} = \frac{\$125{,}000}{\$25} = 5000$$

The slope of this isocost equation is the same as that computed for the isocost equation in part b. However, the K- and L-intercepts are one-half the value of those computed in part b., when $\overline{C}_1 = \$250{,}000$. Therefore, the isocost equation computed for $\overline{C}_2 = \$125{,}000$ is shifted to the left in a parallel fashion, relative to the isocost equation where $\overline{C}_1 = \$250{,}000$, as shown in the figure in part b.

10.3 a. Minimize C = $\overline{P}_{K,1}K + \overline{P}_{L,1}L$
subject to $\overline{Q}_1 = 64K^2 + 16L^2$

$$\mathcal{L} = \overline{P}_{K,1}K + \overline{P}_{L,1}L + \lambda(\overline{Q}_1 - 64K^2 - 16L^2)$$
$$= \overline{P}_{K,1}K + \overline{P}_{L,1}L + \lambda\overline{Q}_1 - 64\lambda K^2 - 16\lambda L^2$$
$$\frac{\partial \mathcal{L}}{\partial K} = \overline{P}_{K,1} - 128\lambda K = 0$$
$$\frac{\partial \mathcal{L}}{\partial L} = \overline{P}_{L,1} - 32\lambda L = 0$$
$$\frac{\partial \mathcal{L}}{\partial \lambda} = \overline{Q}_1 - 64K^2 - 16L^2 = 0$$
$$128\lambda K = \overline{P}_{K,1}$$
$$32\lambda L = \overline{P}_{L,1}$$
$$\frac{4K}{L} = \frac{\overline{P}_{K,1}}{\overline{P}_{L,1}}$$
$$K = \frac{\overline{P}_{K,1}L}{4\overline{P}_{L,1}}$$
$$\overline{Q}_1 - 64\left(\frac{\overline{P}_{K,1}L}{4\overline{P}_{L,1}}\right)^2 - 16L^2 = 0$$
$$\overline{Q}_1 - \frac{4\overline{P}_{K,1}{}^2L^2}{\overline{P}_{L,1}{}^2} - 16L^2 = 0$$
$$\overline{Q}_1 = 16L^2 + \frac{4\overline{P}_{K,1}{}^2L^2}{\overline{P}_{L,1}{}^2}$$
$$\overline{Q}_1 = L^2\left(16 + \frac{4\overline{P}_{K,1}{}^2}{\overline{P}_{L,1}{}^2}\right)$$
$$L^2 = \frac{\overline{Q}_1}{\left(16 + \frac{4\overline{P}_{K,1}{}^2}{\overline{P}_{L,1}{}^2}\right)}$$
$$L = \frac{\overline{Q}_1{}^{.5}}{\left(16 + \frac{4\overline{P}_{K,1}{}^2}{\overline{P}_{L,1}{}^2}\right)^{.5}}$$

Substituting $\overline{Q}_1 = 14{,}400, \overline{P}_{K,1} = \$120$ and $\overline{P}_{L,1} = \$80$ in the above equation yields

$$L^* = \frac{(14{,}400)^{.5}}{\left(16 + \frac{4(120)^2}{(80)^2}\right)^{.5}}$$
$$= \frac{120}{\left(16 + \frac{57{,}600}{6{,}400}\right)^{.5}}$$
$$= \frac{120}{(16+9)^{.5}}$$
$$= \frac{120}{(25)^{.5}}$$
$$= \frac{120}{5}$$
$$= 24.$$

To determine the optimal value of K, substitute $L^* = 24$, $\overline{P}_{K,1} = \$120$, and $\overline{P}_{L,1} = \$80$, into the equation for K as follows.

$$K^* = \frac{\overline{P}_{K,1}L^*}{4\overline{P}_{L,1}} = \frac{(120)(24)}{(4)(80)} = \frac{2880}{320} = 9.$$

b. To determine the minimum value of cost incurred by the firm, substitute $K^* = 9$, $L^* = 24$, $\overline{P}_{K,1} = \$120$ and $\overline{P}_{L,1} = \$80$, into the objective function.

$$C^* = \overline{P}_{K,1}K^* + \overline{P}_{L,1}L^* = (120)(9) + (80)(24)$$
$$= 1080 + 1920 = \$3000.$$

10.4 a. To determine the optimal value of λ, substitute $K^* = 9$, $L^* = 24$, $\overline{P}_{K,1} = \$120$, and $\overline{P}_{L,1} = \$80$ into the equations for either $\frac{\partial \mathcal{L}}{\partial K}$ or $\frac{\partial \mathcal{L}}{\partial L}$ as follows.

$$\frac{\partial \mathcal{L}}{\partial K} = \overline{P}_{K,1} - 128\lambda K = 0$$
$$128\lambda K = \overline{P}_{K,1}$$
$$\lambda^* = \frac{\overline{P}_{K,1}}{128K^*} = \frac{120}{128(9)} = 0.104$$

b. The value of λ* indicates that if the pasta maker's predetermined level of output was reduced by one unit from 14,400 to 14,399 units, then the firm's minimum total expenditure on capital and labor decreases by \$0.104, the value of λ*, from \$3000.00 to \$3000.00 - \$0.104 = \$2999.896. Alternatively, if the predetermined level of output increases by one unit from 14,400 to 14,401, then the firm's minimum total expenditure increases by \$0.104, from \$3000.00 to \$3000.00 + \$0.104 = \$3000.104.

10.5 a. Given the production function
$Q = f(K,L) = 200K^{.75} L^{.50}$,
let δ denote the scaling factor, then we can determine the degree of homogeneity as follows.

$$\delta^n Q = f(\delta K, \delta L) = 200 (\delta K)^{.75} (\delta L)^{.50}$$
$$\delta^n Q = 200\delta^{.75} K^{.75} \delta^{.50} L^{.50}$$
$$\delta^n Q = 200\delta^{1.25} K^{.75} L^{.50}$$
$$\delta^n Q = \delta^{1.25} [200K^{.75} L^{.50}]$$
$$\delta^n Q = \delta^{1.25} Q$$

In this case $n = 1.25$, therefore this production function is homogeneous of degree 1.25.

b. This production function is homogeneous of degree 1.25 > 1, therefore it exhibits increasing returns to scale.

c. Beer and wine production processes exhibit increasing returns to scale.

10.6 a. Minimize C = $\bar{P}_{K,1}K + \bar{P}_{L,1}L$
subject to $\bar{Q}_1 = 400K^{.5}L^{.5}$

$$\mathcal{L} = \bar{P}_{K,1}K + \bar{P}_{L,1}L + \lambda(\bar{Q}_1 - 400K^{.5}L^{.5})$$
$$= \bar{P}_{K,1}K + \bar{P}_{L,1}L + \lambda\bar{Q}_1 - 400\lambda K^{.5}L^{.5}$$
$$\frac{\partial \mathcal{L}}{\partial K} = \bar{P}_{K,1} - 200\lambda K^{-.5}L^{.5} = 0$$
$$\frac{\partial \mathcal{L}}{\partial L} = \bar{P}_{L,1} - 200\lambda K^{.5}L^{-.5} = 0$$
$$\frac{\partial \mathcal{L}}{\partial \lambda} = \bar{Q}_1 - 400K^{.5}L^{.5} = 0$$
$$200\lambda K^{-.5} L^{.5} = \bar{P}_{K,1}$$
$$200\lambda K^{.5} L^{-.5} = \bar{P}_{L,1}$$

$$\frac{200\lambda K^{-.5}L^{.5}}{200\lambda K^{.5}L^{-.5}} = \frac{\bar{P}_{K,1}}{\bar{P}_{L,1}}$$
$$\frac{L}{K} = \frac{\bar{P}_{K,1}}{\bar{P}_{L,1}}$$

$$L = \frac{\overline{P}_{K,1}K}{\overline{P}_{L,1}}.$$

Substitute the above equation for L into the constraint as follows.

$$\overline{Q}_1 - 400K^{.5}L^{.5} = 0$$

$$\overline{Q}_1 - 400K^{.5}\left(\frac{\overline{P}_{K,1}K}{\overline{P}_{L,1}}\right)^{.5} = 0$$

$$\overline{Q}_1 - 400K\left(\frac{\overline{P}_{K,1}}{\overline{P}_{L,1}}\right)^{.5} = 0$$

$$400\text{K}\left(\frac{\overline{P}_{K,1}}{\overline{P}_{L,1}}\right)^{.5} = \overline{Q}_1$$

$$\text{K} = \frac{\overline{Q}_1}{(400)\left(\frac{\overline{P}_{K,1}}{\overline{P}_{L,1}}\right)^{.5}}$$

By substituting $\overline{P}_{K,1} = \$2500, \overline{P}_{L,1} = \$25,$ and $\overline{Q}_1 = 8000$ into the above equation we can determine the optimal value of K.

$$\text{K}^* = \frac{\overline{Q}_1}{(400)\left(\frac{\overline{P}_{K,1}}{\overline{P}_{L,1}}\right)^{.5}} = \frac{8000}{(400)\left(\frac{2500}{25}\right)^{.5}} = \frac{8000}{(400)(10)} = \frac{8000}{4000} = 2 \text{ units.}$$

By substituting $\text{K}^* = 2$, $\overline{P}_{K,1} = \$2500$, and $\overline{P}_{L,1} = \$25$, into the equation for L, we can determine the optimal level of labor use, L^*.

$$\text{L}^* = \frac{\overline{P}_{K,1}K^*}{\overline{P}_{L,1}} = \frac{(2500)(2)}{25} = \frac{5000}{25} = 200 \text{ units.}$$

b. We can determine the minimum cost of producing 8000 units of green beans by substituting $\text{K}^* = 2$, $\text{L}^* = 200$, $\overline{P}_{K,1} = \$2500$, and $\overline{P}_{L,1} = \$25$, into the objective function.

$$\text{C}^* = \overline{P}_{K,1}K^* + \overline{P}_{L,1}L^* = (\$2500)(2) + (\$25)(200) = \$5000 + \$5000 = \$10{,}000$$

10.7 a. The necessary condition for a constrained cost minimum for the problem in exercise 10.6 was determined to be

$$\frac{L}{K} = \frac{\overline{P}_{K,1}}{\overline{P}_{L,1}}$$

or

$$\frac{K}{L} = \frac{\overline{P}_{L,1}}{\overline{P}_{K,1}}.$$

Solving the above equation for K we can derive the expansion path as follows.

$$K = \frac{\overline{P}_{L,1}L}{\overline{P}_{K,1}}.$$

Substituting the input prices from exercise 10.6, $\overline{P}_{K,1} = \$2500$ and $\overline{P}_{L,1} = \$25$, into the above equation yields the expansion path specifically for the constrained cost minimization problem in exercise 10.6.

$$K = \frac{\overline{P}_{L,1}L}{\overline{P}_{K,1}} = \frac{25L}{2500} = \frac{L}{100}.$$

b. If L = 500 units then by substituting this value for L into the expansion path, derived in part a., we can determine the amount of capital that must be used with 500 units of labor to minimize the farmer's total expenditures on the inputs necessary to produce 8000 units of green beans.

$$K = \frac{L}{100} = \frac{500}{100} = 5 \text{ units}.$$

10.8 a. Given the fixed coefficient production function

$$\text{Q} = \text{minimum}\left(\frac{K}{1}, \frac{L}{4}\right),$$

the firm must use capital and labor inputs in a fixed proportion of one unit of capital to four units of labor, or mathematically stated,

$$\frac{K}{L} = \frac{1}{4}$$

or

$$\text{K} = \frac{L}{4}.$$

In order to determine the amounts of capital and labor necessary to produce the predetermined level of output, $\overline{Q}_1 = 400$, set the production function equal to 400 as follows.

$$\overline{Q}_1 = \text{minimum}\left(\frac{K}{1}, \frac{L}{4}\right) = 400.$$

If K = 400 and L = 1600 then

$$\overline{Q}_1 = \text{minimum}\left(\frac{400}{1}, \frac{1600}{4}\right) = \text{minimum } (400, 400) = 400.$$

Therefore, the optimal amounts of capital and labor the baker will purchase to produce 400 donuts are $K^* = 400$ and $L^* = 1600$.

b. To determine the minimum cost the baker incurs to produce 400 units of donuts, substitute $K^* = 400$, $L^* = 1600$, $\overline{P}_{K,1} = \$100$, and $\overline{P}_{L,1} = \$10$ into the firm's total expenditure function as follows.

$$\begin{aligned} C^* &= \overline{P}_{K,1}K^* + \overline{P}_{L,1}L^* \\ &= (\$100)\ (400) + (\$10)\ (1600) \\ &= \$40{,}000 + \$16{,}000 \\ &= \$56{,}000 \end{aligned}$$

c. To plot the optimal isocost equation for this problem determine the slope and intercept values for the function as follows.

$$\text{Slope of isocost equation} = \frac{-\overline{P}_{L,1}}{\overline{P}_{K,1}} = \frac{-\$10}{\$100} = \frac{-1}{10}$$

$$\text{K-intercept of isocost equation} = \frac{C^*}{\overline{P}_{K,1}} = \frac{\$56{,}000}{\$100} = 560 \text{ units}$$

$$\text{L-intercept of isocost equation} = \frac{C^*}{\overline{P}_{L,1}} = \frac{\$56{,}000}{\$10} = 5600 \text{ units.}$$

To plot the isoquant associated with the fixed coefficient production function, $Q = \text{minimum}\left(\frac{K}{1}, \frac{L}{4}\right)$, where $\overline{Q}_1 = 400$ units, recall that the isoquant is L-shaped with its vertex at the optimal (cost minimizing) input combination, $L^* = 1600$ and $K^* = 400$, as shown in the figure on the following page.

Figure 10.2

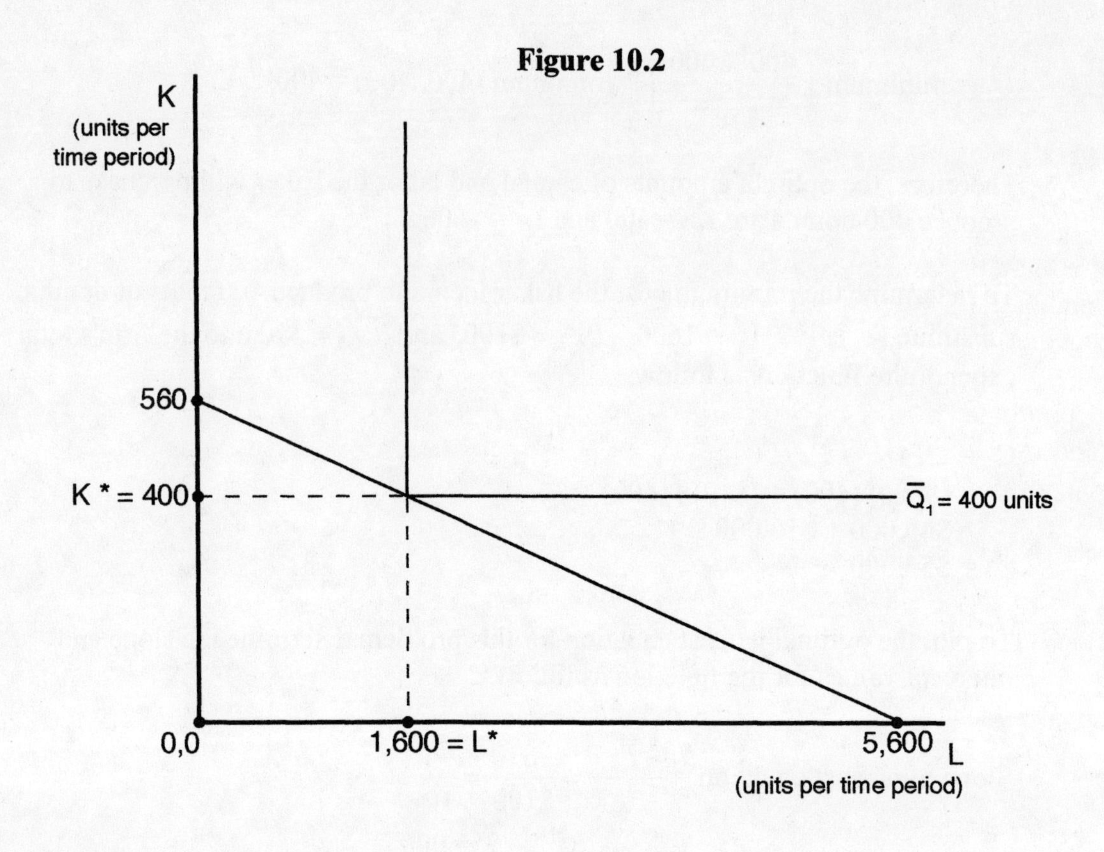
K
(units per
time period)
560
K * = 400
$\bar{Q}_1$ = 400 units
0,0
1,600 = L*
5,600
L
(units per time period)

SOLUTIONS

Chapter 11

11.1 Conceptually, economists define a firm's costs as the summation of its explicit and implicit, or opportunity, costs. The implicit costs for the owner of the firm are the summation of the opportunity costs associated with her labor and capital inputs that are devoted to the firm, or

Opportunity cost of labor = \$40,000
and
Opportunity cost of capital = .05 (100,000) = \$5,000.

Thus, the overall costs are

Costs = \$100,000 + \$40,000 + \$5,000 = \$145,000.

11.2 a. The firm's isocost equation is

$$C = \overline{P}_{K,1}K + \overline{P}_{L,1}L.$$

Therefore

$$\text{Min: } C = \overline{P}_{K,1}K + \overline{P}_{L,1}L.$$

$$\text{Subject to: } \overline{Q} - 4K^{\frac{1}{4}}L^{\frac{1}{4}} = 0$$

$$\mathcal{L} = \overline{P}_{K,1}K + \overline{P}_{L,1}L + \lambda\left(\overline{Q}_1 - 4K^{\frac{1}{4}}L^{\frac{1}{4}}\right)$$

$$= \overline{P}_{K,1}K + \overline{P}_{L,1}L + \lambda\overline{Q}_1 - 4\lambda K^{\frac{1}{4}}L^{\frac{1}{4}}$$

$$\frac{\partial\mathcal{L}}{\partial K} = \overline{P}_{K,1} - \lambda K^{-\frac{3}{4}}L^{\frac{1}{4}} = 0$$

$$\frac{\partial\mathcal{L}}{\partial L} = \overline{P}_{L,1} - \lambda K^{\frac{1}{4}}L^{-\frac{3}{4}} = 0$$

$$\frac{\partial\mathcal{L}}{\partial \lambda} = \overline{Q}_1 - 4K^{\frac{1}{4}}L^{\frac{1}{4}} = 0$$

$$\frac{\overline{P}_{L,1}}{\overline{P}_{K,1}} = \frac{\lambda K^{\frac{1}{4}}L^{-\frac{3}{4}}}{\lambda K^{-\frac{3}{4}}L^{\frac{1}{4}}}$$

$$\frac{\overline{P}_{L,1}}{\overline{P}_{K,1}} = \frac{K}{L}$$

$$K = \frac{\overline{P}_{L,1}}{\overline{P}_{K,1}}L = \frac{8}{2}L = 4L,$$

or alternatively

$$L = \frac{1}{4}K.$$

Either of the two equations

$$K = 4L$$

or

$$L = \frac{1}{4}K,$$

can be interpreted as the firm's expansion path.

b. $Q = 4K^{\frac{1}{4}}L^{\frac{1}{4}}$

Thus

$$Q = 4\,(4L)^{\frac{1}{4}}\,L^{\frac{1}{4}} = 4(4)^{\frac{1}{4}}\,L^{\frac{1}{2}}$$

$$L^{\frac{1}{2}} = \frac{Q}{4(4)^{\frac{1}{4}}}$$

$$L = \frac{Q^2}{16(4)^{\frac{1}{2}}} = \frac{Q^2}{16(2)} = \frac{Q^2}{32}$$

and

$$Q = 4K^{\frac{1}{4}}\left(\frac{1}{4}K\right)^{\frac{1}{4}}$$

$$= 4\left(\frac{1}{4}\right)^{\frac{1}{4}}K^{\frac{1}{2}}$$

$$K^{\frac{1}{2}} = \frac{Q}{4\left(\frac{1}{4}\right)^{\frac{1}{4}}}$$

$$K = \frac{Q^2}{16\left(\frac{1}{4}\right)^{\frac{1}{2}}} = \frac{Q^2}{16\left(\frac{1}{2}\right)} = \frac{Q^2}{8}.$$

$$C = \overline{P}_{K,1}K + \overline{P}_{L,1}L$$

$$= 2\left(\frac{Q^2}{8}\right) + 8\left(\frac{Q^2}{32}\right)$$

$$= \frac{1}{4}Q^2 + \frac{1}{4}Q^2 = \frac{1}{2}Q^2,$$

or

$$\text{LRTC} = \frac{1}{2}Q^2,$$

since all inputs are variable.

11.3 a. $$\text{LRMC} = \frac{dLRTC}{dQ} = \frac{d\left(\frac{1}{2}Q^2\right)}{dQ} = Q.$$

$$\text{LRAC} = \frac{LRTC}{Q} = \frac{\frac{1}{2}Q^2}{Q} = \frac{1}{2}Q.$$

b. **Figure 11.1**

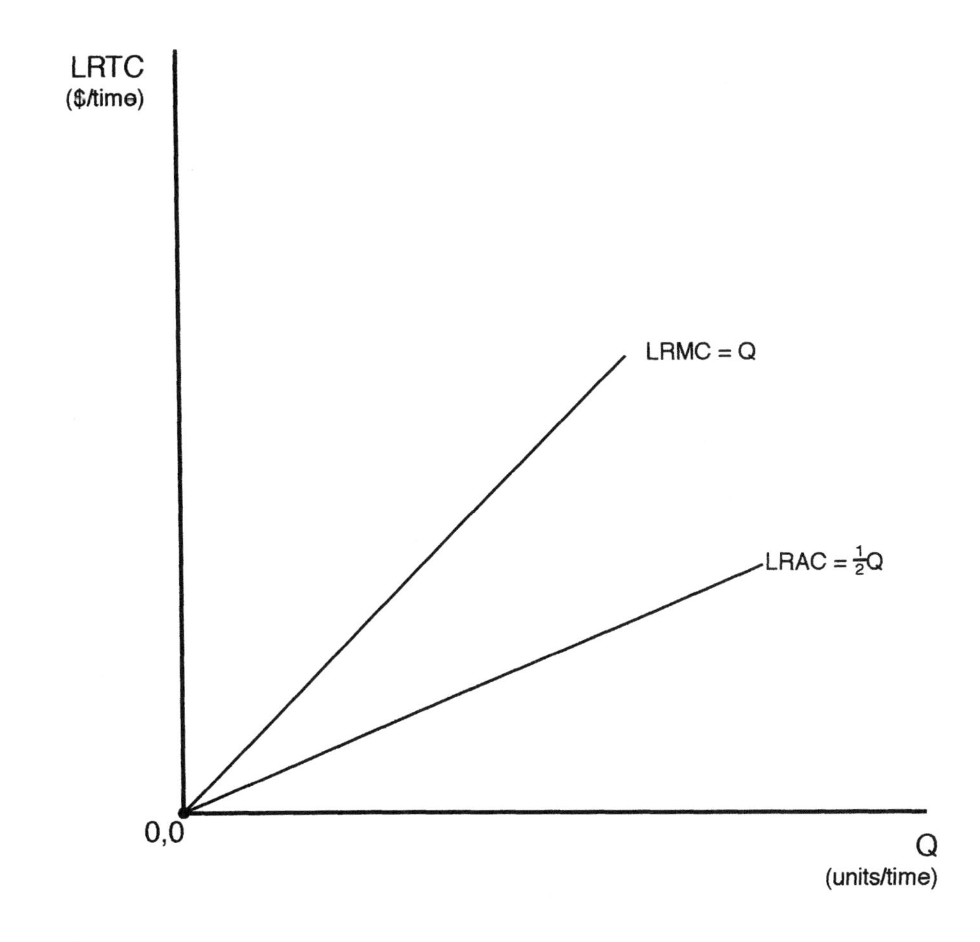

c. $\text{LRTC} = \frac{1}{2}(4)^2 = \$8$

$\text{LRAC} = \frac{1}{2}(4) = \$2$

$\text{LRMC} = Q = \$4$

11.4 a. $C = 0.05\,Q^3 - 2Q^2 + 50Q - 2KQ + 2K^2$

$$\frac{\partial C}{\partial K} = -2Q + 4K = 0$$
$$4K = 2Q$$
$$K = \frac{1}{2}Q.$$

b. $\text{LRTC} = C = 0.05Q^3 - 2Q^2 + 50Q - 2\left(\frac{1}{2}Q\right)Q + 2\left(\frac{1}{2}Q\right)^2$

$= 0.05Q^3 - 2Q^2 - 50Q - Q^2 + \frac{1}{2}Q^2$
$= 0.05Q^3\ \ 2.5Q^2 + 50Q.$

11.5 a. $\text{LRMC} = \frac{dLRTC}{dQ}$
$= 0.15Q^2 - 5Q + 50$
and
$\text{LRAC} = \frac{LRTC}{Q} = \frac{0.05Q^3 - 2.5Q^2 + 50Q}{Q}$
$= 0.05Q^2 - 2.5Q + 50.$

b. To minimize LRAC

$$\frac{dLRAC}{dQ} = \frac{d\left(0.05Q^2 - 2.5Q + 50\right)}{dQ} = 0$$

$= 0.10Q - 2.5 = 0$

$Q = \frac{2.5}{0.10} = 25$ units.

$\text{LRAC} = 0.05\,(25)^2 - 2.5\,(25) + 50 = 31.25 - 62.5 + 50 = \$18.75.$

c. $K = \frac{1}{2}Q = \frac{1}{2}(25) = 12.5$ units.

d. Q = 25 units, is that level of output at which the firm realizes all economies of scale, but experiences no diseconomies of scale. Thus, the firm is using the ideal plant size, K = 12.5 units, in this situation.

11.6 a. When LRAC is at its minimum value, LRMC = LRAC. We have demonstrated that this result occurs at Q = 25 units. Thus

$$\begin{aligned} LRMC &= 0.15Q^2 - 5Q + 50 \\ &= 0.15\,(25)^2 - 5\,(25) + 50 \\ &= 93.75 - 125 + 50 \\ &= \$18.75, \end{aligned}$$

or the same value as LRAC, computed above, when LRAC is at its minimum value.

b. Since LRMC = LRAC, when LRAC achieves a minimum value, we can compute the corresponding output level as

$$0.15Q^2 - 5Q + 50 = 0.05\,Q^2 - 2.5Q + 50$$

$$0.10Q^2 - 2.5Q = 0$$

$$Q\,(.10Q - 2.5) = 0$$

$$.10Q = 2.5$$
$$Q = \frac{2.5}{10} = 25.$$

c. **Figure 11.2**

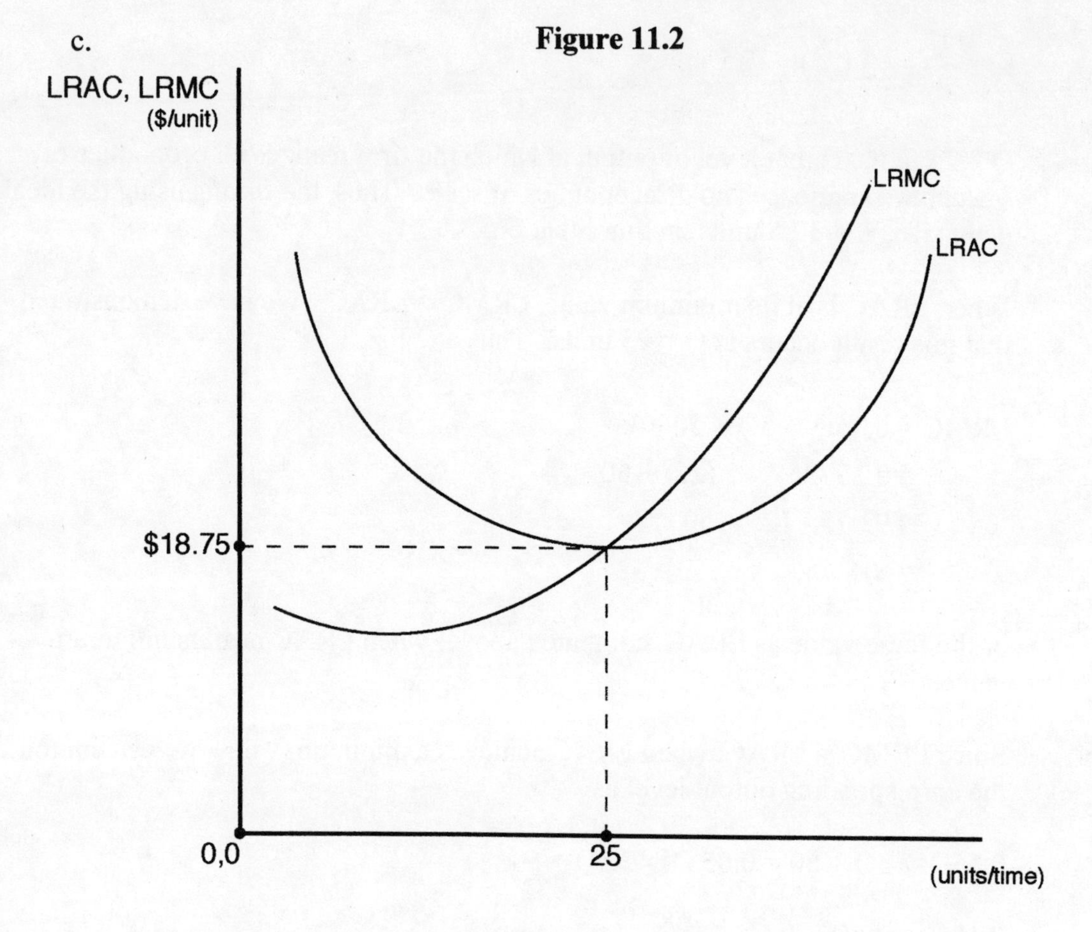

11.7 a. Letting θ be the scale factor, then

$$Q^* = 8(\theta K)^{\frac{1}{4}}(\theta L)^{\frac{3}{4}}$$
$$= 8\,\theta^{\frac{1}{4}}K^{\frac{1}{4}}\theta^{\frac{3}{4}}L^{\frac{3}{4}}$$
$$= \theta^1 8K^{\frac{1}{4}}L^{\frac{3}{4}}$$
$$= \theta^1 Q$$

Thus, the degree of homogeneity, n, is

$$n = 1,$$

indicating that this firm experiences constant returns to scale. Specifically, there are no advantages nor disadvantages associated with increasing or decreasing its level of output. For example, if this firm should double its use of both inputs, it will just double its production of output.

b. The corresponding LRAC curve will be horizontal, indicating constant returns to scale.

11.8 Private and social costs can diverge if there are externalities present. An externality of production occurs when a firm's production of a good or service generates an uncompensated cost or benefit, depending whether the externality is negative or positive, respectively, for another producer. For the firm generating the externality, the private costs will be less than the social costs if the externality is negative. Conversely, the firm's private costs will exceed the social costs if the externality is positive.

SOLTUIONS

Chapter 12

12.1 a. $Q = 4K^{\frac{1}{4}}L^{\frac{1}{4}} = 4\overline{K}_1^{\frac{1}{4}}L^{\frac{1}{4}}$

$= 4(2)^{\frac{1}{4}}L^{\frac{1}{4}}$

$L^{\frac{1}{4}} = \dfrac{Q}{4(2)^{\frac{1}{4}}}$

$L = \dfrac{Q^4}{256(2)} = \dfrac{Q^4}{512}.$

The isocost equation is

$C = \overline{P}_{K,1}K + \overline{P}_{L,1}L,$

and if K is fixed at $\overline{K}_1 = 2$ units, then

C = SRTC = $\overline{P}_{K,1}(2) + \overline{P}_{L,1}L$

= 2 (2) + 8L

= 4 + 8L.

Thus

$\text{SRTC} = 4 + 8\left(\dfrac{Q^4}{512}\right)$

$= 4 + \dfrac{Q^4}{64}.$

b. $\text{ATC} = \dfrac{SRTC}{Q} = \left(4 + \dfrac{Q^4}{64}\right)/Q$

$= \dfrac{4}{Q} + \dfrac{Q^3}{64}.$

$\text{SRMC} = \dfrac{dSRTC}{dQ} = \dfrac{d\left(4 + \dfrac{Q^4}{64}\right)}{dQ}$

$= \dfrac{4Q^3}{64} = \dfrac{Q^3}{16}.$

12.2 a. $\text{SRTC} = 4 + \dfrac{(4)^4}{64}$

$$= 4 + \frac{256}{64} = 4 + 4 = \$8$$

$$\text{ATC} = \frac{4}{4} + \frac{4^3}{64} = 1 + \frac{64}{64} = 1 + 1 = \$2$$

$$\text{SRMC} = \frac{4^3}{16} = \frac{64}{16} = \$4.$$

b. The short run values for SRTC, ATC, and SRMC are all equal to their long run counterparts, LRTC, LRAC, and LRMC, respectively, at Q = 4 units of output.

These results reflect the fact that K = 2 units is an optimal level of capital, even in the short run, when producing Q = 4 units of output.

c. To verify the conclusion drawn in part b, we can develop the equation for the optimal level of capital as follows. Recall

$$C = \overline{P}_{K,1}K + \overline{P}_{L,1}L$$
$$= 2K + 8L$$

and

$$Q = 4K^{\frac{1}{4}}L^{\frac{1}{4}}$$

$$L^{\frac{1}{4}} = \frac{Q}{4K^{\frac{1}{4}}}$$

$$L = \frac{Q^4}{256K}.$$

Thus

$$C = 2K + 8\left(\frac{Q^4}{256K}\right)$$

$$= 2K + \frac{Q^4}{32K}$$

$$= 2K + \frac{1}{32}Q^4K^{-1}.$$

Therefore

$$\frac{\partial C}{\partial K} = 2 - \frac{1}{32}Q^4K^{-2} = 0$$

$$2 - \frac{Q^4}{32K^2} = 0$$

$$64K^2 - Q^4 = 0$$

$$K^2 = \frac{Q^4}{64}$$

$$K = \frac{Q^2}{8}.$$

Thus, if Q = 4, then

$$K = \frac{4^2}{8} = \frac{16}{8} = 2 \text{ units.}$$

12.3

Figure 12.1

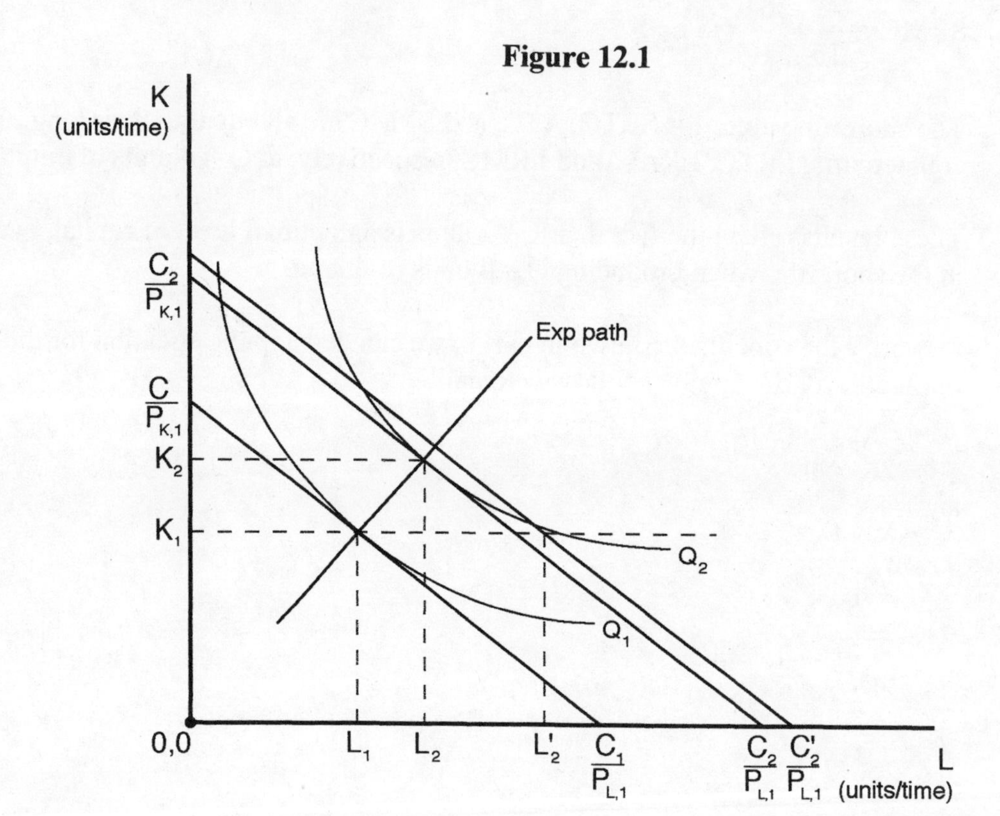

In the long run, where capital can vary, the firm produces Q_1 units of output using input combination (L_1, K_1) and produces Q_2 using combination (L_2, K_2). These L-K combinations lie on the firm's expansion path and the corresponding costs are the constrained cost minimum values of C_1 and C_2, respectively.

When the firm's capital is fixed at $\overline{K}_1$ units, then in the short run, if the firm increases its production of output to Q_2 units, it can only do so by using L'_2 units of labor. This input combination (L'_2, K_1) is not optimal and thus the firm's corresponding short run cost, C'_2, associated with producing Q_2 units, in the short run, is greater than the long run cost, C_2, associated with producing this level of output.

12.4 a. $C = 0.05\,Q^3 - 2Q^2 + 50Q - 2KQ + 2K^2$

If capital is fixed at $\overline{K}_1 = 12.5$ units, then

$$C = SRTC = 0.05Q^3 - 2Q^2 + 50Q - 2(12.5)Q + 2(12.5)^2$$
$$= 0.05Q^3 - 2Q^2 + 50Q - 25Q + 312.50$$
$$= 0.05Q^3 - 2Q^2 + 25Q + 312.50$$

b. FC = $312.50
$VC = 0.05Q^3 - 2Q^2 + 25Q$

12.5 a. $AFC = \frac{FC}{Q} = \frac{\$312.50}{Q}$

$$AVC = \frac{VC}{Q} = \left(0.05Q^3 - 2Q^2 + 25Q\right)/Q$$
$$= 0.05\,Q^2 - 2Q + 25$$

$$ATC = \frac{SRTC}{Q} = AFC + AVC$$
$$= \frac{312.50}{Q} + 0.05Q^2 - 2Q + 25$$

$$SRMC = \frac{dSRTC}{dQ} = 0.15Q^2 - 4Q + 25$$

b. $ATC = \frac{312.50}{25} + 0.05(25)^2 - 2(25) + 25$
$= 12.5 + 31.25 - 50 + 25 = \$18.75$

$SRMC = 0.15(25)^2 - 4(25) + 25$
$= 93.75 - 100 + 25 = \$18.75.$

12.6 a. These results for ATC and SRMC, computed in exercise 12.5, are equal to those computed for LRAC and SRMC, respectively, in exercise 11.6.

b. The short and long run cost values are equal at Q = 25 units of output. The reason for these results is that if K = 12.5 units of capital, Q = 25 units necessitates a level of labor that makes the input combination optimal, or constrained cost minimizing, even in the short run.

c. No, for levels of output different from Q = 25 units, short run costs will exceed those for the long run. The reason is that, if the firm has K = 12.5 units of fixed capital, then producing Q > 25 units necessitates suboptimally high amounts of labor, combined with what will be a suboptimally low amount of capital. If Q < 25, then the firm will be using a suboptimally high level of capital combined with suboptimally low levels of labor. For the long run, both inputs are variable and therefore, the firm will always use optimal, or constrained cost minimizing, input combinations to produce its output.

12.7 Diminishing marginal productivity describes the fact that, as additional units of an input are used in a production process, holding all other inputs constant, the resulting increments in output become successively smaller. Thus, diminishing marginal productivity is a short run concept. Decreasing returns to scale, on the other hand, describes the fact that, as more units of all inputs are used in a production process, the resulting increments to output are proportionally smaller. Thus, the long run average cost curve will rise with increases in the production of output. This result is a long run concept because no inputs are being held constant. Some reasons for this outcome are the problems of coordination and control, as well as disproportionally increasing transportation costs associated with increases in the production of output.

12.8 Recall

$$\text{SRMC} = \frac{\overline{P}_{L,1}}{MP_L}.$$

Thus, if

$$Q = \overline{K}_1^{\frac{3}{4}} L^{\frac{1}{4}}$$

then

$$\text{MP}_L = \frac{\partial Q}{\partial L} = \frac{1}{4}\overline{K}_1^{\frac{3}{4}} L^{-\frac{3}{4}} = \frac{\overline{K}_1^{\frac{3}{4}}}{4L^{\frac{3}{4}}}$$

$$\text{SRMC} = \frac{\overline{P}_{L,1}}{\frac{\overline{K}_1^{\frac{3}{4}}}{4L^{\frac{3}{4}}}} = \frac{4\overline{P}_{L,1}L^{\frac{3}{4}}}{\overline{K}_1^{\frac{3}{4}}}$$

$$= 4(9)\left(\frac{16^{\frac{3}{4}}}{81^{\frac{3}{4}}}\right) = 36\left(\frac{8}{27}\right) = \$10\frac{2}{3}.$$

SOLUTIONS

Chapter 13

13.1 a. The structural characteristics attributed to a perfectly competitive market are:

1. a large number of insignificantly small buyers and sellers
2. homogeneous products
3. no barriers to entry
4. equal access to complete information

b. A perfectly own-price elastic demand curve indicates that, for any change in price, there will be an infinite response in the quantity demanded of the good. This result, which pertains to a perfectly competitive firm, follows from the characteristics listed in part a. Specifically, the major determinant of own-price elasticity is the number and closeness of available substitutes for a good. Thus, for a perfectly competitive firm's good, there exist many perfect substitutes. This fact follows from the conditions of no barriers to entry and thus, the result that there are many sellers of the good. Also, the goods are homogeneous, or identical, and consumers have access to enough information to be aware of this fact. The overall result of these characteristics is that the firm has no discretion over the price of its good.

13.2 a. In equilibrium the market quantity demanded of a good is equal to the market quantity supplied, or

$Q^d = Q^S$.

Thus, the equilibrium price is

$500 - 6P = -40 + 3P$

$9P = 540$

$P = \$60$.

The equiliburm quantities demanded and supplied are

$Q^d = 500 - 6\,(60) = 140$ units

and

$Q^S = -40 + 3\,(60) = 140$ units.

b. If $P = \$80$, then

$Q^d = 500 - 6\,(80) = 20$ units

and

$Q^S = -40 + 3(80) = 200$ units.

Thus, at $P = \$80$, $Q^S > Q^d$, or there is an excess supply of

$Q^S - Q^d = 200 - 20 = 180$ units.

This excess supply will put a downward pressure on the price.

c. If P = $40, then

$Q^d = 500 - 6(40) = 260$ units
and
$Q^S = -40 + 3\ (40) = 80$ units.

Thus, at P = $40, $Q^d > Q^S$, or there is an excess demand of

$Q^d - Q^S = 260 - 80 = 180$ units.

13.3

Figure 13.1

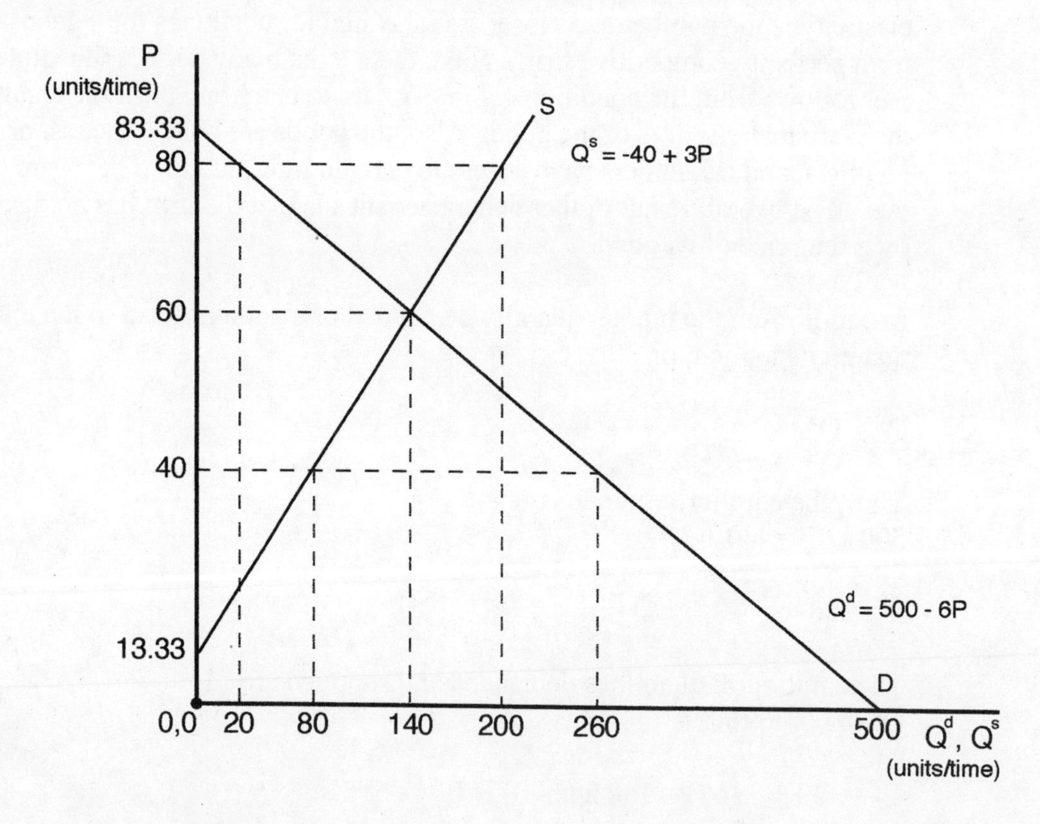

13.4 a.

$$ATC = \frac{SRTC}{Q}$$

$$= (0.05Q^3 - 2Q^2 + 25Q + 312.50)/Q$$

$$= 0.05Q^2 - 2Q + 25 + \frac{312.50}{Q}.$$

$$AVC = 0.05Q^2 - 2Q + 25$$

$$AFC = \frac{312.50}{Q}$$

$$SRMC = \frac{dSRTC}{dQ} = \frac{d\left(0.05Q^3 - 2Q^2 + 25Q + 312.50\right)}{dQ}$$

$$= 0.15Q^2 - 4Q + 25.$$

b. $P = SRMC$

$18.75 = 0.15Q^2 - 4Q + 25$

$0.15Q^2 - 4Q + 6.25 = 0.$

Dividing by 0.15 yields

$$Q^2 - 26\frac{2}{3}Q \,|\, 41\frac{2}{3} = 0$$

or

$$Q^2 - \frac{80}{3}Q + \frac{125}{3} = 0$$

$3Q^2 - 80Q + 125 = 0$

$(3Q - 5)\ (Q - 25) = 0.$

The roots are

$Q = 25$

and

$3Q = 5$

$Q = \frac{5}{3}.$

If $Q = 25$, the short run profit, $SR\pi$, is

$$\begin{aligned} SR\pi &= TR - SRTC \\ &= PQ - (0.05Q^3 - 2Q^2 + 25Q + 312.50) \\ &= 18.75\ (25) - 0.05\ (25)^3 + 2(25)^2 - 25(25) - 312.50 \\ &= 468.75 - 781.25 + 1250 - 625 - 312.50 \\ &= \$0. \end{aligned}$$

If $Q = \frac{5}{3}$, then

$$\begin{aligned} SR\pi &= 18.75\ (1.67) - 0.05\ (1.67)^3 + 2\ (1.67)^2 - 25\ (1.67) - 312.50 \\ &= 31.31 - .23 + 5.58 - 41.75 - 312.50 \\ &= -\$317.59. \end{aligned}$$

Thus, the profit maximizing level of output is Q = 25 units.

c. $\text{SR AVE}\pi = \frac{\text{SR}\pi}{Q} = \frac{0}{25} = 0.$

13.5 a. If P = 5, then

$P = SRMC$
$5 = 0.15\,Q^2 - 4Q + 25$
$0.15Q^2 - 4Q + 20 = 0$
$Q^2 - 26\frac{2}{3}Q + 133\frac{1}{3} = 0$
$Q^2 - \frac{80Q}{3} + \frac{400}{3} = 0$
$3Q^2 - 80Q + 400 = 0$
$(3Q - 20)(Q - 20) = 0,$
yielding the roots Q = 20 and

$3Q = 20,$
or
$Q = \frac{20}{3}.$
If Q = 20, then

$\text{SR}\pi = 5(20) - [0.05(20)^3 - 2(20)^2 + 25(20) + 312.50]$

$= 100 - 400 + 800 - 500 - 312.50 = \$-312.50.$

If $Q = \frac{20}{3} = 6.67$, then

$\text{SR}\pi = 5(6.67) - 0.05(6.67)^3 + 2(6.67)^2 - 25(6.67) - 312.50.$
$33.35 - 296.74 + 88.98 - 166.75 - 312.50 = \$-653.66.$

Thus, the profit maximizing (loss minimizing) level of output is

Q = 20 units.

b. $\text{SR AVE}\pi = \frac{\text{SR}\pi}{Q} = \frac{-312.50}{20} = \$-15.62.$

c. Since the firm's profit, $-312.50, is just equal to its fixed cost, then P = $5 represents the price at which the firm will shut down its production of output.

d. The firm's short run supply curve is equal to its short run marginal cost curve, or

$$SRS = SRMC = 0.15Q^2 - 4Q + 25,$$

provided P ≥ \$5. For prices less than \$5, the short run supply curve is

$$Q^S = 0.$$

13.6

Figure 13.2

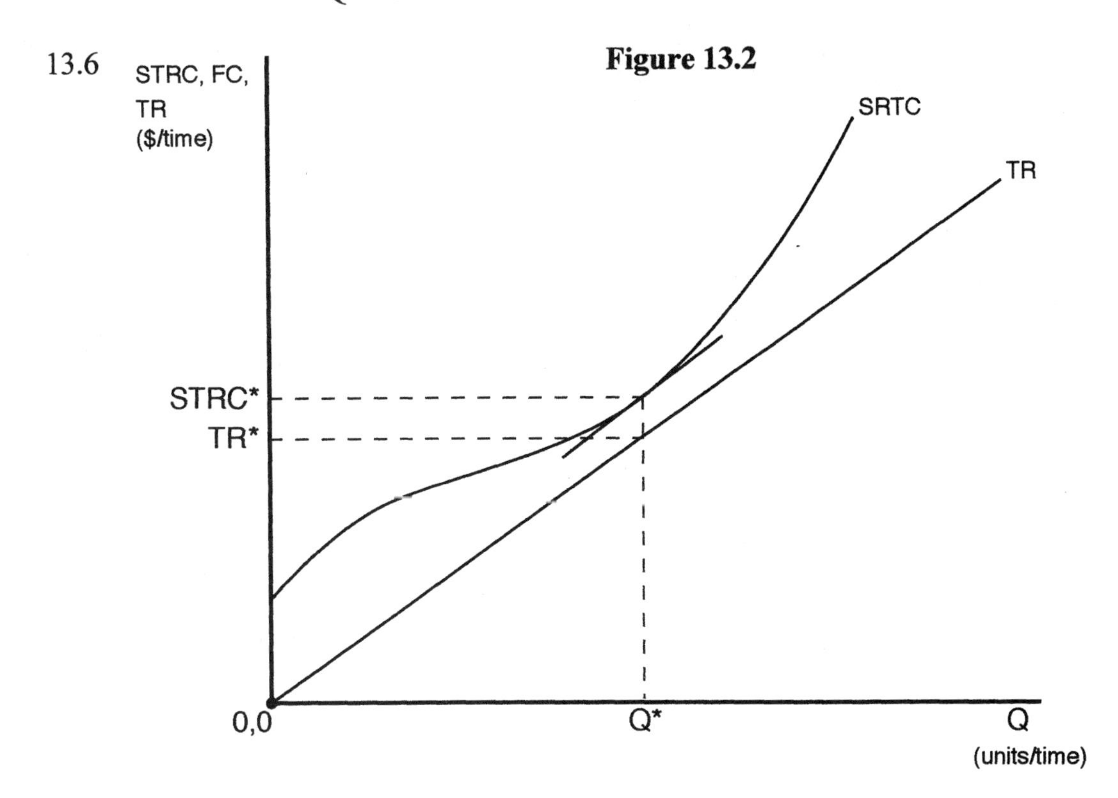

The firm maximizes its short run profit at Q^* units, where P = MR = SRMC. In this case the profit is negative, or $TR^* - SRTC^* < 0$, but it represents the best result the firm can achieve.

13.7 $SRTC = 0.025Q^3 - Q^2 + 12.5Q + 156.25$

$SRMC = 0.075\,Q^2 - 2Q + 12.5$

$P = SRMC$

$9.375 = 0.075Q^2 - 2Q + 12.5$

$0.075Q^2 - 2Q + 3.125 = 0$

$Q^2 - 26\frac{2}{3}Q + 41\frac{2}{3} = 0$

$Q^2 - \frac{80}{3} + \frac{125}{3} = 0$

$3Q^2 - 80 \;+ 125 = 0$

$(3Q - 5)\,(Q - 25) = 0,$

yielding roots of Q = 25 and

$3Q = 5$

$Q = \frac{5}{3}.$

If Q = 25, then

$SR\pi = PQ - (0.025Q^3 - Q^2 + 12.5Q + 156.25)$

$= 9.375\ (25) - 0.025\ (25)^3 + (25)^2 - 12.5\ (25) - 156.25$

$= 234.375 - 390.625 + 625 - 312.50 - 156.25$

$= \$0.$

If $Q = \frac{5}{3} = 1.67$ units, then

$SR\pi = 9.375\ (1.67) - 0.025\ (1.67)^3 + (1.67)^2 - 12.5\ (1.67) - 156.25$

$= 15.66 - .12 + 2.79 - 20.88 - 156.25$

$= \$-158.80.$

The profit maximizing level of output is Q = 25 units.

b. $SR\ AVE\pi = \frac{SR\pi}{Q} = \frac{0}{25} = \$0.$

13.8 If P = \$50, then

$Q^S = -50 + 3P = -50 + 3\ (50) = 100$ units.

Short run elasticity of supply, $E_{Q^S,P}$ is represented as

$$E_{Q^S,P} = \frac{\%\Delta Q^S}{\%\Delta P} = \frac{\partial Q^S}{\partial P}\frac{P}{Q^S}.$$

$$\frac{\partial Q^S}{\partial P} = \frac{\partial(-50 + 3P)}{\partial P} = \frac{\partial(-50)}{\partial P} + \frac{\partial(3P)}{\partial P} = 3.$$

Thus

$$E_{Q^S,P} = (3)\left(\frac{50}{100}\right) = \frac{150}{100} = \frac{3}{2} = 1.5.$$

This result indicates that, at this point on the short run market supply curve, a 1 percent change in the market price results in a 1.5 percent response in the market quantity supplied of the good, in the same direction.

SOLUTIONS

Chapter 14

14.1 a. If $LRTC = Q^3 - 4Q^2 + 80Q$ then

$$LRAC = \frac{LRTC}{Q} = \frac{Q^3 - 4Q^2 + 80Q}{Q} = Q^2 - 4Q + 80$$

b. At long-run equilibrium, the perfectly competitive firm produces that level of output associated with its minimum long-run average cost. To determine this level of output, take the derivative of long-run average cost, LRAC, with respect to the firm's output, Q, set this derivative equal to zero, and solve for the associated value of Q. Recall from part a.,

$LRAC = Q^2 - 4Q + 80.$

$$\frac{dLRAC}{dQ} = 2Q - 4 = 0$$

$2Q = 4$

$Q = 2$ units

Therefore, when the perfectly competitive firm produces 2 units of output its long-run average cost is minimized, which is consistent with a long-run competitive equilibrium.

c. To determine the minimum value of the firm's long-run average cost, substitute Q = 2 units into the firm's long-run average cost curve as follows.

$LRAC = Q^2 - 4Q + 80$

Minimum $LRAC = 2^2 - 4(2) + 80 = 4 - 8 + 80 = \$76$

14.2 a. When the firm is at long-run equilibrium, the price in the market must equal the minimum value of long-run average cost, which was determined in part c. of exercise 14.1 to be $76.

b. When a perfectly competitive firm is in long-run equilibrium, it earns zero profit. To verify that the perfectly competitive firm earns zero profit we can compute the level of profit earned when the firm produces the level of output associated with its long-run equilibrium. In exercise 14.1, we determined that the firm's long-run average cost is minimized when it produces two units of output. In part a. of this exercise we found that market price is $76 when the firm is at a long-run competitive equilibrium. Therefore, when P = $76, Q = 2 and the firm's long-run total cost function is

$LRTC = Q^3 - 4Q^2 + 80Q$

then long-run profit, LRπ, is

$$
\begin{aligned}
LR\pi &= TR - LRTC \\
&= PQ - [Q^3 - 4Q^2 + 80Q] \\
&= (76)(2) - [2^3 - 4(2)^2 + 80(2)] \\
&= 152 - 152 \\
&= \$0
\end{aligned}
$$

c.

Figure 14.1

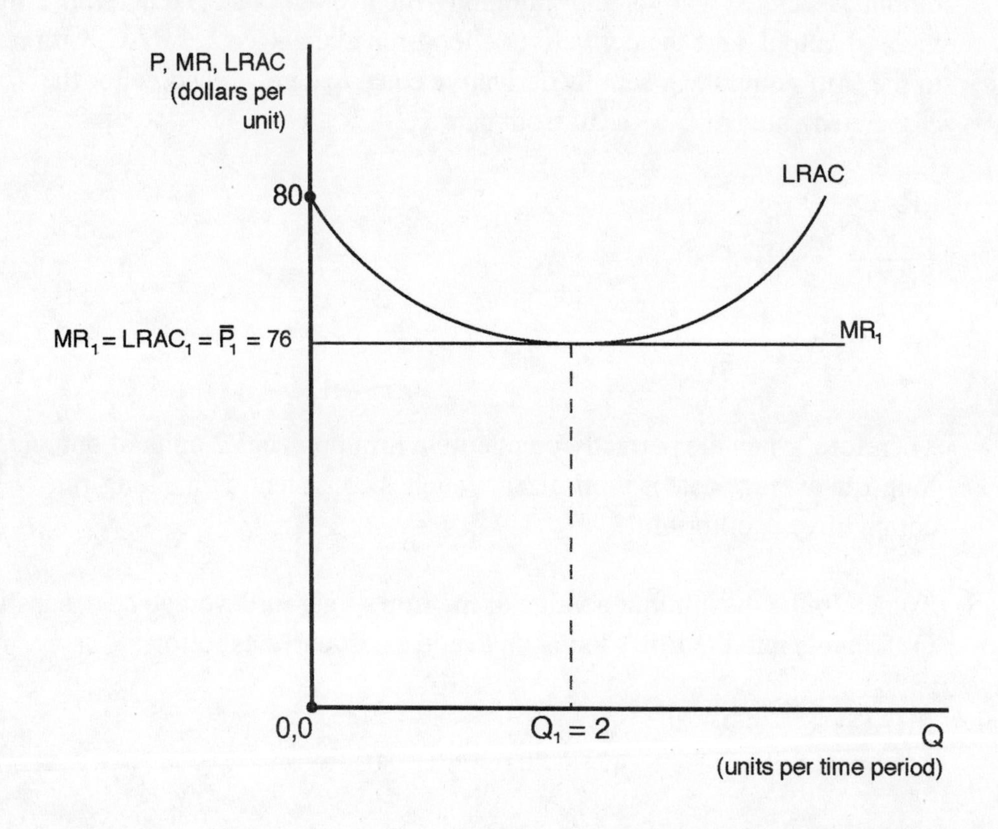

14.3 a. If $C = \frac{1}{3}Q^3 - 4Q^2 + 20Q - 2KQ + 0.50K^2$, then the mathematical equation for determining the optimal level of capital use for alternative levels of output is determined as follows.

$$\frac{\partial C}{\partial K} = -2Q + K = 0$$

$K = 2Q$.

b. The perfectly competitive firm's long-run total cost curve is determined by substituting the relationship between Q and K found in part a., $K = 2Q$, into the equation representing the basis of the firm's cost curves, C = $\frac{1}{3}Q^3 - 4Q^2 + 20Q - 2KQ + 0.50K^2$, as follows.

$$\text{LRTC} = \frac{1}{3}Q^3 - 4Q^2 + 20Q - 2(2Q)Q + 0.50(2Q)^2$$
$$= \frac{1}{3}Q^3 - 4Q^2 + 20Q - 4Q^2 + 2Q^2$$
$$= \frac{1}{3}Q^3 - 6Q^2 + 20Q$$

14.4 a. To determine the long-run marginal cost curve, take the derivative of the long-run total cost curve, found in part b. of exercise 14.3, with respect to Q as follows.

$$\text{LRTC} = \frac{1}{3}Q^3 - 6Q^2 + 20Q$$

$$\text{LRMC} = \frac{dLRC}{dQ} = \frac{d\left(\frac{1}{3}Q^3 - 6Q^2 + 20Q\right)}{dQ} = Q^2 - 12Q + 20$$

b. To determine the profit maximizing level of output, set the market price, P = \$9, equal to the long-run marginal cost curve. If P = \$9 and LRMC = Q^2 - 12Q + 20 then

Q^2 - 12Q + 20 = 9
Q^2 - 12Q + 11 = 0
(Q - 11) (Q - 1) = 0

The two roots to this problem are Q = 11 and Q = 1. To determine which level of output maximizes the firm's long-run profit substitute each value of Q into the firm's long-run profit function and compare the associated values of long-run profit.

If Q = 11 and P = \$9 then long-run profit is computed as follows.

$$\text{LR}\pi = \text{PQ - LRTC}$$
$$= \text{PQ} - [\frac{1}{3}Q^3 - 6Q^2 + 20Q]$$
$$= (\$9)(11) - [\frac{1}{3}(11)^3 - 6(11)^2 + 20(11)]$$
$$= 99 - [443.67 - 726 + 220]$$
$$= 99 - [-62.33]$$

$= \$161.33$

If Q = 1 and P = \$9 then long-run total profit is computed as follows.

$$LR\pi = (9)(1) - [\frac{1}{3}(1)^3 - 6(1)^2 + 20(1)]$$
$$= 9 - [0.33 - 6 + 20]$$
$$= 9 - 14.33$$
$$= \$-5.33$$

Therefore, the optimal level of production is Q = 11 units and the maximum amount of long-run profit earned by the firm is \$161.33.

c. Since the firm is earning a positive profit when the market price is \$9 and the firm produces 11 units of output, this level of output does not constitute a stable long-run competitive equilibrium for the firm. The positive profit earned by the firm will encourage other firms to enter the market in the long run. As a result of the entry of new firms into the market, the market price of the good will decrease and, subsequently, the firm under analysis will reduce its level of output.

14.5 a. If $C = \frac{1}{3}Q^3 - 2Q^2 + 40Q - 2KQ + 0.25K^2$ then the mathematical equation for determining the optimal level of capital use for alternative levels of output is determined as follows.

$$\frac{\partial C}{\partial K} = -2Q + 0.50K = 0$$
$$0.50K = 2Q$$
$$K = 4Q.$$

b. The perfectly competitive firm's long-run total cost curve is determined by substituting the relationship between Q and K found in part a, K = 4Q, into the equation representing the basis of the firm's cost curves, $C = \frac{1}{3}Q^3 - 2Q^2 + 40Q - 2KQ + 0.25K^2$, as demonstrated below.

$$LRTC = \frac{1}{3}Q^3 - 2Q^2 + 40Q - 2(4Q)Q + 0.25(4Q)^2$$
$$= \frac{1}{3}Q^3 - 2Q^2 + 40Q - 8Q^2 + 4Q^2$$
$$= \frac{1}{3}Q^3 - 6Q^2 + 40Q$$

c. The firm's long-run marginal cost curve is determined by taking the derivative of the long-run total cost curve, determined in part b., with respect to the firm's level of output, Q.

Given LRTC = $\frac{1}{3}Q^3 - 6Q^2 + 40Q$,

then LRMC = $\frac{dLRTC}{dQ} = \frac{d\left[\frac{1}{3}Q^3 - 6Q^2 + 40Q\right]}{dQ} = Q^2 - 12Q + 40$

14.6 a. To derive the long-run average cost curve divide the long-run total cost curve, determined in part b. of exercise 14.5, by Q, the firm's level of output, as demonstrated below.

Given LRTC = $\frac{1}{3}Q^3 - 6Q^2 + 40Q$

then LRAC = $\frac{LRTC}{Q} = \frac{\frac{1}{3}Q^3 - 6Q^2 + 40Q}{Q} = \frac{1}{3}Q^2 - 6Q + 40$

b. To determine the level of output at which the firm's long-run average cost is minimized take the derivative of long-run average cost, LRAC, with respect to the firm's output, Q, set this derivative equal to zero, and solve for the associated value of Q as we have demonstrated below. Recall, from part a.we know

LRAC = $\frac{1}{3}Q^2 - 6Q + 40Q$

therefore

$$\frac{dLRAC}{dQ} = \frac{2}{3}Q - 6 = 0$$
$$\frac{2}{3}Q = 6$$
Q = 9 units.

c. A perfectly competitive firm is producing a level of output associated with a long-run competitive equilibrium if at that level of output its long-run average cost is minimized. At this level of output the firm earns zero profit in the long-run, therefore, there is no incentive for new firms to enter the industry in the long-run. In part b. we determined that the firm's long-run average cost is minimized when it produces 9 units of output. Substitute Q = 9 into the firm's long-run average cost curve, derived in part a., to determine the minimum value of long-run average cost. When Q = 9 units,

$$
\begin{aligned}
\text{LRAC} &= \frac{1}{3}Q^2 - 6Q + 40 \\
&= \frac{1}{3}(9)^2 - 6(9) + 40 \\
&= 27 - 54 + 40 \\
&= \$13
\end{aligned}
$$

Thus, the market price be $13, which is equal to the minimum LRAC, for this firm to produce a level of output, specifically Q = 9 units, that is consistent with a long-run competitive equilibrium outcome.

d. When the firm is at a long-run competitive equilibrium it produces 9 units of output, as we determined in part b. To determine the optimal, cost minimizing, amount of capital the firm uses to produce this level of output, substitute Q = 9 into the mathematical relationship between the firm's level of output and its optimal level of capital derived in part a. of exercise 14.5, specifically K = 4Q. Therefore, if Q = 9 then

$$
\begin{aligned}
K &= 4Q \\
&= 4\,(9) \\
&= 36 \text{ units.}
\end{aligned}
$$

The firm optimally employs 36 units of capital when it produces 9 units of output and has achieved a long-run competitive equilibrium when the market price is $13.

Figure 14.2

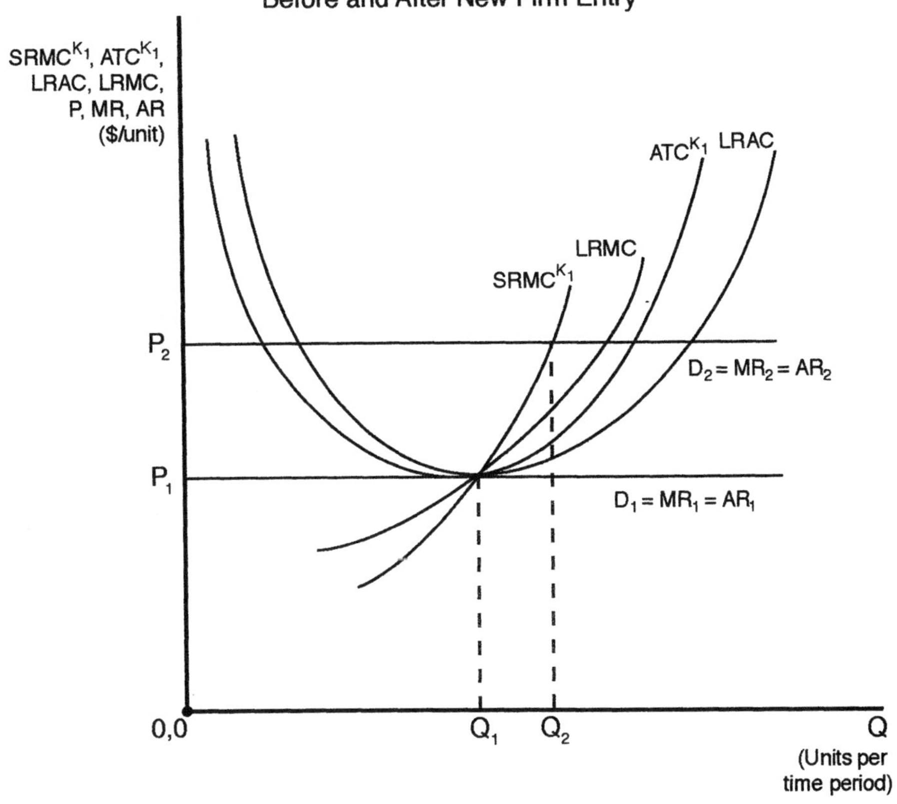
Panel (A)
Perfectly Competitve Firm
Before and After New Firm Entry
SRMC^K1, ATC^K1, LRAC, LRMC, P, MR, AR ($/unit)
ATC^K1
LRAC
LRMC
SRMC^K1
P2
P1
D2 = MR2 = AR2
D1 = MR1 = AR1
0,0
Q1
Q2
Q
(Units per time period)

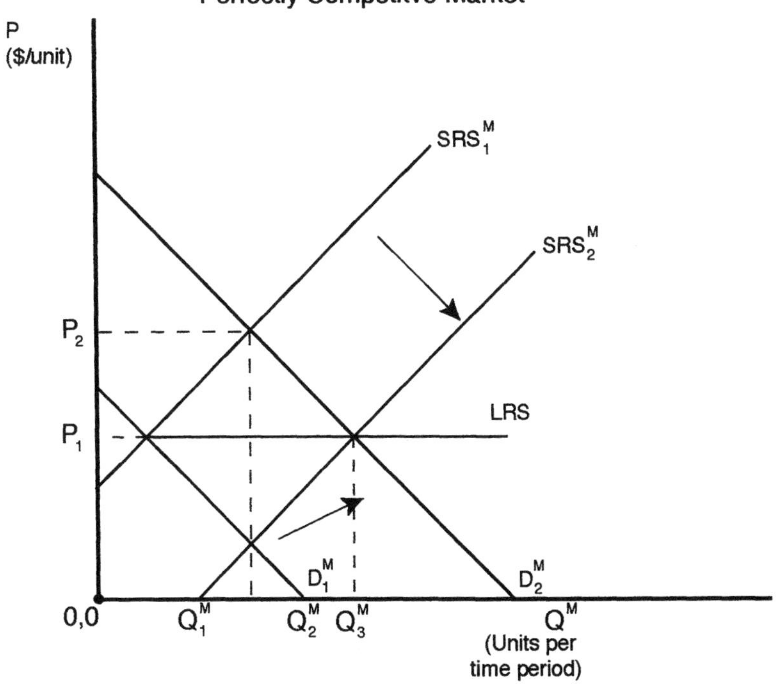
Panel (B)
Perfectly Competitve Market
P ($/unit)
SRS1M
SRS2M
P2
P1
LRS
D1M
D2M
0,0
Q1M
Q2M
Q3M
QM
(Units per time period)

Since the inputs used in the housesitting services industry are described as unspecialized and, therefore, are plentiful in supply, this industry is characterized as a constant cost industry. As a result, any change in the number of firms in this industry will not change the cost structures of the firms operating in this industry. In panel (B) in the figure above, assume that the initial short-run market supply curve is SRS_1^M, and the initial market demand curve is D_1^M, resulting in P_1 as the initial equilibrium price and Q_1^M as the initial equilibrium level of output in the market for housesitting services. A typical perfectly competitive firm produces Q_1 units of output, determined where $SRMC_1^{\overline{K}_1} = MR_1 \equiv P_1$ and earns zero profit, as shown in panel (A). Assume that market demand for housesitting services increases from D_1^M to D_2^M. A new short-run market equilbirum is established at (Q_2^M, P_2) in panel (B). The perfectly competitive firm depicted in panel (A) reacts to the higher market price of P_2 by increasing its output from Q_1 to Q_2, where its $SRMC^{\overline{K}_1} = MR_2 \equiv P_2$, and now earns positive profit. The existence of positive profit is the incentive for new firms to enter the market and, therefore, cause the market supply curve to shift to the right from SRS_1^M to SRS_2^M. This increase in the market supply causes the price of housesitting services to decrease, however, since this is a constant cost industry, the firms' costs of production are not affected by the entry of new firms into the industry. Entry of new firms into the industry ceases when the market price drops to P_1. As the market price drops to P_1 the typical perfectly competitive firm, as shown in panel (A), reduces its level of output to Q_1 and once again earns zero profit. The long-run industry supply curve, LRS, in panel (B) is horizontal and passes through the long-run competitive equilibiria of (Q_1^M, P_1) and (Q_3^M, P_1).

SOLUTIONS

Chapter 15

15.1 This result follows from two characteristics. First, a monopolist's own-price demand curve is the same as the market own-price demand curve for a good. For all good purposes, these own-price demand cures always possess negative slopes, indicating that a monopolist must lower the price of its product in order to sell an additional unit. Further, we generally assume that a monopolist does not price discriminate, meaning that once it determines a profit maximizing price for its good, it charges this same price for all of the units it sells. Thus, if the monopolist lowers the price, in order to sell an additional unit of output, it will also lower the price for all of the units that it was selling at the previously higher price. As a result, the firm's marginal revenue, or extra revenue from selling an additional unit of output, will equal the price of the extra unit multiplied by the one extra unit sold, minus the price reduction multiplied by the units that were sold at the previously higher price.

15.2 The Chicago school believes the main sources of monopoly are the entry barriers created by government intervention. It is these barriers that prevent new firms from entering a market and thus confer a monopoly privilege to an incumbent firm. Some examples of these barriers are such government activities as licensing laws, zoning laws, government franchises, patent laws, and tariffs.

15.3 The structure - conduct - performance school, unlike Chicago school, believes that monopoly is the result of factors inherent to the structure of an industry and the conduct of the firms operating within an industry. Some factors inherent to an industry, that constitute barriers to entry, are large economies of scale and high capital requirements. Some types of firm conduct that might create barriers to entry are such activities as limit pricing, building excess capacity, advertising, or gaining the exclusive control over key inputs necessary to produce a good.

15.4 a. $Q = 200 - 0.2P$

Therefore

$0.2P = 200 - Q$

$P = 1000 - 5Q.$

Total revenue, TR, is

$$TR = PQ = (1000 - 5Q)Q = 1000Q - 5Q^2$$

and marginal revenue, MR, is

$$MR = \frac{dTR}{dQ} = 1000 - 10Q.$$

$$SRTC = 1000 + 5Q^2$$

Therefore, the short run marginal cost, SRMC, curve is

$$\text{SRMC} = \frac{dSRTC}{dQ} = \frac{d(1000 + 5Q^2)}{dQ} = 10Q.$$

The firm determines its profit maximizing level of output where MR = SRMC.

Thus

$1000 - 10Q = 10Q$

$20Q = 1000$

$Q^* = \frac{1000}{20} = 50$ units

and

$P^* = 1000 - 5\,(50) = \$750.$

b. The short run profit, SRπ, is

$SR\pi^* = TR - SRTC$

$= PQ - (1000 + 5Q^2)$

$= 750\,(50) - 1000 - 5\,(50)^2$

$= 37{,}500 - 1000 - 12{,}500 = \$24{,}000.$

15.5 a. $Q = 44 - \frac{1}{2}P$

$\frac{1}{2}P = 44 - Q$

$P = 88 - 2Q.$

b. $TR = PQ = (88 - 2Q)Q$

$= 88Q - 2Q^2$

$$\text{MR} = \frac{dTR}{dQ} = \frac{d(88Q - 2Q^2)}{dQ}$$

$= 88 - 4Q.$

$\text{LRTC} = \frac{2}{3}Q^3 - 12Q^2 + 120Q$

$$\text{LRMC} = \frac{dLRTC}{dQ} = \frac{d\left(\frac{2}{3}Q^3 - 12Q^2 + 120Q\right)}{dQ}$$

$= 2Q^2 - 24Q + 120.$

15.6 MR = LRMC

$88 - 4Q = 2Q^2 - 24Q + 120$

$2Q^2 - 20Q + 32 = 0$

$2 (Q^2 - 10Q + 16) = 0$
$2 (Q - 8) (Q - 2) = 0,$
yielding roots of Q = 8 and Q = 2.

If Q = 8, then
P = 88 - 2(8) = $72.

If Q = 2, then
P = 88 - 2 (2) = $84.

$LR\pi = TR - LRTC$

$$= PQ - \left(\frac{2}{3}Q^3 - 12Q^2 + 120Q\right)$$

$$= PQ - \frac{2}{3}Q^3 + 12Q^2 - 120Q.$$

If Q = 8 and P = $72, then

$$LR\pi = 72 (8) - \frac{2}{3} (8)^3 + 12 (8)^2 - 120 (8)$$

$= 576 - 341.33 + 768 - 960$
= $42.67.

If Q = 2 and P = $84, then

$$LR\pi = 84(2) - \frac{2}{3} (2)^3 + 12 (2)^2 - 120 (2)$$

$= 168 - 5.33 + 48 - 240$
= $-29.33.

Thus, the profit maximizing levels of output and price are Q = 8 units and P = $72. The corresponding long run profit is $42.67.

15.7 a.

$$C = \frac{2}{3}Q^3 - 10Q^2 + 120Q - 2KQ + 0.50K^2$$

$$\frac{\partial C}{\partial K} = -2Q + 1.0K = 0$$

K = 2Q.

Therefore, if Q = 8, then
K = 2 (16) = 16 units.

b.

$$SRTC = \frac{2}{3} Q^3 - 10Q^2 + 120Q - 2 (16) Q + 0.50 (16)^2$$

$= \frac{2}{3}Q^3 - 10Q^2 + 120Q - 32Q + 128$

$= \frac{2}{3}Q^3 - 10Q^2 + 88Q + 128.$

c. $\text{ATC} = \frac{SRTC}{Q} = \left(\frac{2}{3}Q^3 - 10Q^2 + 88Q + 128\right)/Q$

$= \frac{2}{3}Q^2 - 10Q + 88 + \frac{128}{Q}.$

$$\text{SRMC} = \frac{dSRTC}{dQ} = \frac{d\left(\frac{2}{3}Q^3 - 10Q^2 + 88Q + 128\right)}{dQ}$$

$=2Q^2 - 20Q + 88.$

d. $Q = 44 - \frac{1}{2}P$

Therefore

$\frac{1}{2}P = 44 - Q$

$P = 88 - 2Q$

$TR = PQ = (88 - 2Q)Q = 88Q - 2Q^2$

$$MR = \frac{dTR}{dQ} = \frac{d(88Q - 2Q^2)}{dQ} = 88 - 4Q.$$

The firm determines its profit maximizing level of output, in the short run, by the rule

MR = SRMC.

Thus

$88 - 4Q = 2Q^2 - 20Q + 88$

$2Q^2 - 16Q = 0$

$2Q(Q - 8) = 0$

$Q^* = 8$

Thus

$P^* = 88 - 2(8) = \$72$

and

$SR\pi = TR - SRTC$

$= PQ - \left(\frac{2}{3}Q^3 - 10Q^2 + 88Q + 128\right)$

$$= 72(8) - \frac{2}{3}(8)^3 + 10\,(8)^2 - 88\,(8) - 128$$
$$= 576 - 341.33 + 640 - 704 - 128$$
$$= \$42.67.$$

This is the same value as the long run profit computed in exercise 15.6.

15.8 **Figure 15.1**

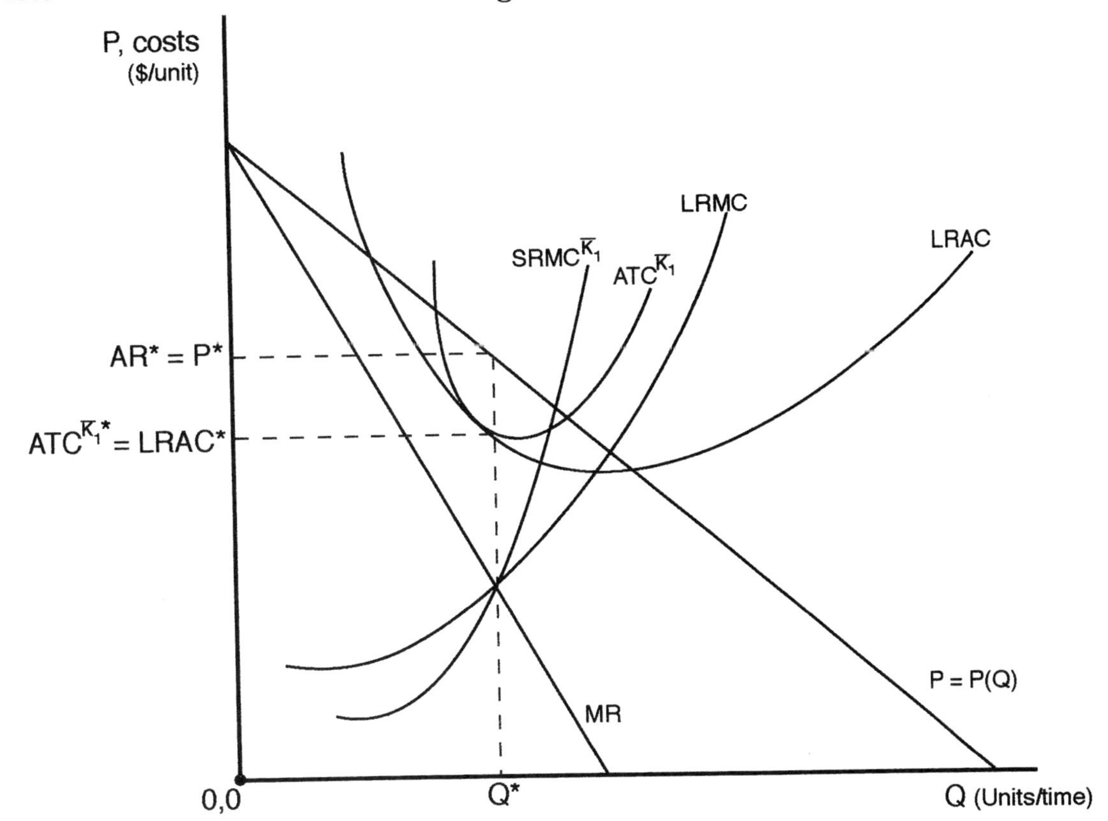

The profit maximizing levels of output and price are Q* and P*, respectively. The corresponding long and short run average profit levels are

$$\text{LRave}\pi^* = P^* - \text{LRAC}^* = \text{SRave}\pi^* - P^* - \text{ATC}^{\overline{K_1}^*}.$$

SOLUTIONS

Chapter 16

16.1 A deadweight welfare loss is the amount of consumer and producer surplus that is lost due to a monopolist's restriction of the output it sells. This concept is defined as a deadweight loss in that no one receives it. Specifically, it does not refer to a transfer of surplus from consumers to a firm, rather it is a complete loss of some consumer and producer surplus.

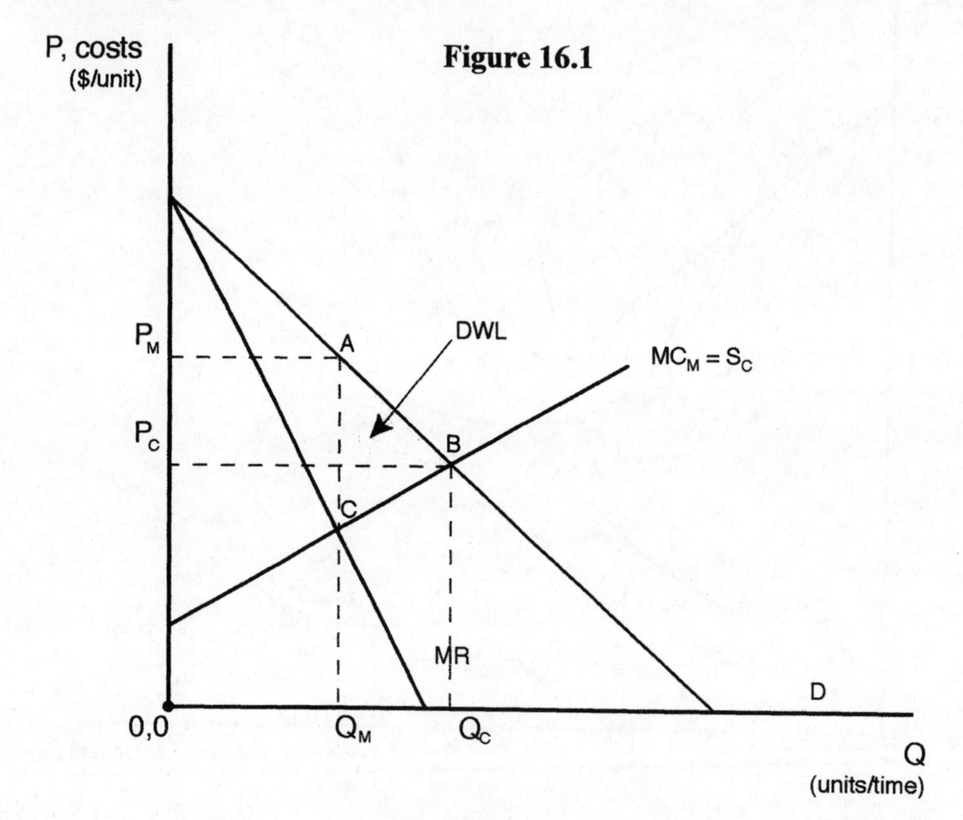

The deadweight welfare loss is the area of the triangle, ABC.

16.2 a. $Q = 200 - \frac{1}{4}P,$

and thus

$$\frac{1}{4}P = 200 - Q$$
$$P = 800 - 4Q.$$
$$LRTC = 80Q.$$

Therefore

$$\text{LRMC} = \frac{dLRTC}{dQ} = 80$$

and

$$\text{LRAC} = \frac{LRTC}{Q} = \frac{80Q}{Q} = 80.$$

For perfect competition, the level of output is determined where price, P, is equal to marginal cost, or

$P = MC$.

Thus, the perfectly competitive price, P_C, is

$P_C = MC = \$80$,

and the quantity sold is

$P = 800 - 4Q$

$80 = 800 - 4Q$

$4Q = 720$

$Q_C = 180$.

b. $LR\pi_C = TR - LRTC$

$= P_C Q_C - 80 Q_C$

$= 80\ (180) - 80\ (180) = \$0$.

c. Consumer surplus, CS_C, for the perfectly competitive market is

$$CS_C = \frac{1}{2}\ (180 - 0)\ (800 - 80)$$

$$= \frac{1}{2}\ (180)\ (720)$$

$= \$64{,}800$.

16.3 a. $TR = PQ$

$= (800 - 4Q)\ Q$

$= 800Q - 4Q^2$.

Therefore

$$MR = \frac{dTR}{dQ} = \frac{d(800Q - 4Q^2)}{dQ} = 800 - 8Q.$$

$MR = LRMC$

$800 - 8Q = 80$

$8Q = 720$

$Q_M = 90$.

$P_M = 800 - 4\ Q_M$

$= 800 - 4\ (90)$

$= 800 - 360 = \$440$.

b. $LR\pi_M = TR - LRTC$
$= P_M Q_M - 80\ Q_M$
$= 440\ (90) - 80\ (90)$
$= 39{,}600 - 7200 = \$32{,}400.$

c. $CS_M = \frac{1}{2}\ (90 - 0)\ (800 - 440)$
$= \frac{1}{2}\ (90)\ (360) = \$16{,}200.$

d. $DWL = \frac{1}{2}\ (Q_C - Q_M)\ (P_M - P_C)$
$= \frac{1}{2}\ (180 - 90)\ (440 - 80)$
$= \frac{1}{2}\ (90)\ (360) = \$16{,}200.$

16.4 a. The first degree price discriminating monopolist will determine its profit maximizing level of output, Q_M^{Dis} where
$P = MC.$
Thus,
$800 - 4Q = 80$
$4Q = 720$
$Q_M^{Dis} = \frac{720}{4} = 180.$
This level of output is equal to the amount sold, if the market is perfectly competitive.

b. The firm does not charge the same price for all of the units it sells. Thus, if it sells 180 units of the good, as in the case of first degree price discrimination, it will charge 180 different prices, in descending order. For the first unit sold, it will charge
$P_1 = 800 - 4(1) = \$796.$
For the second unit
$P_2 = 800 - 4(2) = \$792,$
and so forth, until
$P_{180} = 800 - 4(180) = \$80.$

c. In this case, the monopolist's long run profit, $LR\pi$, is
$LR\pi = TR - LRTC,$
where total revenue, TR is
$TR = P_C Q_C + CS_C,$
since the firm extracts all of the consumer surplus attributed to the perfectly competitive outcome. Thus

$LR\pi = 80\ (180) + 64{,}800 - 80\ (180)$
$= 14{,}400 + 64{,}800 - 14{,}400$
$= \$64{,}800.$

Alternatively, this profit can be computed as the summation of the monopolist's profit and the consumer surplus for monopoly, without price discrimination, plus the deadweight welfare loss, or

$LR\pi = \$32{,}400 + 16{,}200 + \$16{,}200$
$= \$64{,}800.$

16.5 a. For submarket 1

$$Q_1 = 50 - \frac{1}{2} P_1$$

$$\frac{1}{2} P_1 = 50 - Q_1$$

$$P_1 = 100 - 2Q_1$$

and for submarket 2

$$Q_2 = 36 - \frac{1}{5} P_2$$

$$\frac{1}{5} P_2 = 36 - Q_2$$

$$P_2 = 180 - 5Q_2.$$

b. For submarket 1

$TR_1 = P_1 Q_1 = (100 - 2Q_1)\ Q_1$
$= 100\ Q_1 - 2\ Q_1^2.$

Therefore

$$MR_1 = \frac{dTR_1}{dQ_1} = \frac{d(100Q_1 - 2Q_1^2)}{dQ_1}$$

$$= 100 - 4Q_1.$$

$MR_1 = MC$
$100 = 4Q_1 = 40$
$4Q_1 = 60$

$$Q_1 = \frac{60}{4} = 15,$$

and therefore

$P_1 = 100 - 2\ (15) = \$70.$

For submarket 2

$TR_2 = P_2 Q_2 = (180 - 5Q_2) Q_2$
$= 180 Q_2 - 5 Q_2^2$.
Therefore

$$MR_2 = \frac{dTR_2}{dQ_2} = \frac{d(180Q_2 - 5Q_2^2)}{dQ_2}$$
$= 180 - 10Q_2$.

$MR_2 = MC$
$180 = 10Q_2 = 40$
$10Q_2 = 140$
$Q_2 = 14$,

and therefore

$P_2 = 180 - 5 (14) = \$110$.

c. The firm's profit, π, is
$\pi = TR_1 + TR_2 - TC$
$= P_1Q_1 + P_2Q_2 - MC (Q_1 + Q_2)$
$= 70 (15) + 110 (14) - 40 (15 + 14)$
$= 1050 + 1540 - 1160 = \$1430$.

16.6 We can select any price that is common to both own-price demand curves. Thus, say if $P_1 = P_2 = \$10$, the corresponding quantities demanded can be computed as

$$Q_1 = 50 - \frac{1}{2} P_1 = 50 - \frac{1}{2} (10) = 45$$

and

$$Q_2 = 36 - \frac{1}{5} (P_2) = 36 - \frac{1}{5} (10) = 34.$$

$$\frac{\partial Q_1}{\partial P_1} = \frac{\partial\left(50 - \frac{1}{2} P_1\right)}{\partial P_1} = -\frac{1}{2}$$

and

$$\frac{\partial Q_2}{\partial P_2} = \frac{\partial\left(36 - \frac{1}{5} P_2\right)}{\partial P_2} = -\frac{1}{5}.$$

Thus

$$E_{Q_1,P_1} = \left|\frac{\partial Q_1}{\partial P_1}\frac{P_1}{Q_1}\right| = \left|\left(-\frac{1}{2}\right)\left(\frac{10}{45}\right)\right| = \left|\frac{-10}{90}\right| = .11$$

and

$$E_{Q_2,P_2} = \left|\frac{\partial Q_2}{\partial P_2}\frac{P_2}{Q_2}\right| = \left|\left(-\frac{1}{5}\right)\left(\frac{10}{34}\right)\right| = \left|\frac{-10}{170}\right| = .06.$$

Submarket 2 possesses the less elastic, or more inelastic, own-price demand curve. Thus, we would expect the firm to charge the higher price in submarket 2, which is the case.

16.7 a. Allocative efficiency is the allocation of resources to their most highly valued uses.

b. A perfectly competitive market outcome is considered to be allocatively efficient because the firms determine their profit maximizing levels of output where price equals marginal cost, or P = MC. This outcome reflects the fact that, for the last unit of output produced, society values the unit exactly equal to the cost of producing it. This result is considered to be allocatively efficient in the sense that the desired amount of the good is produced and sold. On the other hand, the monopolist determines its profit maximizing level of output where P > MR = MC, and thus P > MC. This outcome reflects the fact that society values the last unit produced more than the cost of producing it. This result is not allocatively efficient because the good is being under produced.

16.8 a. $TR = PQ = (1000 - 10Q)\,Q = 1000Q - 10Q^2$

$$MR = \frac{dTR}{dQ} = \frac{d(1000Q - 10Q^2)}{dQ}$$

$= 1000 - 20Q.$

Thus

$MR = MC$

$1000 - 20Q = 400$

$20Q = 600$

$$Q = \frac{600}{20} = 30$$

and

$P = 1000 - 10\,(30) = \$700.$

b. $\pi = TR - TC$

$= PQ - AC\,(Q)$

$= 700\,(30) - 400\,(30)$

$= 21{,}000 - 12{,}000 = \$9{,}000.$

c. The firm will sell the perfectly competitive level of output, or

$P = MC$

$1000 - 10Q = 400$

$10Q = 600$

$Q = 60.$

d. Since the two blocks of units are equal in size, then it will sell two blocks of 30 units each. Thus, the price, P_1, of the first 30 units is

$$P_1 = 1000 - 10\ (30)$$
$$= 1000 - 300 = \$700$$

and the price, P_2, of the second 30 units is

$$P_2 = 1000 - 10\ (60)$$
$$= 1000 - 600 = \$400.$$

e. $\pi = TR - TC,$

where total revenue, TR, is equal to the sum of the total revenue amounts, TR_1 and TR_2, associated with blocks one and two, respectively, or

$$TR = TR_1 + TR_2.$$

Thus

$$TR = P_1Q_1 + P_2Q_2$$
$$= 700\ (30) + 400\ (30)$$
$$= 21{,}000 + 12{,}000 = \$33{,}000.$$

Therefore

$$\pi = 33{,}000 - AC\ (Q_1 + Q_2)$$
$$= 33{,}000 - 400\ (30 + 30)$$
$$= 33{,}000 - 24{,}000 = \$9{,}000.$$

Note, the firm's profit is the same value, in this example, whether or not it price discriminates.

SOLUTIONS

Chapter 17

17.1 An oligopoly is a market structure consisting of a few sellers of a general product, where the specific products sold by the firms can be either homogeneous or slightly differentiated. The central characteristic associated with an oligopoly and thus found, to some degree, in all oligopoly models is that of interdependent behavior. This interdependence affects the firms' determination of the values of their output and price, as well as other strategic variables such as advertising. The underlying reason as to why interdependent behavior is so paramount in oligopoly follows from the fact that there are so few sellers of the product. Thus, each firm's behavior measurably affects the market quantity demanded of the good and correspondingly, the profits of the other firm's comprising the oligopoly. Further, because of a small number of firms, it is virtually impossible for each firm to be unaware of its rival's behavior.

17.2 A reaction function expresses a firm's profit maximizing level of output in terms of its rivals' levels of output. Thus, a reaction function shows how the firm will react to different levels of its rivals' output sold, in a manner that maximizes its profit. Conjectural variations represent how one firm thinks its rivals will react to its own output levels. The reason these concepts of reaction functions and conjectural variations are relevant to oligopoly, follows from the fact that there are so few sellers of the good. As a result, each firm's actions impact the other firms' profits. These concepts are not relevant to perfect competition because each firm comprising the market is so small that it has no perceptible influence over the market quantity and price of the good. Thus, in this case, the firms are all price takers. In the case of monopoly, there are no other sellers of the good. Therefore, without any rivals, the concepts of reaction functions and conjectural variations are not relevant.

In the Cournot model, it is assumed that the conjectural variations are equal to zero. Specifically, no firm believes that the others will react to its own changes in output. Reaction functions, however, are central to the Cournot model as each firm is assumed to react to its rivals' changes in output. Stackleberg broadens the Cournot model by allowing for the possibility of nonzero conjectural variations. As a result, those firms that employ these conjectural variations are treated as leaders and those that do not are treated as followers.

17.3 a. $Q_T = 800 - 2P$

Thus, in inverse form

$2P = 800 - Q_T$

$$P = 400 - \frac{1}{2} Q_T.$$

Since $Q_T = Q_1 + Q_2$, then

$$P = 400 - \frac{1}{2} (Q_1 + Q_2).$$

The cartel's profit, π, is

$\pi = TR_1 + TR_2 - TC_1 - TC_2$

$= PQ_1 + PQ_2 - TC_1 - TC_2$

$= P(Q_1 + Q_2) - TC_1 - TC_2$

$$= \left[400 - \frac{1}{2}(Q_1 + Q_2)\right](Q_1 + Q_2) - 200 - 10Q_1 - 400 - \frac{1}{2}Q_2^2$$

$$= 400(Q_1 + Q_2) - \frac{1}{2}(Q_1 + Q_2)^2 - 200 - 10Q_1 - 400 - \frac{1}{2}Q_2^2$$

$$= 400Q_1 + 400Q_2 - \frac{1}{2}\left(Q_1^2 + 2Q_1Q_2 + Q_2^2\right) - 200 - 10Q_1 - 400 - \frac{1}{2}Q_2^2$$

$$= 400Q_1 + 400Q_2 - \frac{1}{2}Q_1^2 - Q_1Q_2 - \frac{1}{2}Q_2^2 - 200 - 10Q_1 - 400 - \frac{1}{2}Q_2^2$$

$$\frac{\partial \pi}{\partial Q_1} = 400 - Q_1 - Q_2 - 10 = 0$$

$Q_1 = 390 - Q_2$

and

$$\frac{\partial \pi}{\partial Q_2} = 400 - Q_1 - Q_2 - Q_2 = 0$$

$= 400 - Q_1 - 2Q_2 = 0$

$2Q_2 = 400 - Q_1$

$Q_2 = 200 - \frac{1}{2}Q_1.$

Thus

$Q_1 = 390 - (200 - \frac{1}{2}Q_1)$

$= 390 - 200 + \frac{1}{2}Q_1$

$\frac{1}{2}Q_1 = 190$

$Q_1^* = 380$

and

$Q_2^* = 200 - \frac{1}{2}(380) = 10.$

Thus

$Q_T^* = Q_1^* + Q_2^* = 380 + 10 = 390.$

b. $P^* = 400 - \frac{1}{2}Q_T$

$= 400 - \frac{1}{2}(390) = 400 - 195 = \$205.$

$\pi = TR_1 + TR_2 - TC_1 - TC_2$

$$= P_1Q_1 + P_2Q_2 - 200 - 10Q_1 - 400 - \frac{1}{2}Q_2^2$$

$$= 205\,(380) + 205\,(10) - 200 - 10\,(380) - 400 - \frac{1}{2}(10)^2$$

$$= 77900 + 2050 - 200 - 3800 - 400 - 50$$

$$= \$75{,}500.$$

17.4 The reaction function for firm one is determined as

$$\pi_1 = TR_1 - TC_1$$
$$= PQ_1 - (200 + 10Q_1)$$
$$= \left[400 - \frac{1}{2}(Q_1 + Q_2)\right]Q_1 - 200 - 10Q_1$$
$$= 400\,Q_1 - \frac{1}{2}Q_1^2 - \frac{1}{2}Q_1Q_2 - 200 - 10Q_1$$
$$\frac{\partial \pi_1}{\partial Q_1} = 400 - Q_1 - \frac{1}{2}Q_2 - 10 = 0$$
$$= 390 - Q_1 - \frac{1}{2}Q_2 = 0$$
$$Q_1 = 390 - \frac{1}{2}Q_2.$$

The reaction function for firm two is determined as

$$\pi_2 = TR_2 - TC_2$$

$$= PQ_2 - (400 + \frac{1}{2}Q_2^2)$$
$$= \left[400 - \frac{1}{2}(Q_1 + Q_2)\right]Q_2 - 400 - \frac{1}{2}Q_2^2$$
$$= 400\,Q_2 - \frac{1}{2}Q_1Q_2 - \frac{1}{2}Q_2^2 - 400 - \frac{1}{2}Q_2^2$$
$$\frac{\partial \pi_2}{\partial Q_2} = 400 - \frac{1}{2}Q_1 - Q_2 - Q_2 = 0$$
$$400 - \frac{1}{2}Q_1 - 2Q_2 = 0$$
$$2Q_2 = 400 - \frac{1}{2}Q_1$$

$$Q_2 = 200 - \frac{1}{4}Q_1.$$

b. $Q_1 = 390 - \frac{1}{2}(200 - \frac{1}{4}Q_1)$

$= 390 - 100 + \frac{1}{8}Q_1$

$\frac{7}{8}Q_1 = 290$

$Q_1^* = 290\left(\frac{8}{7}\right) = 331$

$Q_2^* = 200 - \frac{1}{4}(331) = 117$

$Q_T^* = Q_1^* + Q_2^* = 331 + 117 = 448.$

c. $P^* = 400 - \frac{1}{2}Q_T$

$= 400 - \frac{1}{2}(448) = \$176.$

$\pi_1^* = TR_1 - TC_1$

$= PQ_1 - (200 + 10Q_1)$
$= 176(331) - 200 - 10(331)$
$= 58{,}256 - 200 - 3310 = \$54{,}746.$

$\pi_2^* = TR_2 - TC_2$
$= 176(117) - 400 - \frac{1}{2}(117)^2$
$= 20{,}592 - 400 - 6844.50$
$= \$13{,}347.50.$

The total output level for the Cournot model (448) is greater than that for the cartel (390). The price for the Cournot model (\$176) is lower than that for the cartel (\$205). Finally, the total profit for the Cournot model ($\pi_T^* = 54{,}746 + 13{,}347.50 = \$68{,}093.50$) is less than for the cartel (\$75,500.)

17.5 a. If firm one is a leader, it will incorporate the reaction function for firm two into its own reaction function. This means that the conjectural variation of firm one is no longer equal to zero. Recall

$Q_2 = 200 - \frac{1}{4}Q_1.$

Thus

$\pi_1 = TR_1 - TC_1$
$= PQ_1 - (200 + 10Q_1)$

$$= \left[400 - \frac{1}{2}(Q_1 + Q_2)\right]Q_1 - 200 - 10Q_1$$

$$= 400\ Q_1 - \frac{1}{2}\ Q_1^2 - \frac{1}{2}\ Q_1Q_2 - 200 - 10\ Q_1.$$

Since

$$Q_2 = 200 - \frac{1}{4}\ Q_1,$$

then

$$\pi_1 = 400\ Q_1 - \frac{1}{2}\ Q_1^2 - \frac{1}{2}\ Q_1\ (200 - \frac{1}{4}\ Q_1) - 200 - 10\ Q_1$$

$$= 400\ Q_1 - \frac{1}{2}\ Q_1^2 - 100\ Q_1 + \frac{1}{8}\ Q_1^2 - 200 - 10Q_1$$

$$\frac{\partial \pi_1}{\partial Q_1} = 400 - Q_1 - 100 + \frac{1}{4}Q_1 - 10 = 0$$

$$290 - \frac{3}{4}\ Q_1 = 0$$

$$Q_1^* = 290\left(\frac{4}{3}\right) = 386\frac{2}{3}.$$

$$Q_2^* = 200 - \frac{1}{4}\left(386\frac{2}{3}\right)$$

$$= 103\frac{1}{3}.$$

b. $$P^* = 400 - \frac{1}{2}\ (Q_T)$$

$$= 400 - \frac{1}{2}\left(386\frac{2}{3} + 103\frac{1}{3}\right)$$

$$= 400 - \frac{1}{2}\ (490) = \$155.$$

$\pi_1^* = PQ_1 - TC_1$
$= 155\ (386.67) - 200 - 10\ (386.67)$
$= 59933.85 - 200 - 3866.70$
$= \$55867.15$

$\pi_2^* = PQ_2 - TC_2$
$= 155\ (103.33) - 400 - \frac{1}{2}\ (103.33)^2$
$= 16016.15 - 400 - 5338.54$
$= \$10,277.61.$

17.6 **Figure 17.1**

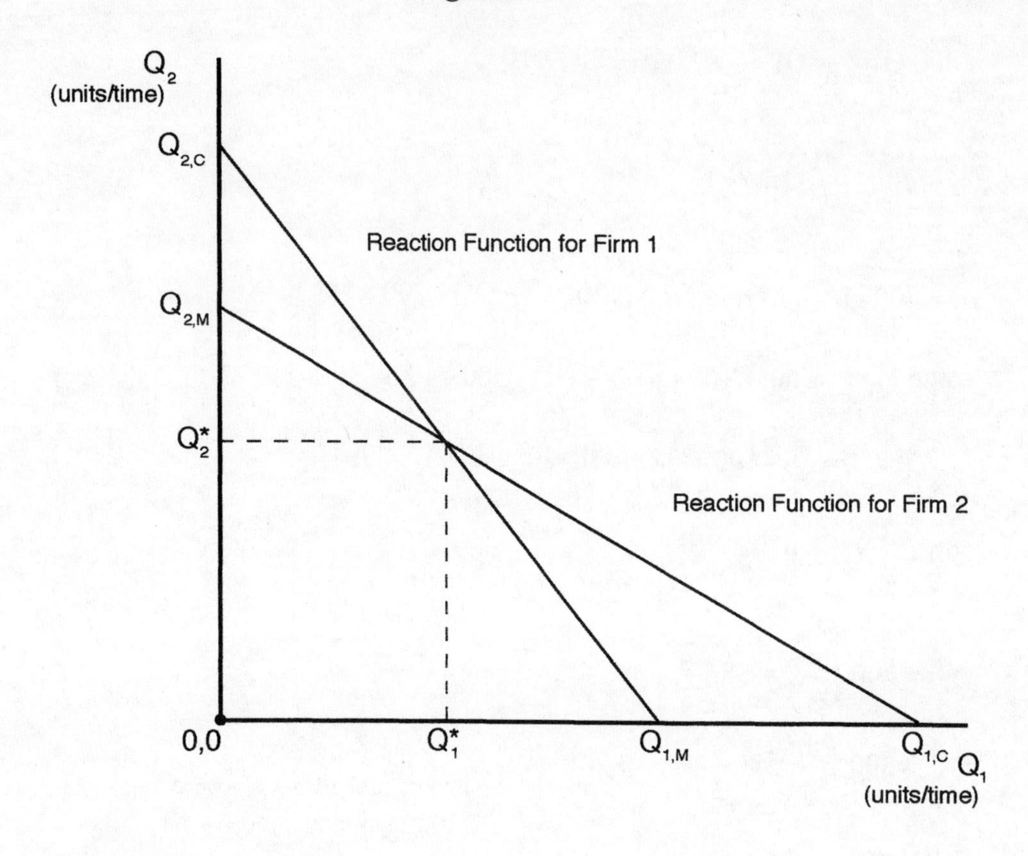

The Q_2, or vertical, intercept of the reaction function for firm one, $Q_{2,C}$, indicates the perfectly competitive market amount that firm two could sell if firm one sells zero output. The Q_2 intercept of the reaction function for firm two, $Q_{2,M}$, is the restricted amount that firm two will actually sell if firm one sells zero units of output. The Q_1 intercept of the reaction function for firm two, $Q_{1,C}$ is the perfectly competitive amount firm one could sell if firm two sells zero units of output. The Q_1 intercept of the reaction function for firm one is the restricted amount that firm one will sell if firm two sells no output. The point (Q_1^*, Q_2^*), where the two reaction functions intersect, represents the level of output for the two firms, where they are both maximizing their profits simultaneously. Thus, (Q_1^*, Q_2^*) is a stable combination that represents the Cournot oligopoly solution.

17.7

Figure 17.2

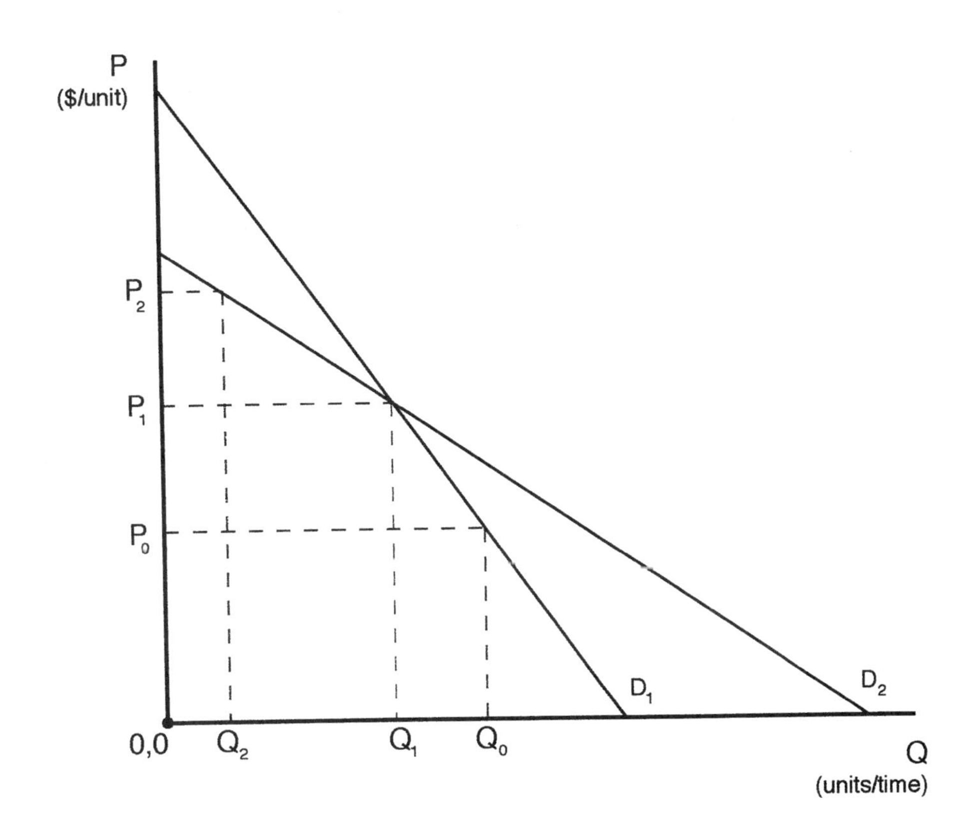

Assume the firm's initial price is P_1. If the firm decreases its price to P_0, it will increase the sales of its output to Q_0, moving down the steeper, or less price elastic, demand curve, D_1. The reason for this result, is the Sweezy assumption that if the firm decreases its price, the rival firms will decrease their prices as well. Accordingly, the increase in the firm's quantity demanded is relatively small. Conversely, if the firm raises its price to P_2, its quantity demanded falls substantially to Q_2, moving up the flatter, or more price elastic, demand curve, D_2. This result reflects the other Sweezy assumption that if a firm increases its price, the rival firms will not increase their prices in response.

17.8 **Figure 17.3**

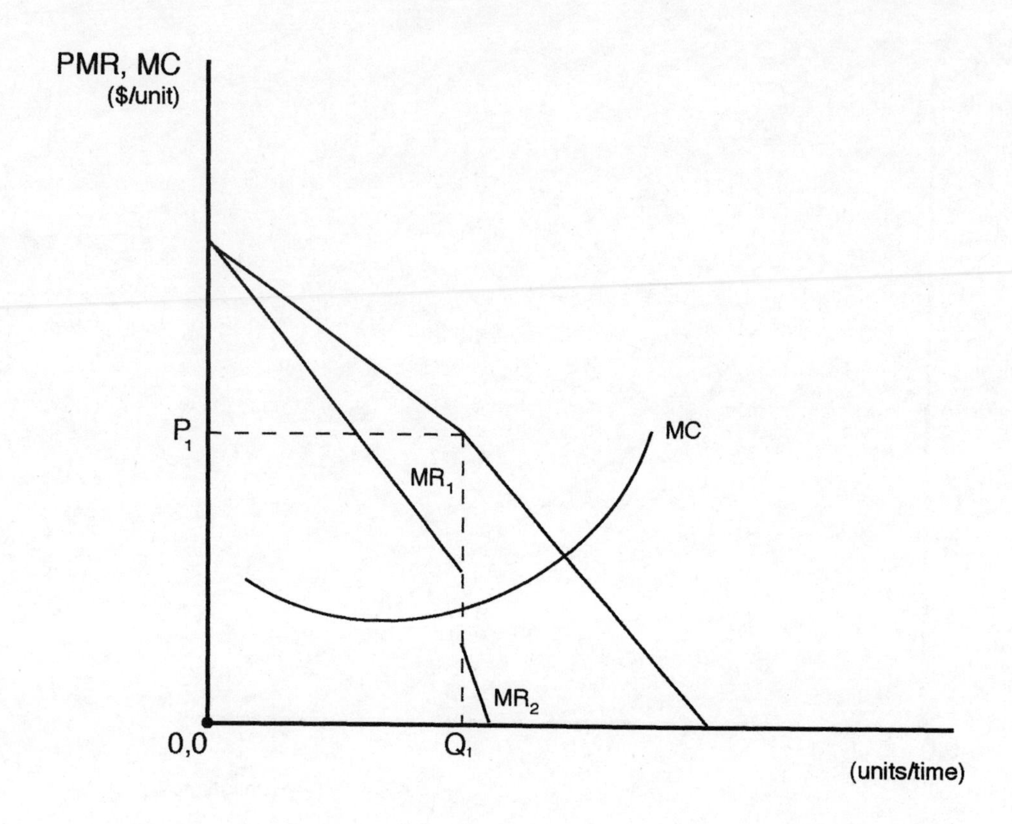

The own-price demand curve for the firm is kinked, where the upper portion is less elastic than the lower portion for the reasons you gave in exercise 17.7. Accordingly, the marginal revenue curves are MR_1 and MR_2, corresponding to the upper and lower portions of the own-price demand curve, respectively. The kink in the demand curve yields a discontinuity in the marginal revenue segments, MR_1 and MR_2. Thus, if the marginal cost curve, MC, passes through this discontinuity, as shown, it can shift up or down, within this range, without resulting in a change in the price of the good.

SOLUTIONS

Chapter 18

18.1 Since OPEC is a cartel it is very concerned with its members abiding by the cartel's production agreement. OPEC member nations typically meet four times a year to formulate their production agreements, which are devised so as to maximize the profit of the cartel as a whole, not the profit of any one member of the cartel. Therefore, a repeated game would be most appropriate for modeling the behavior of OPEC over time. This type of game can capture the retaliatory nature of some OPEC member nations actions, in response to cheating by other member nations on the production agreement. Specifically, tit-for-tat strategies can be used to model the behavior of OPEC member nations production strategies, and their profit, over time.

18.2

Firm Y's Strategies

Firm X's Strategies	Limited Advertising	Extensive Advertising
Limited Advertising	$4 million (Y) / $5 million (X)	$-1 million (Y) / $8 million (X)
Extensive Advertising	$7 million (Y) / $100,000 (X)	$6 million (Y) / $6 million (X)

18.3 a. Firm X does have a dominant strategy. Regardless of the strategy chosen by firm Y, firm X's profit is always higher if it follows a limited advertising strategy.

Firm Y does have a dominant strategy. Regardless of the strategy chosen by firm X, firm Y's profit is always higher if it follows a limited advertising strategy.

18.4 This game possesses a Nash equilibrium when each firm selects its limited advertising strategy. Firm X will receive $5 million in profit and firm Y will receive $4 million in profit. By choosing these strategies, each firm will maximize its profit, given the strategy choice made by the other firm.

18.5

Firm P's Strategies

Firm S's Strategies	**Abide by Production Agreement**	**Cheat on Production Agreement**
Abide by Production Agreement	$400,000 $400,000	$750,000 $15,000
Cheat on Production Agreement	$5,000 $750,000	$75,000 $75,000

18.6 Round 1: Firm S selects Abide by Production Agreement
Round 2: Firm P selects Abide by Production Agreement
Firm S's profit = $400,000 and Firm P's profit = $400,000
Round 3: Firm S selects Cheat on Production Agreement
Round 4: Firm P selects Cheat on Production Agreement
Firm S's profit = $75,000. Firm P's profit = $75,000

18.7 a. This is a constant sum game since the total percentage of market share available is a constant value, 100%. With only two firms comprising the market, the percentage of market share claimed by one firm must also represent the percentage of market share lost by the other firm.

b., c.

		Firm M's Strategies		
		Add Sports Car to Product Line	Add SUV to Product Line	Minimum of Firm L's Row Gains
Firm L's Strategies	Add Sports Car to Product Line	50	80	50 (Maximum)
	Add SUV to Product Line	20	60	20
	Maximum of Firm M's Column Losses	50 (Minimum)	80	

If firm L follows a maximin strategy it will select its strategy to add a sports car to its product line. By doing so its payoff will be 50% of the market share. Note in the column to the right of the payoff matrix above that 50 represents the maximum value of the minimum row gains that firm L can receive in this constant sum game.

If firm M follows a minimax strategy it will select its strategy to add a sports car to its product line. By doing so its payoff will be 50% of the market share. Note in the row at the bottom of the payoff matrix illustrated above that 50 represents the minimum value of the maximum column losses that firm M can receive in this constant sum game.

SOLUTIONS

Chapter 19

19.1 a. In the model of monopolistic competition a typical firm faces both a proportional own-price demand curve and a set of perceived own-price demand curves, although the firm is unaware of the former. A proportional own-price demand curve is a set of quantity-price combinations representing the proportion of the total product group quantity demanded attributed to one firm within the group. By contrast, a perceived own-price demand curve is simply a curve expressing, what a firm believes to be, its quantity demanded as a function of the price of its good.

b. We use both types of demand curves in the model because there is a difference between what a typical firm believes to be the own-price demand for its product and that which actually exists. Specifically, a firm believes that it possesses a greater degree of product differentiation, and therefore price setting discretion, than really exists. Thus, if it changes its price, the firm does not think its actions will be noticed by its rivals. The result of all of this, is that its perceived own-price demand curve is more price elastic than the proportional own-price demand curve.

19.2

Figure 19.1

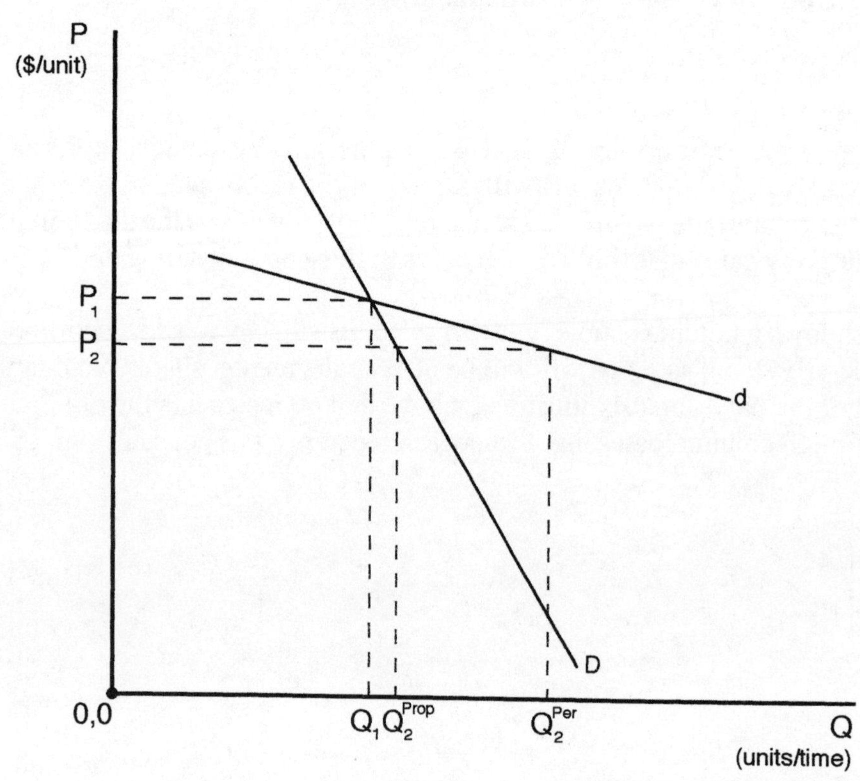

If the firm decreases its price from P_1 to P_2, it believes the quantity demanded of its product will increase from Q_1 to Q_2^{Per}, when in reality, it only increases to Q_2^{Prop}.

19.3 a. The proportional quantity demanded of a firm's good, $Q^{D,P}$, is

$$Q^{D,P} = \frac{1}{400}(Q^{D,G}) = \frac{1}{400}(10{,}000 - 100P)$$
$$= 25 - 0.25P$$

b. No, it will base its decisions on a more elastic perceived own-price demand curve. However, once an equilibrium is achieved, its perceived own-price demand must equal the proportional own-price demand. Thus, the firm is ultimately subjected to the proportional own-price demand curve.

19.4 In order to attain a short run equilibrium a firm's perception and reality must coincide. Thus, its perceived marginal revenue, mr, must be equal to its short run marginal cost, SRMC, and simultaneously, its perceived quantity demanded must equal its actual, or proportional, quantity demanded.

Figure 19.2

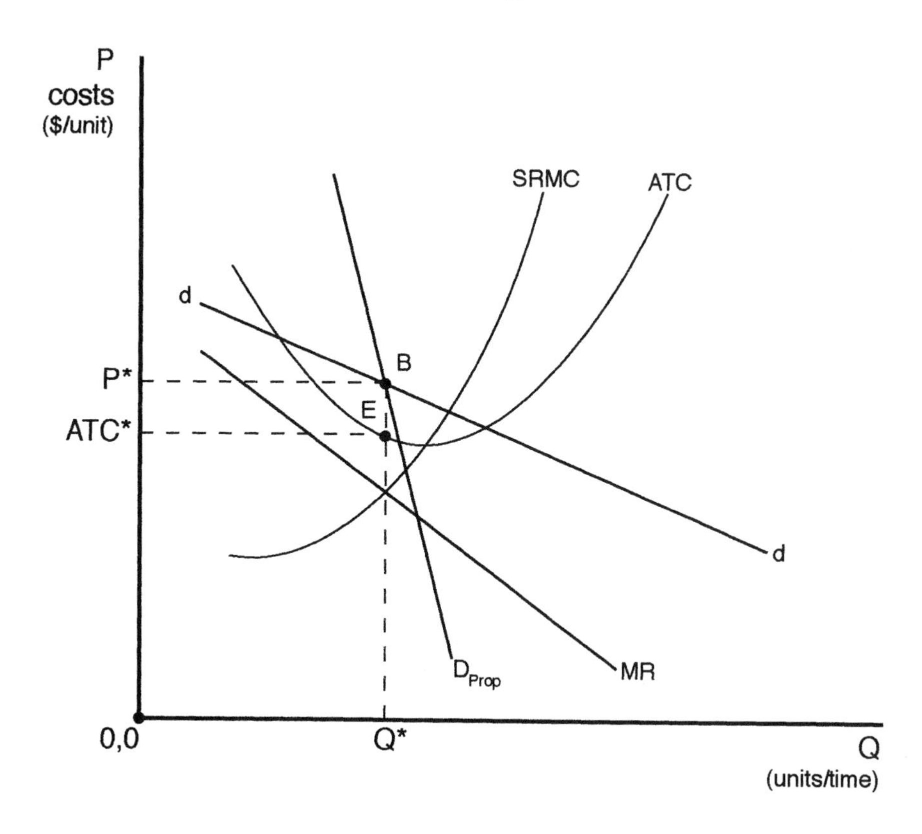

The firm's short run total profit, that is positive in this case, is the area of the rectangle $P^* BEATC^*$.

19.5 In long run equilibrium, the firm's perceived marginal revenue, must equal both its long run marginal cost, LRMC, and the corresponding short run marginal cost, SRMC. Also, its perceived quantity demanded must equal its proportional quantity demanded. Finally, its long run, and corresponding short run, profits must be equal to zero.

Figure 19.3

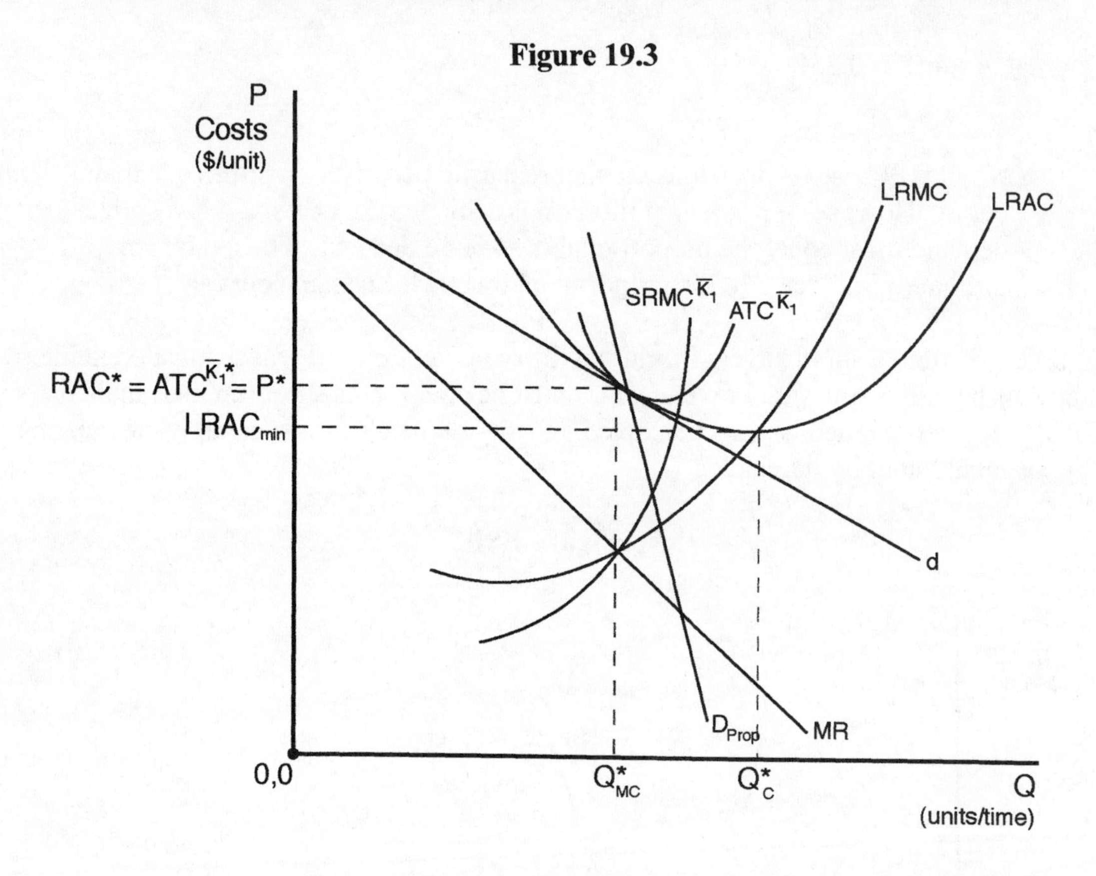

The reason profits must be equal to zero, in the long run, is that the entry of new firms into the product group drives them down by shifting the proportional demand curve, along with the corresponding set of perceived demand curves, to the left.

19.6 Excess capacity is the difference between the level of output produced by a perfectly competitive firm and that produced by a monopolistically competitive firm, when both are in long run equilibrium. In the figure illustrated for exercise 19.5, the excess capacity is represented by the amount $Q^*_C - Q^*_{MC}$. The desirability of excess capacity is debatable. On one hand it results in a level of output for each firm that is not sufficiently high to enable the firm to realize all economies of scale. Thus, costs and prices are higher for monopolistically competitive firms than for perfectly competitive firms. On the other hand, some economists view this excess capacity as simply reflecting the higher costs and prices associated with having a variety of slightly differentiated products.

SOLUTIONS

Chapter 20

20.1 a. The value of the marginal product of labor curve is the change in revenue, TR, due to a change in the amount of labor used. Thus

$$\text{VMP}_\text{L} = \frac{dTR}{dL},$$

where TR = $\overline{P}_1 Q$,

and since Q = $8\overline{K}_1^{\frac{1}{4}} L^{\frac{1}{4}}$, then

$$\text{VMP}_\text{L} = \frac{d(\overline{P}_1 Q)}{dL} = \frac{d(\overline{P}_1 8\overline{K}_1^{\frac{1}{4}} L^{\frac{1}{4}})}{dL}$$

$$= 2\overline{P}_1 \overline{K}_1^{\frac{1}{4}} L^{-\frac{3}{4}}$$

$$= 2(2)(16)^{\frac{1}{4}} L^{-\frac{3}{4}} = 8L^{-\frac{3}{4}} = \frac{8}{L^{\frac{3}{4}}}.$$

b. The marginal expense of labor curve is the change in a firm's total cost due to a change in the amount of labor it hires. Thus

$$\text{MEI}_\text{L} = \frac{dTC}{dL},$$

where

$$\text{TC} = \overline{P}_{K,1}\overline{K}_1 + \overline{P}_{L,1}L.$$

Therefore

$$\text{MEI}_\text{L} = \frac{dTC}{dL} = \frac{d\left(\overline{P}_{K,1}\overline{K}_1 + \overline{P}_{L,1}L\right)}{dL}$$

$$= \frac{d\overline{P}_{L,1}L}{dL} = \overline{P}_{L,1}.$$

20.2 a. $\text{VMP}_\text{L} = \text{MEI}_\text{L}$ at the profit maximizing level of labor. Thus

$$\frac{8}{L^{\frac{3}{4}}} = P_L$$

$$L^{\frac{3}{4}} = \frac{8}{P_L}$$

$$L = \left(\frac{8}{P_L}\right)^{\frac{4}{3}} = \frac{16}{(P_L)^{\frac{4}{3}}}$$

b. $$L^* = \frac{16}{(8)^{\frac{4}{3}}} = \frac{16}{16} = 1 \text{ unit.}$$

$$Q^* = 8\overline{K}_1^{\frac{1}{4}} L^{\frac{1}{4}} = 8(16)^{\frac{1}{4}}(1)^{\frac{1}{4}} = 16 \text{ units.}$$

20.3 a. The firm's profit maximizing level of output is determined where P = SRMC.

Also,

$$TC = \overline{P}_{K,1}\overline{K}_1 + \overline{P}_{L,1}\overline{L}$$

and thus

$$SRMC = \frac{dTC}{dQ} = \frac{d\left(\overline{P}_{K,1}\overline{K}_1 + \overline{P}_{L,1}\overline{L}\right)}{dQ}$$

$$= \overline{P}_{L,1}\frac{dL}{dQ} = \overline{P}_{L,1}\left(\frac{1}{MP_L}\right).$$

By definition

$$MP_L = \frac{dQ}{dL} = \frac{d\left(8\overline{K}_1^{\frac{1}{4}} L^{\frac{1}{4}}\right)}{dL} = 2\overline{K}_1^{\frac{1}{4}} L^{-\frac{3}{4}}$$

$$SRMC = \overline{P}_{L,1}\left(\frac{1}{2\overline{K}_1^{\frac{1}{4}} L^{-\frac{3}{4}}}\right) = \overline{P}_{L,1}\left(\frac{L^{\frac{3}{4}}}{2\overline{K}_1^{\frac{3}{4}}}\right)$$

$$= 8\left(\frac{1^{\frac{3}{4}}}{2(16)^{\frac{1}{4}}}\right) = \frac{8}{4} = \$2,$$

that is equal to the output price of P = \$2.

b. $$P = SRMC = P_L\left(\frac{1}{MP_L}\right)$$

$$P = P_L\frac{L^{\frac{3}{4}}}{2\overline{K}_1^{\frac{1}{4}}}$$

$$L^{\frac{3}{4}} = \frac{2P\overline{K}_1^{\frac{1}{4}}}{P_L}$$

$$L = \left(\frac{2P\bar{K}_1^{\frac{1}{4}}}{P_L} \right)^{\frac{4}{3}}$$

$$= \left(\frac{2(2)(16)^{\frac{1}{4}}}{P_L} \right)^{\frac{4}{3}} = \left(\frac{8}{P_L} \right)^{\frac{4}{3}} = \frac{16}{(P_L)^{\frac{4}{3}}}.$$

20.4 a. $Q = 4K^{\frac{1}{4}} L^{\frac{1}{4}} \bar{Z}_1^{\frac{1}{2}}$

$$TC = \bar{P}_{K,1}K + \bar{P}_{L,1}L + \bar{P}_{Z,1}\bar{Z}_1$$

Short run profit, $SR\pi$, is

$$SR\pi = TR - TC = \bar{P}_1 Q - TC$$

$$= \bar{P}_1\left(4K^{\frac{1}{4}} L^{\frac{1}{4}} \bar{Z}_1^{\frac{1}{2}}\right) - \left(\bar{P}_{K,1}K + \bar{P}_{L,1}L + \bar{P}_{Z,1}\bar{Z}_1\right)$$

$$= 4\bar{P}_1 K^{\frac{1}{4}} L^{\frac{1}{4}} \bar{Z}^{\frac{1}{2}} - \bar{P}_{K,1}K - \bar{P}_{L,1}L - \bar{P}_{Z,1}\bar{Z}_1$$

$$\frac{\partial SR\pi}{\partial K} = \bar{P}_1 K^{-\frac{3}{4}} L^{\frac{1}{4}} \bar{Z}_1^{\frac{1}{2}} - \bar{P}_{K,1} = 0$$

$$\frac{\partial SR\pi}{\partial L} = \bar{P}_1 K^{\frac{1}{4}} L^{-\frac{3}{4}} \bar{Z}_1^{\frac{1}{2}} - \bar{P}_{L,1} = 0$$

$$\frac{\bar{P}_1 K^{\frac{1}{4}} L^{-\frac{3}{4}} \bar{Z}_1^{\frac{1}{2}}}{P_1 K^{-\frac{3}{4}} L^{\frac{1}{4}} \bar{Z}_1^{\frac{1}{2}}} = \frac{\bar{P}_{L,1}}{\bar{P}_{K,1}}$$

$$\frac{K}{L} = \frac{\bar{P}_{L,1}}{\bar{P}_{K,1}}$$

$$K = \frac{\bar{P}_{L,1}}{\bar{P}_{K,1}} L$$

$$\bar{P}_1 \left(\frac{\bar{P}_{L,1}}{\bar{P}_{K,1}} L \right)^{\frac{1}{4}} L^{-\frac{3}{4}} \bar{Z}_1^{\frac{1}{2}} - \bar{P}_{L,1} = 0$$

$$\bar{P}_1 \left(\frac{\bar{P}_{L,1}^{\frac{1}{4}}}{\bar{P}_{K,1}^{\frac{1}{4}}} \right) L^{-\frac{1}{2}} \bar{Z}_1^{\frac{1}{2}} = \bar{P}_{L,1}$$

$$\overline{P}_1\left(\frac{\overline{P}_{L,1}^{\frac{1}{4}}}{\overline{P}_{K,1}^{\frac{1}{4}}}\right)\overline{Z}_1^{\frac{1}{2}} = \overline{P}_{L,1}L^{\frac{1}{2}}.$$

Since $Z_1 = 1$

$$L^{\frac{1}{2}} = \frac{\overline{P}_1}{\overline{P}_{L,1}^{\frac{3}{4}}\overline{P}_{K,1}^{\frac{1}{4}}}$$

$$L^d = \frac{\overline{P}_1^2}{P_L^{\frac{3}{2}}P_{K,1}^{\frac{1}{2}}} = \frac{(512)^2}{P_L^{\frac{3}{2}}(4)^{\frac{1}{2}}}$$

$$= \frac{262{,}144}{P_L^{\frac{3}{2}}(2)} = \frac{131{,}072}{P_L^{\frac{3}{2}}}.$$

b. Recall

$$K = \frac{\overline{P}_{L,1}}{\overline{P}_{K,1}}L$$

Thus

$$K^d = \frac{\overline{P}_{L,1}}{P_K}\left(\frac{\overline{P}_1^2}{\overline{P}_{L,1}^{\frac{3}{2}}P_K^{\frac{1}{2}}}\right) = \frac{P_1^2}{\overline{P}_{L,1}^{\frac{1}{2}}P_K^{\frac{3}{2}}}$$

$$= \frac{(512)^2}{(64)^{\frac{1}{2}}P_K^{\frac{3}{2}}} = \frac{262{,}144}{8P_K^{\frac{3}{2}}}$$

$$= \frac{32{,}768}{P_K^{\frac{3}{2}}}$$

20.5 a.

$$K^* = \frac{32{,}768}{(4)^{\frac{3}{2}}} = \frac{32{,}768}{8} = 4{,}096 \text{ units}$$

$$L^* = \frac{131{,}072}{(64)^{\frac{3}{2}}} = 256 \text{ units}$$

$$Q^* = 4K^{\frac{1}{4}}L^{\frac{1}{4}}\overline{Z}_1^{\frac{1}{2}}$$

$$= 4(4096)^{\frac{1}{4}}(256)^{\frac{1}{4}}(1)^{\frac{1}{2}}$$
$$= 4(8)(4)(1) = 128 \text{ units.}$$

b. $$Q = 4K^{\frac{1}{4}}L^{\frac{1}{4}}\overline{Z}_1^{\frac{1}{2}}$$

$$= 4\left(\frac{P^2}{P_{L,1}^{\frac{1}{2}}P_{K,1}^{\frac{3}{2}}}\right)^{\frac{1}{4}}\left(\frac{P^2}{P_{L,1}^{\frac{3}{2}}P_{K,1}^{\frac{1}{2}}}\right)^{\frac{1}{4}}(1)^{\frac{1}{2}}$$

$$= 4\left(\frac{P^{\frac{1}{2}}}{P_{L,1}^{\frac{1}{8}}P_{K,1}^{\frac{3}{8}}}\right)\left(\frac{P^{\frac{1}{2}}}{P_{L,1}^{\frac{3}{8}}P_{K,1}^{\frac{1}{8}}}\right)$$

$$= \frac{4P}{P_{L,1}^{\frac{1}{2}}P_{K,1}^{\frac{1}{2}}} = \frac{4P}{(64)^{\frac{1}{2}}(4)^{\frac{1}{2}}}$$

$$= \frac{4P}{8(2)} = \frac{1}{4}P.$$

Thus, if P = \$512, then

$$Q^S = \frac{1}{4}(512) = 128 \text{ units,}$$

or the same value as computed above.

20.6

Figure 20.1

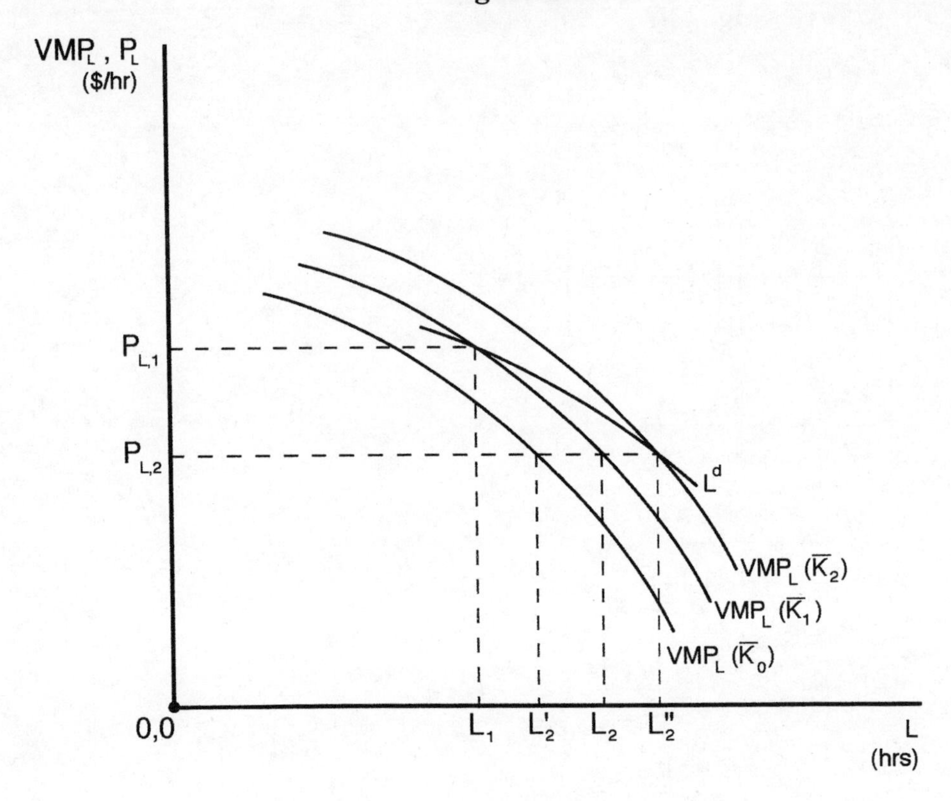

If capital is fixed at $\overline{K}_1$, then the VMP_L ($\overline{K}_1$) curve is the firm's demand for labor curve. Thus, if P_L decreases from $P_{L,1}$ to $P_{L,2}$, the firm increases its demand for labor from L_1 to L_2 units. If capital is allowed to vary, then, as P_L decreases, the firm substitutes labor for capital shifting the VMP_L curve to the left, because labor now has less capital with which to work. The resulting net increase in labor is from L_1 to L_2', representing the substitution effect. However, once the output effect is introduced, the firm is now using more of both inputs due to the decrease in its marginal costs caused by the decrease in P_L. Thus, the total amount of labor the firm demands at $P_{L,2}$ is L_2''.

20.7 Both the VMP and the MRP of an input measure the change in revenue from selling an extra amount of a good, due to a change in the amount of an input used in producing that good. Specifically, the VMP of an input is equal to the predetermined price of a good multiplied by the marginal product of the input. Thus, this concept is appropriate for a firm that behaves as a perfect competitor in its output market. The marginal revenue product of an input is equal to a firm's marginal revenue multiplied by the marginal product of the input. Accordingly, this concept is relevant when a firm behaves as a monopolist in its output market. Broadly speaking, the VMP is simply a special case of the MRP where P = MR, as is the case for a perfectly competitive firm.

SOLUTIONS

Chapter 21

21.1 a. The individual's real income is the product of the price of labor and the number of hours of labor supplied, or

$$y = \overline{P}_{L,1} L.$$

The time period of one week is

$$\overline{T} = (7 \text{ days})\ (24 \text{ hours/day}) = 168 \text{ hours},$$

that is divided between leisure and labor, or

$$\overline{T} = L_e + L,$$

and therefore

$$L = \overline{T} - L_e.$$

Thus

$$y = \overline{P}_{L,1}\left(\overline{T} - L_e\right)$$

$$y = \overline{P}_{L,1}\overline{T} - \overline{P}_{L,1}L_e,$$

and if P_L = \$1/hour and $\overline{T}$ = 168 hours

$$y = (2)\ 168 - (2)\ L_e$$

$$y = 2\ (168) - 2\ L_e$$

$$= 336 - 2\ L_e.$$

b. The y intercept is

$$y = 336 - 2\ (0) = \$336.$$

This value represents the maximum amount of income the individual could earn if he selects zero leisure and supplies labor for the entire week.

The L_e intercept is

$$0 = 336 - 2L_e$$

$$L_e = \frac{336}{2} = 168 \text{ hours}.$$

This value is the maximum amount of leisure the individual can have if he selects zero income. Thus, in this case, he chooses leisure time for the entire week.

The slope of the budget constraint is

$$\frac{dy}{dL_e} = \frac{d(336 - 2L_e)}{dL_e} = -2.$$

Thus, if he gives up \$2 of income, he can have 1 more hour of leisure time or alternatively, if he gives up 1 hour of leisure time, he can have \$2 of additional income.

21.2 a. $y = \overline{P}_{L,1} L$

or

$y \ \overline{P}_{L,1}\overline{T} - \overline{P}_{L,1} L_e$

$= 3\,(168) - 3\, L_e$

$= 504 - 3\, L_e$

The y intercept is

$y = 504 - 3(0) = \$504.$

The L_e intercept is

$0 = 504 - 3L_e$

$$L_e = \frac{504}{3} = 168 \text{ hours.}$$

The slope is

$$\frac{dy}{dL_e} = \frac{d(504 - 3L_e)}{dL_e} = -3.$$

Figure 21.1

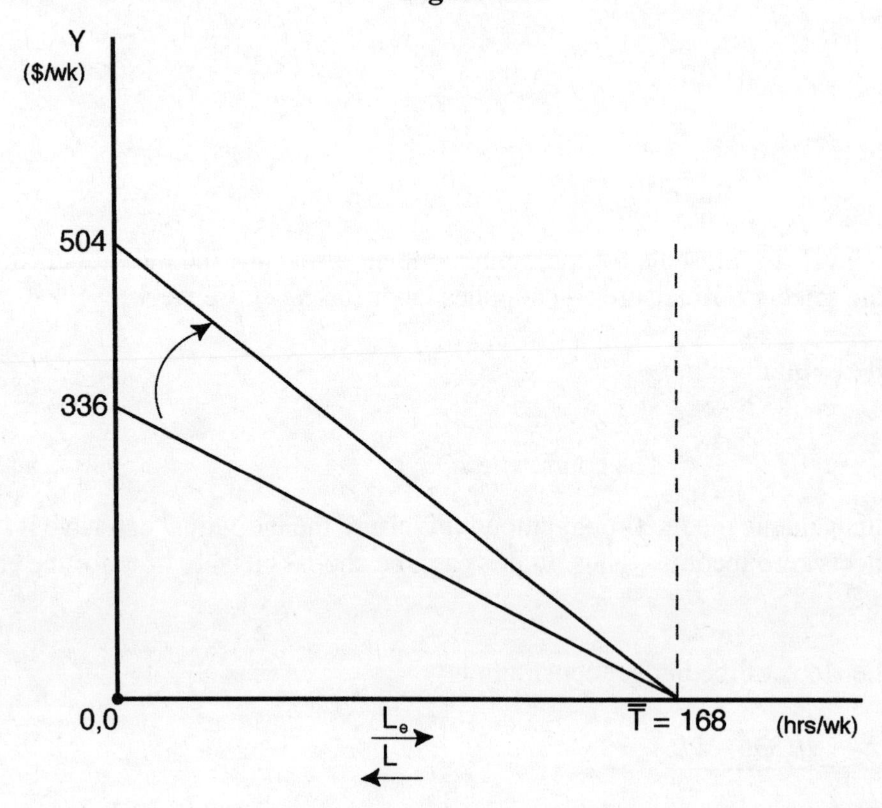

The increase in P_L has caused the budget constraint to rotate clockwise, with the L_e intercept as the pivot point.

21.3 $y = \overline{P}_{L,1}L + \overline{N}$

$= \overline{P}_{L,1}\left(\overline{T} - L_e\right) + \overline{N}$

$= \overline{P}_{L,1}\overline{T} - \overline{P}_{L,1}L_e + \overline{N}$

$= 2\ (168) - 2\ L_e + 12$

$= 348 - 2\ L_e$

The y intercept is
$y = 348 - 2(0) = \$348$.

There is no L_e intercept because the minimum income value is \$12. This occurs when $L_e = 168$, determined as

$12 = 348 - 2\ L_e$

$L_e = \dfrac{336}{2} = 168.$

The slope is $\dfrac{dy}{dL_e} = \dfrac{d(348 - 2L_e)}{dL_e} = -2.$

Figure 21.2

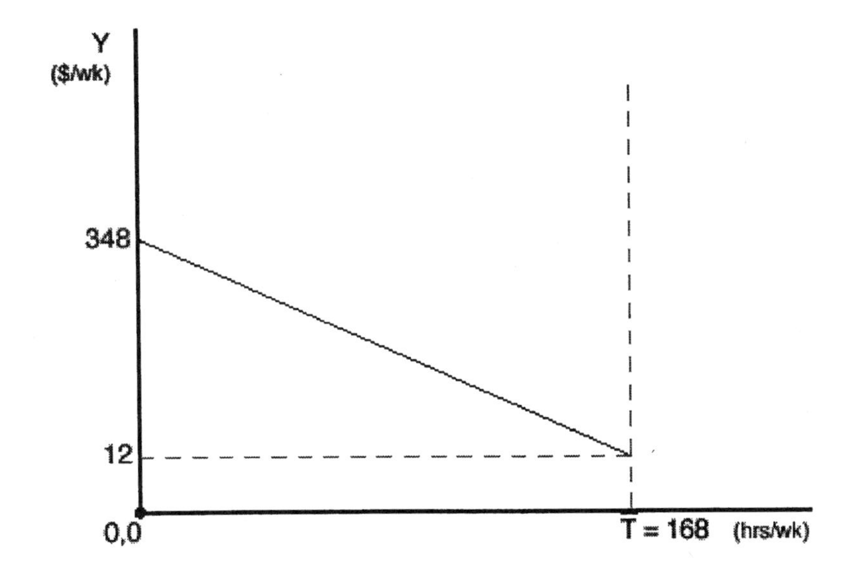

21.4 a. Maximize: $U = 20 L_e^{\frac{1}{2}} + 10y^{\frac{1}{2}}$

Subject to: $y = \overline{P}_{L,1}\overline{T} - \overline{P}_{L,1}L_e$,

or

$y - \overline{P}_{L,1}\overline{T} + \overline{P}_{L,1}L_e$

$$\mathcal{L} = 20L_e^{\frac{1}{2}} + 10y^{\frac{1}{2}} + \lambda(y - \overline{P}_{L,1}\overline{T} + \overline{P}_{L,1}L_e)$$

$$= 20L_e^{\frac{1}{2}} + 10y^{\frac{1}{2}} + \lambda y - \lambda\overline{P}_{L,1}\overline{T} + \lambda\overline{P}_{L,1}L_e$$

$$\frac{\partial\mathcal{L}}{\partial L_e} = 10L_e^{-\frac{1}{2}} + \lambda\overline{P}_{L,1} = 0$$

$$\frac{\partial\mathcal{L}}{\partial y} = 5y^{-\frac{1}{2}} + \lambda = 0$$

$$\frac{\partial\mathcal{L}}{\partial \lambda} = y - \overline{P}_{L,1}\overline{T} + \overline{P}_{L,1}L_e = 0$$

$$\frac{10L_e^{-\frac{1}{2}}}{5y^{-\frac{1}{2}}} = \frac{-\lambda\overline{P}_{L,1}}{-\lambda}$$

$$\frac{2y^{\frac{1}{2}}}{L_e^{\frac{1}{2}}} = \overline{P}_{L,1}$$

$$y^{\frac{1}{2}} = \frac{\overline{P}_{L,1}L_e^{\frac{1}{2}}}{2}$$

$$y = \frac{\overline{P}_{L,1}^{\,2}L_e}{4}$$

$$\frac{\overline{P}_{L,1}^{\,2}L_e}{4} - \overline{P}_{L,1}\overline{T} + \overline{P}_{L,1}L_e = 0$$

$$\frac{\overline{P}_{L,1}^{\,2}L_e}{4} + \overline{P}_{L,1}L_e = \overline{P}_{L,1}\overline{T}$$

$$L_e\left(\frac{1}{4}\overline{P}_{L,1}^{\,2} + \overline{P}_{L,1}\right) = \overline{P}_{L,1}\overline{T}$$

$$L_e^d = \frac{P_L\overline{T}}{\frac{1}{4}P_L^2 + P_L} = \frac{\overline{T}}{\frac{1}{4}P_L + 1},$$

or

$$L_e^d = \frac{4\overline{T}}{P_L + 4}.$$

Since L = $\overline{T}$ - L_e, then

$$L = \overline{T} - \frac{4\overline{T}}{P_L + 4} = \frac{\overline{T}(P_L + 4) - 4\overline{T}}{P_L + 4}$$

b. $$L_e^* = \frac{4\overline{T}}{P_L + 4} = \frac{4(168)}{2+4} = 112 \text{ hours}$$

$$L^* = \frac{P_L\overline{T}}{P_L + 4} = \frac{2(168)}{2+4} = 56 \text{ hours}$$

$y^* = P_L L = 2\,(56) = \$112.$

21.5 Maximize: $U = 20\, L_e^{\frac{1}{2}} + 10y^{\frac{1}{2}}$

Subject to: $y = \overline{P}_{L,1}\overline{T} - \overline{P}_{L,1}L_e + N$

$$\mathscr{L} = 20L_e^{\frac{1}{2}} + 10y^{\frac{1}{2}} + \lambda\left(y - \overline{P}_{L,1}\overline{T} + \overline{P}_{L,1}L_e - \overline{N}\right)$$

$$\frac{\partial\mathscr{L}}{\partial L_e} = 10L_e^{-\frac{1}{2}} + \lambda P_{L,1} = 0$$

$$\frac{\partial\mathscr{L}}{\partial y} = 5y^{-\frac{1}{2}} + \lambda = 0$$

$$\frac{\partial\mathscr{L}}{\partial \lambda} = y - \overline{P}_{L,1}\overline{T} + \overline{P}_{L,1}L_e - \overline{N} = 0$$

$$\frac{10L_e^{-\frac{1}{2}}}{5y^{-\frac{1}{2}}} = \frac{\lambda\overline{P}_{L,1}}{\lambda}$$

$$\frac{2y^{\frac{1}{2}}}{L_e^{\frac{1}{2}}} = \overline{P}_{L,1}$$

$$y^{\frac{1}{2}} = \frac{\overline{P}_{L,1}L_e^{\frac{1}{2}}}{2}$$

$$y = \frac{\overline{P}_{L,1}^{\,2}L_e}{4}$$

$$\frac{\overline{P}_{L,1}^{\,2}L_e}{4} - \overline{P}_{L,1}\overline{T} + \overline{P}_{L,1}L_e - \overline{N} = 0$$

$$\frac{(2)^2 L_e}{4} - 2(168) + 2L_e - 12 = 0$$

$L_e - 336 + 2L_e - 12 = 0$

$3L_e = 348$

$L_e^* = 116$ hours

$L^* = \overline{T} - L_e^* = 168 - 116 = 52$ hours

labor income, y_L, is

$y_L^* = \overline{P}_{L,1} L = 2\,(52) = \$104$,

and total income is

$y^* = y_L + \overline{N} = 104 + 12 = \$116$.

b. Comparing the values computed in this exercise to those obtained in exercise 21.4, we find that, with non-labor income included in the constraint, Le is higher, L is lower, labor income is lower, and total income is higher. Intuitively, the reason the individual chooses more leisure and less labor, as well as less labor income, is that the inclusion of non-labor income in the budget constraint creates only an income effect regarding the selection of leisure time. Since leisure is assumed to be a normal good, he subsequently consumes more of it.

21.6

Figure 21.3

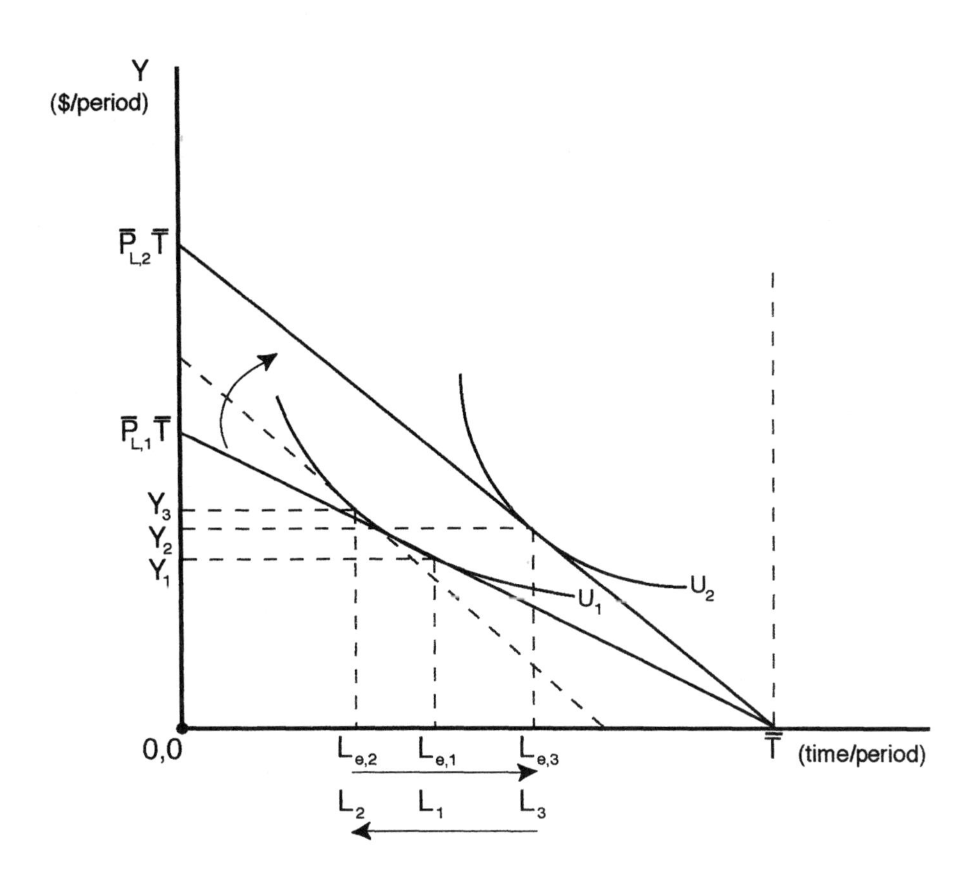

Substitution effect = $L_{e,2} - L_{e,1}$
Income effect = $L_{e,3} - L_{e,2}$
Total effect = $L_{e,3} - L_{e,1}$

21.7 A monopsonist is the sole buyer of a particular input. Thus, the supply of labor curve for the industry is also the supply of labor curve for the firm. Since these curves are generally positively sloped, the firm must pay a higher wage in order to attract greater amounts of the labor input. If we assume that the firm does not wage discriminate, then as it increases the wage to hire the extra unit of labor, it will increase the wage for the other labor units that it could hire at a lower wage. As a result, the extra cost due to hiring an extra unit of labor, or the MEI_L, will exceed the wage rate.

SOLUTIONS

Chapter 22

22.1 There are several reasons as to why developing a firm's demand for capital function is more complex than developing its demand for labor function. Generally, a firm purchases units of labor that it uses entirely in the present time period. However, when the firm purchases capital, it generally expects to receive services from this input for several periods into the future, as well as for the present time period. Thus, this capital will be used to generate output, revenue, and profits for these future time periods. The decision to purchase the capital, however, must be made in the present time period. As a result, it is necessary to discount the contribution made by the capital to the firm's future profits in order to determine this value in the present. In addition, due to including the time dimension, other factors must also be taken into account, such as the depreciation of the capital and the fact that, if the firm should choose to sell the capital at some point in the future, its price may have changed.

22.2 The present value of the $200,000, due three years in the future, is

$$PV = \frac{FV}{(1+r)^3} = \frac{200{,}000}{(1+.20)^3} = \$115{,}740.74.$$

Thus, the offer of $120,000 exceeds the present value of $115,740.73. Definitely, take the offer!

22.3 a. $PV = \sum_{i=1}^{n} \frac{FVi}{(1+r)^i}$, where n = 3 years.

Thus

$$PV = \frac{2000}{(1+.05)^1} + \frac{2000}{(1+.05)^2} + \frac{2000}{(1+.05)^3} + \frac{20{,}000}{(1+.05)^3}$$

= 1904.76 + 1814.06 + 1727.68 + 17,276.75

= $22,723.25.

This present value is also the current price of the bond.

b. $$PV = \frac{2000}{(1+.10)^1} + \frac{2000}{(1+.10)^2} + \frac{2000}{(1+.10)^3} + \frac{20{,}000}{(1+.10)^3}$$

= 1818.18 + 1652.89 + 1502.63 + 15,026.30

= $20,000.

Note, in this case the present value, or price of the bond, is equal to its face value, or \$20,000. This result follows because an interest rate of 10% is the same rate that was used to compute the coupon payments, C, or

C = .10 (20,000) = \$2,000.

22.4 a. $P_B = PV = \sum_{i=1}^{n} \frac{FV_i}{(1+r)^i}$

If you hold it for one year, the bond has two years left to maturity. Thus

$$PV = \frac{500}{(1+.05)^1} + \frac{500}{(1+.05)^2} + \frac{10{,}000}{(1+.05)^2}$$

$= 476.19 + 453.51 + 9070.29$

$= 10{,}000.$

This price is the same as the face value because the interest rate of 5% is the same as that used to compute the coupon payments, or

C = .05 (10,000) = \$500.

b. If, after one year, interest rates are 10%, then

$$P_B = PV = \frac{500}{(1+.10)^1} + \frac{500}{(1+.10)^2} + \frac{10{,}000}{(1+.10)^2}$$

$= 454.54 + 413.22 + 8264.46$

$= \$9132.22.$

In this case, the price of the bond has fallen due to the rise in interest rates.

22.5 a. $\dot{P}_{00} = \frac{P_{00} - P_{99}}{P_{99}} = \frac{1.75 - 1.50}{1.50}$

$= \frac{0.25}{1.50} = .1667 = 16.67\%$

b. $\dot{P}_{00}^* = \dot{P}_{00} = 16.67\%$

Therefore, using the simplified Fisher equation, the nominal interest rate, r_n, is equal to the real interest rate, r_r, plus the expected inflation rate, or

$r_n = r_r + \dot{P}^*$

$= 4\% + 16.67\% = 20.67\%.$

22.6 The more complex version of the Fisher equation takes the compounding of the inflation rate into account, or

$$r_n = r_r + \dot{P}^* + r_r \dot{P}^*$$

$$=4\% + 16.67\% + 4\% \,(16.67\%)$$
$$= .04 + .1667 + .04\,(.1667)$$
$$= .04 + .1667 + .0067$$
$$= .2134 = 21.34\%.$$

22.7 The intertemporal budget constraint equates the individual's consumption for the two time periods to the overall amount of income for the two periods, or

$$C_2 + (1+\bar{r}_1)C_1 = \bar{I}_2 + (1+\bar{r}_2)\bar{I}_1.$$

Solving for C_2 yields

$$C_2 = \bar{I}_2 + (1+\bar{r}_1)\bar{I}_1 - (1+\bar{r}_1)C_1,$$

thus the C_2 intercept is

$$C_2 = \bar{I}_2 + (1+\bar{r}_1)\bar{I}_1$$

representing the total amount of consumption that is possible in period two. To consume this amount, the individual would have to save all of his income in period one. Letting $C_2 = 0$ and solving for C_1 yields the C_1 intercept as

$$(1+\bar{r}_1)C_1 = \bar{I}_2 + (1+\bar{r}_1)\bar{I}_1$$

$$C_1 = \frac{(1+\bar{r}_1)\bar{I}_1}{(1+\bar{r}_1)} + \frac{\bar{I}_2}{(1+\bar{r}_1)}$$

$$= \bar{I}_1 + \frac{\bar{I}_2}{(1+\bar{r}_1)},$$

representing the total amount of consumption that is possible in period one. To consume this amount, the individual would have to borrow, in period one, all of his income earned in period two.

The slope of the constraint is

$$\frac{dC_2}{dC_1} = -(1+\bar{r}_1),$$

representing the rate at which the individual is able to trade off consumption between the two periods.

Figure 22.1

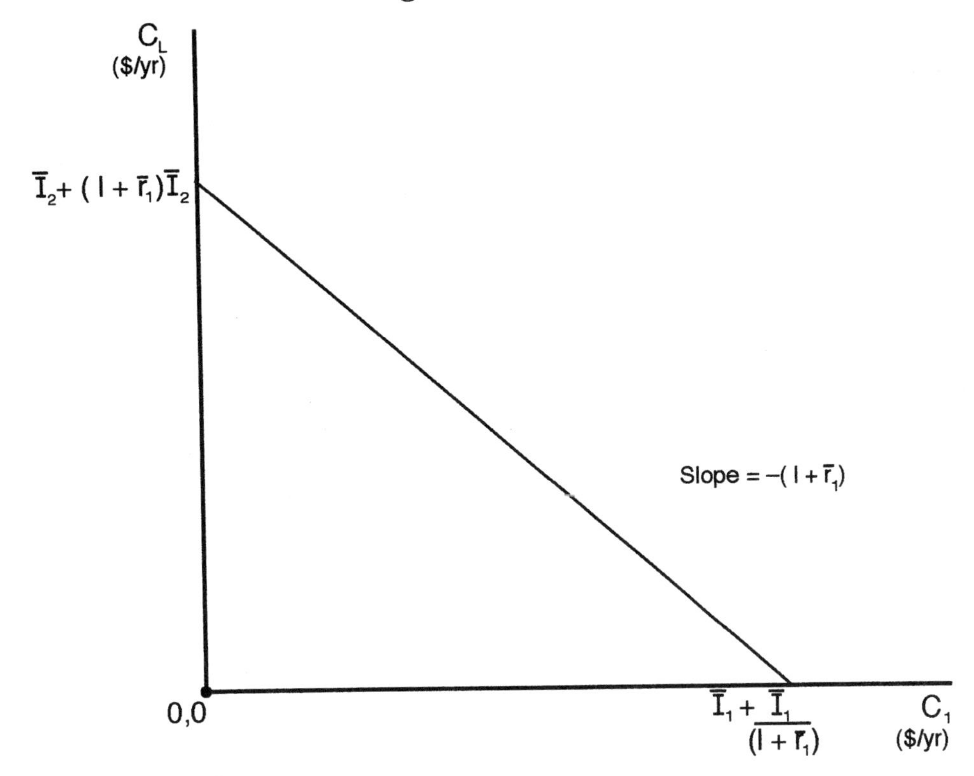

22.8 If $\bar{I}_1 = \bar{I}_2 = \$40{,}000$ and $\bar{r}_1 = 5\%$, then the C_2 intercept is

$$C_2 = \bar{I}_2 + (1 + \bar{r}_1)\bar{I}_1$$

$= 40{,}000 + (1+ .05)\ 40{,}000$

$= 40{,}000 + 40{,}000 + 2{,}000$

$= \$82{,}000.$

The C_1 intercept is

$$C_1 = \bar{I}_1 + \frac{\bar{I}_2}{1 + \bar{r}_2}$$

$$= 40{,}000 + \frac{40{,}000}{1+.05}$$

$= 40{,}000 + 38{,}095.24 = \$78{,}095.24.$

The slope is

$$\frac{dC_2}{dC_1} = -(1+\bar{r}_1) = 1(1+.05) = -1.05.$$

If r = 10%, then

$C_2 = 40{,}000 + (1 + .10)\ 40{,}000$
$= 40{,}000 + 40{,}000 + 4{,}000$
$= \$84{,}000.$

$$C_1 = 40{,}000 + \frac{40{,}000}{1+.10}$$
$= 40{,}000 + 36{,}363.64 = \$76{,}363.64.$
and

$$\frac{dC_2}{dC_1} = -(1+.10) = -1.10.$$

Figure 22.2

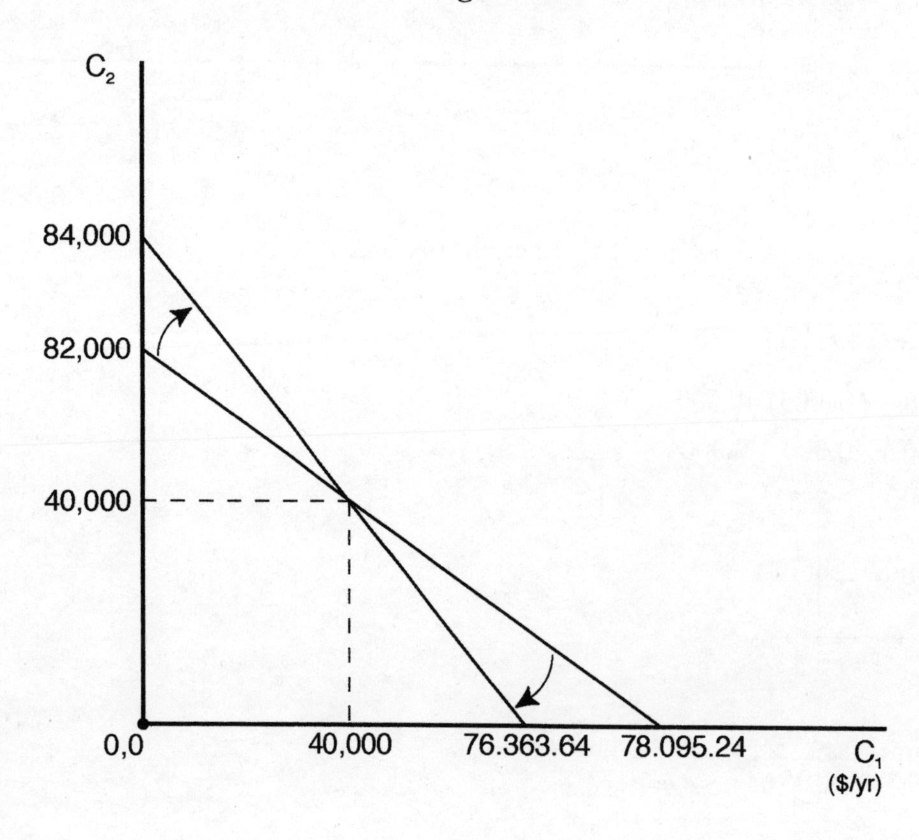

The increase in the interest rate causes the intertemporal budget constraint to rotate clockwise, increasing the C_2 intercept and decreasing the C_1 intercept. Conceptually, this result occurs because a higher interest rate increases the future value of present income saved and lent, thus enhancing potential future consumption. At the same time this increase in interest rates decreases the present value of future income that is borrowed.

SOLUTIONS

Chapter 23

23.1 General equilibrium analysis of consumer exchange focuses on the simultaneous attainment of equilibrium by all consumers in the economy. It differs from partial equilibrium analysis in that partial equilibrium analysis focuses on the attainment of equilibrium by one consumer at a time.

23.2 General equilibrium analysis of consumer exchange behavior is similar to partial equilibrium analysis of consumer behavior in that both methods of analysis use indifference curves to indicate consumers' preferences toward combinations of two goods. Also in both methods of analysis consumer optimization occurs when each persons' marginal rate of substitution of good X for good Y equals the ratio of the unit price of good X to the unit price of good Y.

23.3

Figure 23.2

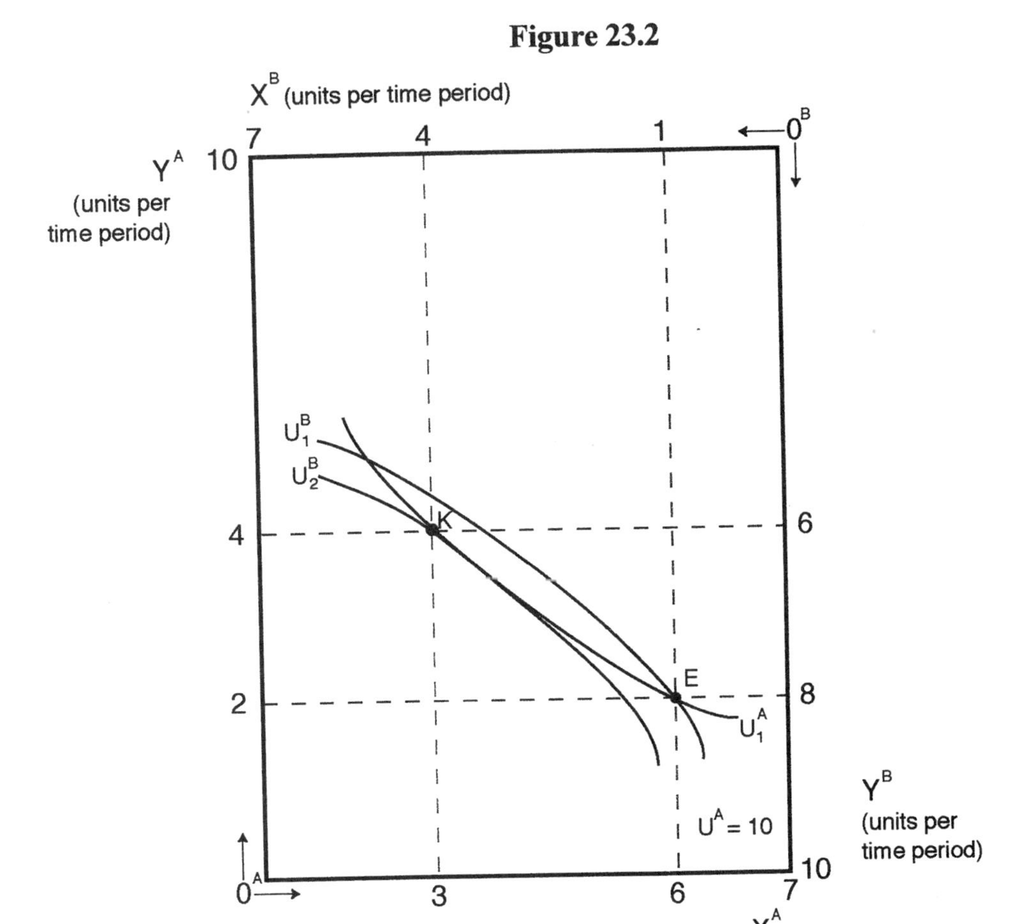

23.4 See figure for exercise 23.3. Consumer A will trade three units of good X to consumer B in return for two units of good Y from consumer B. The Pareto optimal allocation of goods is depicted at point K, where consumer A receives three units of good X and four units of good Y, and consumer B receives four units of good X and six units of good Y. Consumer B's utility increases from $U^B{}_1$ to $U^B{}_2$ after engaging in trade with consumer A, however consumer A's utility remains unchanged at $U^A{}_1$ due to the fact that consumer B is a better negotiator than consumer A.

23.5 a. The initial endowment does not constitute a competitive equilibrium. Recall that in order for an allocation of goods to be a competitive equilibrium in a general equilibrium exchange economy each consumer's marginal rate of substitution must equal the ratio of the unit prices of the goods. In this case, at the initial endowment

$$MRS^{Samantha} = 0.10,$$
$$MRS^{Matt} = 0.50$$

and

$$\frac{P_{\text{chicken wings}}}{P_{\text{steak}}} = \frac{\$2.00}{\$8.00} = 0.25.$$

Since

$$MRS^{Samantha} = 0.10 \neq \frac{P_{\text{chicken wings}}}{P_{\text{steak}}} = \frac{\$2.00}{\$8.00} = 0.25$$

therefore, Samantha's initial endowment is not a competitive equilibrium.

Since

$$MRS^{Matt} = 0.50 \neq \frac{P_{\text{chicken wings}}}{P_{\text{steak}}} = \frac{\$2.00}{\$8.00} = 0.25$$

therefore, Matt's initial endowment is not a competitive equilibrium.

b. Matt and Samantha can exchange these goods so that each person's marginal rate of substitution of chicken wings for steak is equal to the ratio of the unit price of chicken wings to the unit price of steak, or

$$MRS^{Matt} = MRS^{Samantha} = \frac{P_{\text{chicken wings}}}{P_{\text{steak}}} = \frac{\$2.00}{\$8.00} = 0.25.$$

In this case Matt will exchange some of his steak for some of Samantha's chicken wings. By doing so Matt's marginal rate of substitution of chicken wings for steak will decrease and Samantha's marginal rate of substitution of chicken wings for steaks will increase. Exchange will cease when a Pareto optimal allocation is achieved where $MRS^{Matt} = MRS^{Samantha}$.

23.6

Figure 23.3

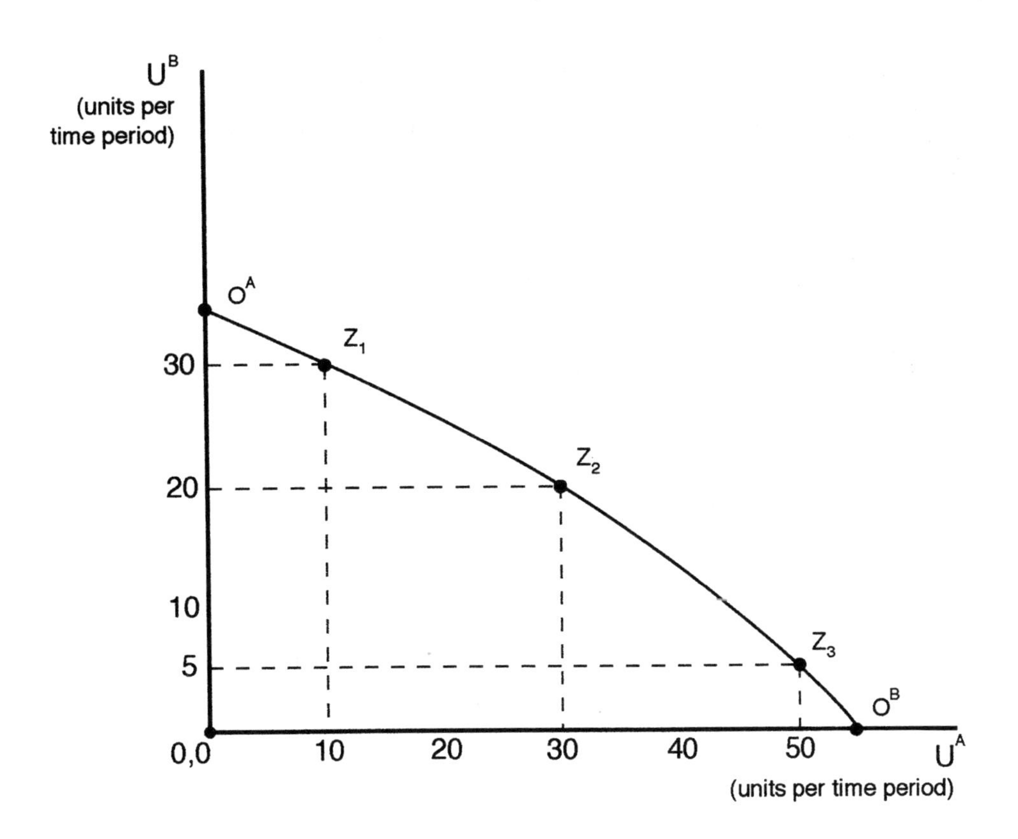

SOLUTIONS

Chapter 24

24.1 When the amounts of capital and labor available in the economy are doubled the Edgeworth production box is twice as long and twice as high as its original dimensions. The production contract curve is longer after the amounts of inputs are doubled since there are more technically efficient input combinations over the larger range of inputs available in the economy. In the example illustrated below the amount of labor available in the economy increased from 10 units to 20 units, and the amount of capital available increased from 7 units to 14 units.

Figure 24.1

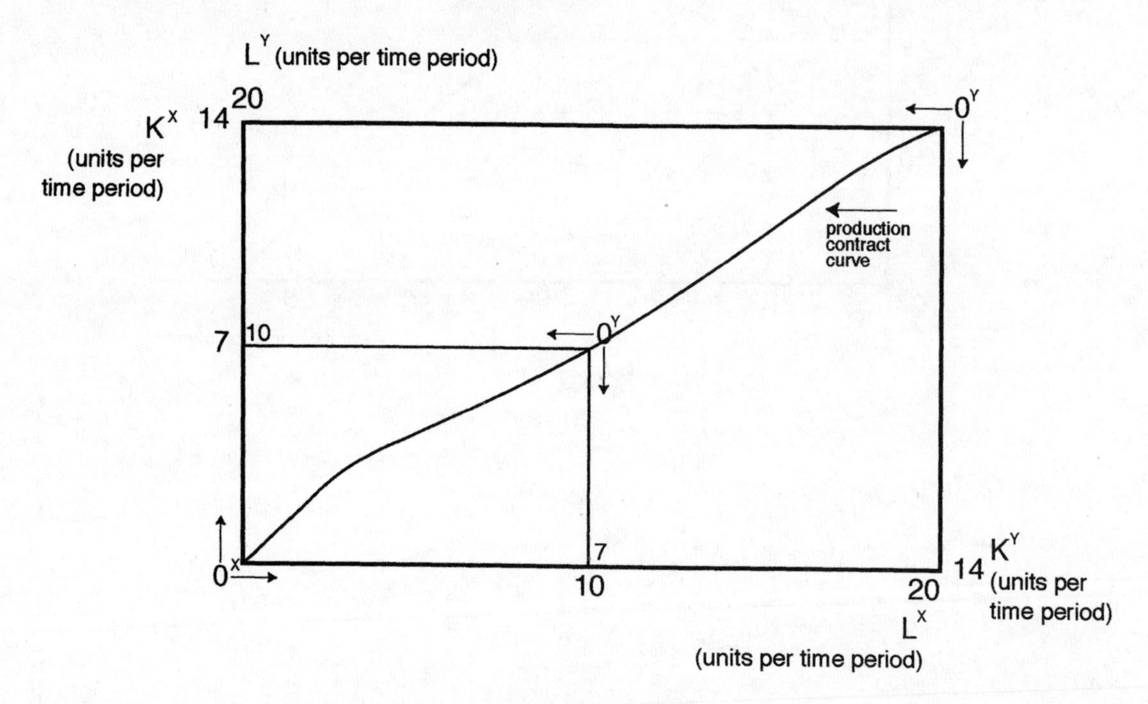

24.2 The production possibilities frontier will shift to the right, from PPF_1 to PPF_2 in the figure below, when the amounts of capital and labor available in the economy double. It will be possible to produce greater amounts of the two goods in the economy due to the increase in the amounts of inputs available for use in their production.

Figure 24.2

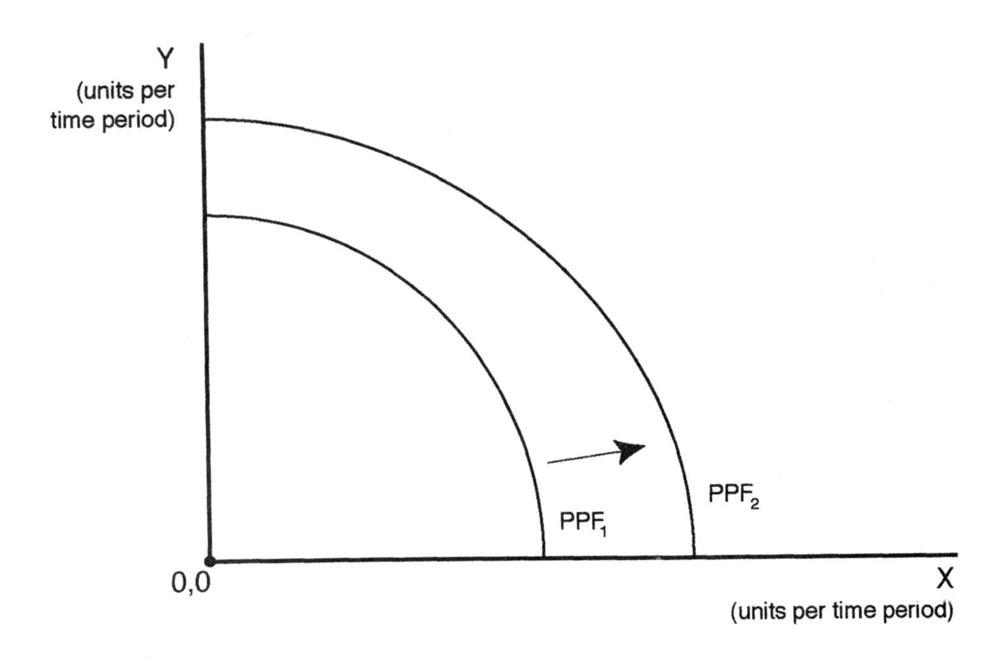

24.3 In general, Ella's MRS = $\dfrac{\dfrac{\partial U^E}{\partial X}}{\dfrac{\partial U^E}{\partial Y}} = \dfrac{10X^{-.5}Y^{.5}}{10X^{.5}Y^{-.5}} = \dfrac{Y}{X}$.

Therefore, when Ella consumes 20 units of good X and 10 units of good Y her marginal rate of substitution of good X for good Y is

$$MRS^{Ella} = \frac{Y}{X} = \frac{10}{20} = 0.50.$$

In general, Lisa's MRS = $\dfrac{\dfrac{\partial U^L}{\partial X}}{\dfrac{\partial U^L}{\partial Y}} = \dfrac{7.5X^{-.5}Y^{.5}}{7.5X^{.5}Y^{-.5}} = \dfrac{Y}{X}$.

Therefore, when Lisa consumes 2 units of good X and 1 unit of good Y her marginal rate of substitution of good X for good Y is

$$MRS^{Lisa} = \frac{Y}{X} = \frac{1}{2} = 0.50.$$

The combination of goods consumed by Ella and Lisa will be a competitive equilibrium if at that combination of goods:

$$MRS^{Ella} = MRS^{Lisa} = \frac{P_X}{P_Y}.$$

In this case, $MRS^{Ella} = 0.50 = MRS^{Lisa} = 0.50 = \frac{P_X}{P_Y} = \frac{\$75}{\$150} = 0.50$,

therefore this combination of goods consumed by Ella and Lisa is a competitive equilibrium.

24.4 In exercise 24.3 we determined that when Ella consumes 20 units of good X and 10 units of good Y her marginal rate of substitution of good X for good Y is 0.50. We also determined that when Lisa consumes 2 units of good X and one unit of good Y her marginal rate of substitution for good X for good Y is 0.50. In order for this allocation of goods in the economy to represent general equilibrium in both production and exchange then each consumer's marginal rate of substitution of good X for good Y must equal the marginal rate of transformation between goods X and Y. Therefore, in this case the marginal rate of transformation must equal 0.50 since,

$MRS^{Ella} = MRS^{Lisa} = 0.50 = MRT$.

24.5 $$MRTS^B = \frac{\frac{\partial Q^B}{\partial L}}{\frac{\partial Q^B}{\partial K}} = \frac{K^{.5}L^{-.5}}{K^{-.5}L^{.5}} = \frac{K}{L}$$

When 50 units of labor and 26 units of capital are used to produce bread, the marginal rate of technical substitution of labor for capital is

$$MRTS^B = \frac{K}{L} = \frac{26}{50} = 0.52$$

$$MRTS^C = \frac{\frac{\partial Q^C}{\partial L}}{\frac{\partial Q^C}{\partial K}} = \frac{4K^{.5}L^{-.5}}{4K^{-.5}L^{.5}} = \frac{K}{L}$$

When 70 units of labor and 34 units of capital are used to produce cheese, the marginal rate of technical substitution of labor for capital is

$$MRTS^C = \frac{K}{L} = \frac{34}{70} = 0.486$$

In order for an input combination to be technically efficient

$MRTS^B = MRTS^C$.

In this case,

$MRTS^B = 0.52 \neq MRTS^C = 0.486$

therefore this input combination is not technically efficient.

24.6 From the solution to exercise 24.5 we know that, in general, the marginal rate of technical substitution between labor and capital used in the production of bread is $MRTS^B = \frac{K}{L}$. We also know that there are 120 units of labor and 60 units of capital available in the economy. When the inputs are exchanged on the basis of their competitively determined prices, a competitive equilibrium in the input markets will exist and this input combination will lie on the production contract curve. Therefore, in this case,

$$MRTS^B = MRTS^C = \frac{K}{L} = \frac{P_L}{P_K} = \frac{\$15}{\$30} = 0.50.$$

Let L^B denote the amount of labor used in the production of bread and $(120 - L^B)$ indicate the amount of labor used in the production of cheese, since the total amount of labor available in the economy is 120 units. Similarly, let K^B denote the amount of capital used in the production of bread and $(60 - K^B)$ indicate the amount of capital used in the production of cheese, since the total amount of capital available in the economy is 60 units. Therefore,

$$MRTS^B = \frac{K^B}{L^B} = \frac{P_L}{P_K} = \frac{\$15}{\$30} = MRTS^C = \frac{(60 - K^B)}{(120 - L^B)},$$

when an allocation of capital and labor used in the production of bread and cheese is a competitive equilibrium in these input markets and lies on the production contract curve.

Thus,

$$MRTS^B = \frac{K^B}{L^B} = \frac{P_L}{P_K} = \frac{\$15}{\$30} = 0.50$$

or $\frac{K^B}{L^B} = 0.5$

and $K^B = 0.5L^B$,

indicating, in general, that the amount of capital used in the production of bread must be one half the amount of labor used in the production of bread. For example, if

$L^B = 30$

then

$K^B = 0.50\,(30) = 15$,

$L^C = (120\text{-}L^B) = (120\text{-}30) = 90$

and

$K^C = (60 - K^B) = (60 - 15) = 45.$

To determine the amount of bread produced when 30 units of labor and 15 units of capital are allocated in the production of bread, substitute L = 30 and K = 15 into the bread production as follows.

$$Q^B = 2K^{.5} L^{.5}$$

$$Q^B = 2\,(15)^{.5}\,(30)^{.5} = 42.426.$$

To determine the amount of cheese produced when 90 units of labor and 45 units of capital are allocated to the production of cheese substitute L = 90 and K = 45 into the cheese production function as follows.

$$Q^C = 8K^{.5} L^{.5}$$

$$Q^C = 8(45)^{.5}\,(90)^{.5} = 509.117.$$

SOLUTIONS

Chapter 3AW

3AW.1

Figure 3AW.1

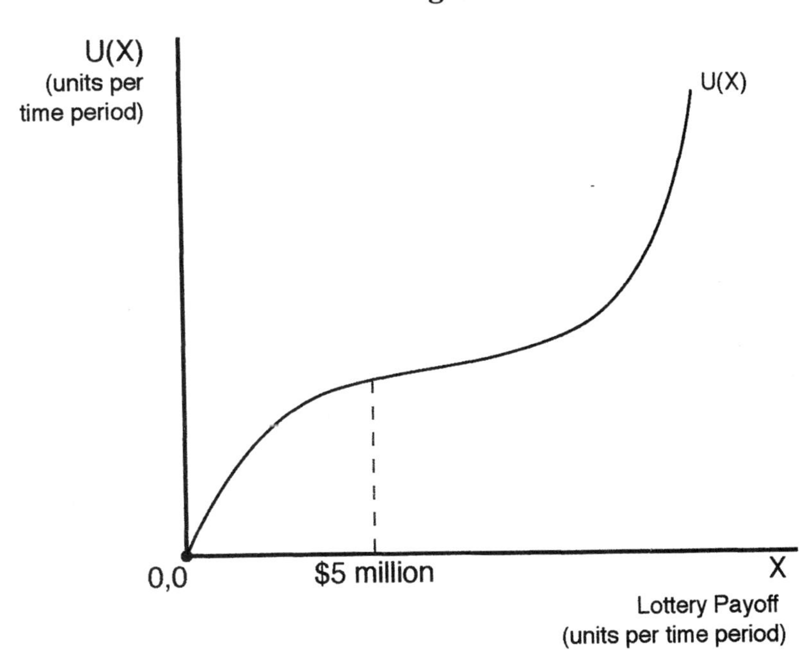

3AW.2 a. When the value of the lottery jackpot increases from $1 million to $2 million Clifford is risk averse, therefore his utility function in this payoff range is concave. This means that the slope of his utility function in this payoff range, which measures his marginal utility from a lottery payoff, decreases as the value of the lottery payoff increases.

b. When the value of the lottery jackpot increases from $6 million to $7 million Clifford is risk preferring, therefore his utility function in this payoff range is convex. This means that the slope of his utility function, which measures his marginal utility from a lottery payoff, increases as the value of the lottery payoff increases.

Figure 3AW.2

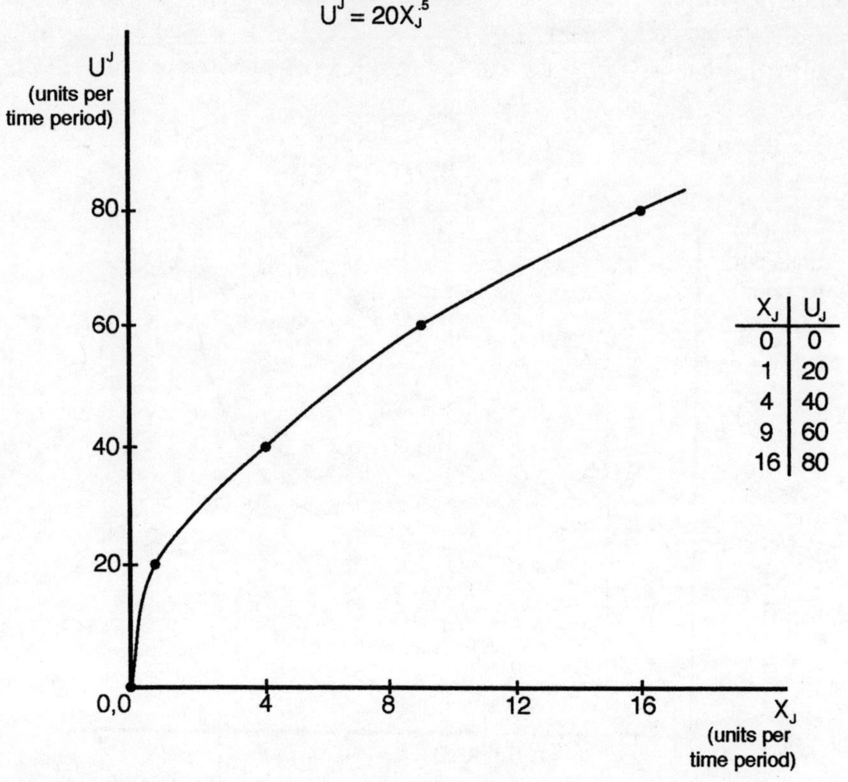

X_J	U_J
0	0
1	20
4	40
9	60
16	80

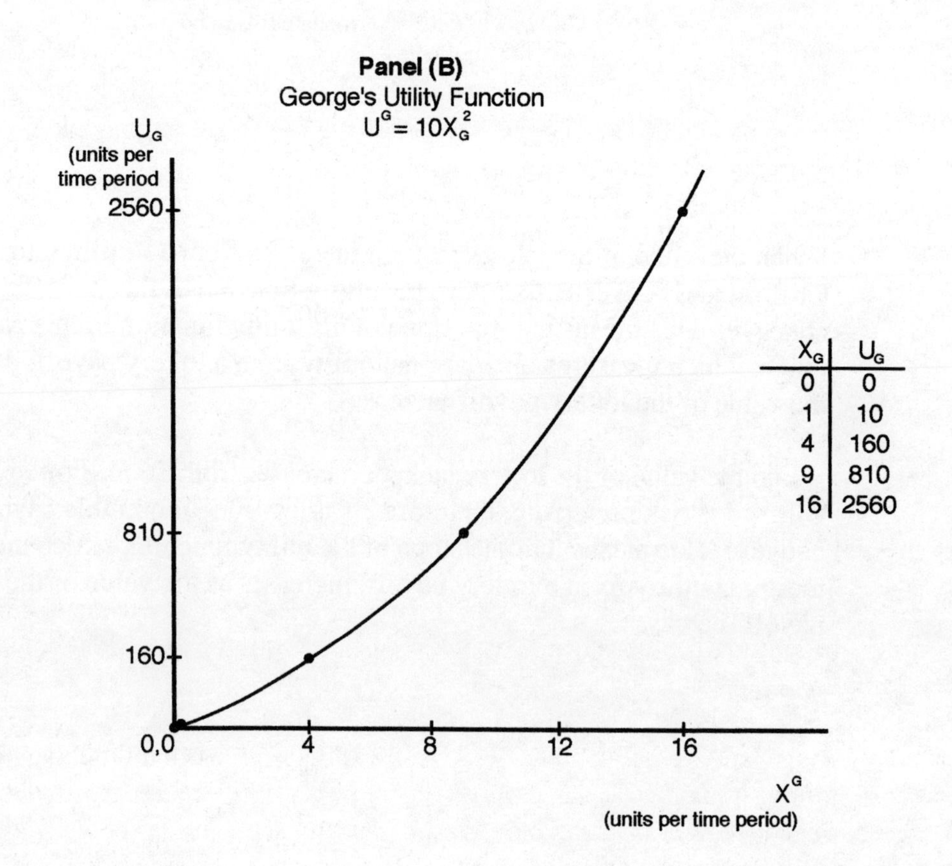

X_G	U_G
0	0
1	10
4	160
9	810
16	2560

3AW.4 John's utility function is concave indicating that he is risk averse. George's utility function is convex indicating that he is risk preferring. Therefore, if both men acted rationally, John would be more likely than George to insure his coin collection.

3AW.5 a. The expected value of stock J is determined as follows.

$$E(X^J) = Pr_G^J \cdot X_G^J + Pr_B^J \cdot X_B^J$$
$$= (0.45)\ (\$6900) + (0.55)\ (\$4900)$$
$$= \$3105 + \$2695$$
$$= \$5800$$

b. The expected value of stock V is determined as follows.

$$E(X^V) = Pr_G^V \cdot X_G^V + Pr_B^V \cdot X_B^V$$
$$= (0.30)\ (\$10{,}000) + (0.70)\ (\$4000)$$
$$= \$3000 + \$2800$$
$$=\$5800$$

3AW.6 a. The expected utility Olga would receive if she invested in stock J is computed as follows.

$$E\ [U(X^J)] = Pr_G^J \cdot U\ (X_G^J) + Pr_B^J \cdot U\ (X_B^J)$$
$$= Pr_G^J \cdot (8(X_G^J)^{.5}) + Pr_B^J \cdot (8(X_B^J)^{.5})$$
$$= (0.45)\ (8(6900)^{.5}) + (0.55)\ (8(4900)^{.5})$$
$$= 299.04 + 308$$
$$= 607.04$$

b. The expected utility Olga would receive if she invested in stock V is computed as follows.

$$E\ [U(X^V)] = Pr_G^V{}_G \cdot U\ (X^V{}_G) + Pr_B^V \cdot U\ (X^V{}_B)$$
$$= Pr_G^V \cdot (8(X^V{}_G)^{.5} + Pr_B^V \cdot (8(X^V{}_B)^{.5}$$
$$= (0.30)\ (8(10{,}000)^{.5}) + (0.70)\ (8\ (4000)^{.5})$$
$$= 240 + 354.175$$
$$= 594.175$$

c. If Olga acts rationally she would invest in stock J since the expected utility she would receive from investing in this stock is 607.04 units, which is greater than the expected utility she would receive if she invested in stock V.

3AW.7 a. A risk premium is the amount of money a consumer is willing to forgo in order to make her indifferent between a risky investment and one with a certain return.

b. In the solution to exercise 3AW.6 it was determined that Olga would choose to invest in stock J, since the expected utility she receives from investing in this stock is greater than the expected utility she would receive from investing in stock V. Specifically, when Olga invests in stock J her expected utility is